W9-BTB-306

PRAISE FOR *Sacred Voices*

"In reading it, I feel as if long-vanished and suppressed parts of my own soul are being restored."

— ANDREW HARVEY, author of *The Direct Path*

"A magnificent resource that not only informs but inspires and encourages us to find our own wisdom, our own voice."

— ORIAH MOUNTAIN DREAMER, author of
The Invitation and *The Dance*

"These visions comprise an unbroken thread woven through five millennia and remain vibrant to this day."

— LARRY DOSSEY, M.D., author of *Reinventing Medicine,*
Healing Words, and *Healing Beyond the Body*

"This marvelous book is a brimming well of empowering knowledge. How miraculous it is to hear, for the first time, the full range of the long-silenced voices of the sacred feminine singing together."

— ERYK HANUT, author of *The Road to Guadalupe* and Director
of the San Francisco Center for the Divine Feminine

"Too long have these stories, visions, and voices announcing the revelation of the Divine Feminine been ignored, trampled on, or condemned. Let the floodgates open now! Let the Divine Feminine Wisdom in this book flood our minds, hearts, and ailing patriarchal institutions!"

— MATTHEW FOX, author of *Original Blessing*

"*Sacred Voices* strikes the missing notes in the music of the earth's spiritual heritage—the voices of women, ancient and modern, that our hearts have been longing to hear. Congratulations to Mary Ford-Grabowsky!"

— NEIL DOUGLAS-KLOTZ, author of *Prayers of the Cosmos*
and *The Hidden Gospel*

"In a brilliant marriage of scholarship and love, Mary Ford-Grabowsky presents a breathtaking chorus of women's voices, celebrating the full range of female experience from exaltation to despair, from the everyday to moments of transcendence. The editor's introduction adds a further dimension, tracing with eloquence and grace the forces that shaped her own life as a woman seeking to discover her true identity in a world fashioned mainly by men. This volume is a triumph, an exciting exploration of the palpable reality that rests behind the notion of the 'divine feminine'."

— DOROTHY WALTERS, PH.D., author, *Marrow of Flame:*
Poems of the Spiritual Journey and *Unmasking the Rose:*
An Account of a Kundalini Initiation

"This superb collection of life-affirming writings sounds a call that men and women alike need to hear. It awakens our ancient connections to each other and the Earth and celebrates our greater humanity, helping us reclaim the whole of ourselves. *Sacred Voices* could well serve as a bridge between our modern-day hunger for communion and a crucial feminine wisdom submerged far too long in the flood of patriarchy."

— K. LAUREN DE BOER, Executive Editor, *EarthLight Journal*

"A much-needed collection of women's wisdom—vibrant, expressive, and vital."

— JACK CANFIELD, editor, *Chicken Soup for the Woman's Soul*

"It is good to hear these blessed women's voices raised at last. This is a soulful wake-up call to the sacred feminine energy within us all. I heartily commend Ford-Grabowsky on gathering all this delightful material."

— LAMA SURYA DAS, spiritual teacher, author of *Awakening the*
Buddha Within, and founder of the Dzogchen Center

"A bedside book to reach for during the darkest nights, as well in times of grace and glory."

— NANCY STEINBECK, author of *The Other Side*
of Eden: Life with John Steinbeck

SACRED VOICES

Essential Women's Wisdom
Through the Ages

MARY FORD-GRABOWSKY

HarperSanFrancisco
A Division of HarperCollins*Publishers*

WITHDRAWN
EDWIN O. SMITH HIGH SCHOOL
LIBRARY MEDIA CENTER
1235 STORRS RD., STORRS, CT 06268

200.8?
SAC

9/02

Sonia Delaunay (1885–1979)
Study of Portugal, ca. 1937 (detail)
Gouache on paper
14 1/4 x 37 in.
The National Museum of Women in the Arts
Gift of Wallace and Wilhelmina Holladay

SACRED VOICES: *Essential Women's Wisdom Through the Ages.* Copyright © 2002 by Mary Ford-Grabowsky. All rights reserved. Printed in the United States of America. No part of this book may be used or reproduced in any manner whatsoever without written permission except in the case of brief quotations embodied in critical articles and reviews. For information address HarperCollins Publishers, Inc., 10 East 53rd Street, New York, NY 10022.

HarperCollins books may be purchased for educational, business, or sales promotional use. For information please write: Special Markets Department, HarperCollins Publishers, Inc., 10 East 53rd Street, New York, NY 10022.

HarperCollins Web site: http://www.harpercollins.com

HarperCollins®, ▉®, and HarperSanFrancisco™ are trademarks of HarperCollins Publishers, Inc.

FIRST EDITION

Designed by Lindgren/Fuller Design

Library of Congress Cataloging-in-Publication Data
Ford-Grabowsky, Mary.
    Sacred voices : essential women's wisdom through the ages /
    Mary Ford-Grabowsky.—1st ed.
        p.   cm.
    Includes bibliographical references.
    ISBN 0–06–251702–3 (cloth)
    ISBN 0–06–251703–1 (paper)
        1. Women—Religious life. I. Title.
BL625.7.F67   2002
200'.82—dc21   2001039731

02 03 04 05 06 ❖ RRD(H) 10 9 8 7 6 5 4 3 2 1

To

La Nuestra Señora de Guadalupe

And to

Tara Grabowsky
Tory Ford
Helen Ford
Karin Grabowsky
Ida Broughton Ford
Charlotte Broughton Winchester
Mary Catherine Broughton
Rosa Reissman Grabowsky
Mary Joan Potts
Mary Elizabeth Broughton
Mary Louise Ford

CONTENTS

FOREWORD BY ANDREW HARVEY / xix

SPECIAL ACKNOWLEDGMENTS / xxi

EDITOR'S INTRODUCTION / 1

VOICES OF HISTORY

Anonymous Hymn in Praise of Inanna, Mesopotamia, Second
or Third Millennium B.C.E. / 9
She Made the Night Come Forth like the Moonlight
A Priestess of Inanna, Sumea, c. 2000 B.C.E. / 10
Bridegroom, beloved of my heart
Hashepsowe, Egypt, Ruled 1503–1482 B.C.E. / 11
Hail King ... Female Sun!
Anonymous Love Song, Egypt, Between 1300 and 1100 B.C.E. / 13
My Hand Is in Your Hand
Sappho, Lesbos, Greece, Seventh Century B.C.E. / 13
Thank You, My Dear
Leave Crete
Patacara, India, Sixth or Fifth Century B.C.E. / 15
I've Done What I Was Taught
Canda, India, Sixth or Fifth Century B.C.E. / 16
I Was Lost
Mettika, India, Sixth or Fifth Century B.C.E. / 18
Psalm
Sumangalamata, India, Sixth or Fifth Century B.C.E. / 18
At Last Free!

Praxilla, Greece, c. 450 B.C.E. / 19
    Cucumbers, Apples, and Pears
The Book of Ruth, Palestine, First Millennium B.C.E. / 20
    Where You Go Will I Go
Judith, Palestine, Second Half of the Second Century B.C.E. / 21
    In Praise of Judith's Courage
Anonymous Lament, Mesopotamia, Ancient Oral
   Tradition, B.C.E. / 22
    Lament of the Flutes for Tammuz
Mary the Mother of Jesus, Palestine, First Century C.E. / 23
    The Magnificat
The Gospel of Mary, Palestine, First Century C.E. / 24
    From *The Gospel of Mary: The Sacredness of Mary Magdalen to*
      Jesus
Perpetua, Carthage (Tunisia, North Africa), c. 182–202 or 203 / 26
    From *Perpetua's Diary*
A Court Record, Saloniki (Greece), 304 / 30
    The Trial and Sentencing of Agape, Chione, Irene, and Four
      of Their Friends
Egeria, Western Europe, Late Fourth to Early Fifth Century / 32
    Journey to Jerusalem
Hypatia, Egypt, d. 415 / 36
    Such Are My Gods!
Anonymous Lament of Mary, Syria, Sixth Century / 38
    Lament of Mary for Her Son
Yamatohime, Japan, Seventh Century / 39
    Others May Forget You
Lady Kasa, Japan, Eighth Century / 39
    I Dreamed I Held a Sword
Rabia Al-Adawiyya, Persia (Iraq), 717–801 / 40
    Stars Are Shining
    A Dream
    You Are Sufficient
    Without You
    From *Her Biography*
    My Joy
    Teachings on Prayer

Mandarava of Zahor, India, Eighth Century / 43
   The Leave-Taking
Rayhana, Today's Iraq?, Eighth to Ninth Century / 45
   You Are My Longing
Dhuodana, Septimania (South of France), 803–843 / 46
   From *A Manual for William*
Umm Abdallah, Tirmidh (Central Asia), Ninth Century / 49
   The Second Dream
   The Third Dream
Bhiksuni Laksmi, Kashmir, Tenth or Eleventh Century / 52
   From *The Chant to Accompany Her Fasting Practice*
Anonymous Love Song, Spain, c. 1042 / 53
   So Much Loving
Christina of Markyate, England, c. 1096-c. 1166 / 54
   You Cannot Make Me Forget
Heloise, France, c. 1100–1163 / 56
   From *A Letter to Abelard*
Hildegard of Bingen, Germany, 1098–1179 / 58
   A Vision of the Sacred Feminine
   Vision of the Shadow of the Living Light
   A Vision of the Living Light
   Antiphon for Divine Wisdom
   From *Antiphon for the Angels*
   From *Antiphon for the Holy Spirit*
   I, God, Am in Your Midst
Sun Bu-er, China, 1124–? / 62
   Cut brambles long enough
Mahadevi, India, Twelfth Century / 63
   The Whole Forest Is You
   I Wear the Morning Light
   I Am Watching All the Roads
Clare of Assisi, Italy, 1194–1253 / 65
   Go Forward Securely
   Contemplation
   From *The "Way" of Saint Clare*
Beatrice of Nazareth, Brabant (Netherlands and Belgium),
   c. 1200–1268 / 68

A Waterfall of Ineffable Delight
Vision of the World as a Wheel
Mechthild of Magdeburg, Germany, c. 1212–1282 / 70
That Prayer Has the Greatest Power
I Cannot Dance, O Lord
Would You Know My Meaning?
Lord, You Are My Lover
Lord, Now I Am Naked
Muktabai, India, Thirteenth Century / 73
Where the Eyes See Nothing
Fire in My Mind
Angela of Foligno, Italy, 1248–1309 / 74
An Experience of Oneness
Gertrude the Great, Germany, 1265–1301 / 76
Divine Birth in the Soul
Through a Desert Without a Path
I Find All My Joy in You
Marguerite Porete, France, c. 1277–1310 / 78
The Empty Mirror
The Soul Speaks to the Beloved
Hadewijch, Flanders (Belgium), c. 1250–? / 80
God Be with You, Dear Friend
If I Desire Something
Love Has Subjugated Me
The Mind Can Never Understand
Irene Eulogia, Constantinople, 1291–1355 / 82
A Thirteenth-Century Search for Spiritual Guidance
Catherine of Siena, Italy, 1347–1380 / 84
A Soul Rises Up
A Prayer of Praise
Praying in the Spirit
The Bridge: God Speaks to the Soul
On Corruption in the Fourteenth-Century Church
Lalleshwari, Kashmir, Fourteenth Century / 87
Wild Longing
Why Lalla Stopped Wearing Clothes
Live in the Soul!

Go Beyond Experience
Moonlight Full of Knowledge
Hidden in My Body
Cutting Through the Six Forests
Gently, Gently, I Trained My Mind
Julian of Norwich, England, 1342–c. 1423 / 91
   The Hazelnut
   Be a Gardener
   Our Sensuality
   God Is Our Mother
   All Shall Be Well
Christine de Pisan, Italy, 1365–c. 1429 / 94
   How a Wise Woman, in the Year 1405, Works for Peace
Margery Kempe, England, 1373–1439 / 96
   The Archbishop Puts Her in Chains
Catherine of Genoa, Italy, 1447–1510 / 99
   Commitment
   Transparency
   Three Teachings
Mirabai, India, 1498–c. 1550 / 101
   Why Mira Can't Go Back
   O Friends, I Am Mad
   The Dark One Is Here Inside
   The City Seeks Its Lord
   I Put Bells on My Ankles
   O Friend, Understand
Teresa of Avila, Spain, 1515–1582 / 104
   Two Fountains, Two Ways of Prayer
Rose of Lima, Peru, 1586–1617 / 107
   Mosquitoes in Praise
Anonymous Pawnee Chant, Native America, Oral Tradition / 108
   Anointing with Sacred Ointment
Anne Bradstreet, England, 1612–1672 / 109
   On the Burning of Our House, July 10, 1666
Margaret Mary Alacoque, France, 1647–1690 / 111
   From *A Vision of the Divine Heart*
   Prayer to the Sacred Heart

Sor Juana Inés de la Cruz, Mexico, c. 1648–1695 / 113
   Selections
Rwala Bedouin Women, Arabian Peninsula, Oral Tradition / 115
   O Mother of Rain, Rain upon Us!
Ann Lee, England, 1736–1784 / 116
   'Tis the Gift to Be Simple
   The Lord of the Dance
Sojourner Truth, New York, c. 1799–1883 / 118
   Ar'n't I a Woman?
   In Defense of Eve
   I Am Going to Stay Right Here and Stand the Fire!
Pygmy Women, Zaire (Today's Democratic Republic of the Congo),
   Oral Tradition / 120
   Women's Morning Song
   Chant for a Sick Child
Ashanti Women, Ghana, Oral Tradition / 121
   From *The Menstrual Rite of Passage*
   Let One Remain
   In Desperation of Grief
   Cover Me with the Night
Bibi Hayati, Persia (Iraq), ?–1853 / 123
   Is this darkness the night of power?
Eskimo Prayer, West Greenland, Oral Tradition / 125
   Thanks for the Birth of a Baby Girl
A Hopi Creation Story, Native America, Oral Tradition / 125
   In the Womb of Earth-Mother
Harriet A. Jacobs, North Carolina, 1813–1897 / 126
   From *Incidents in the Life of a Slave Girl*
Florence Nightingale, England, 1820–1910 / 128
   From *A Letter on Women's Stagnation in the Nineteenth Century*
Emily Dickinson, Massachusetts, 1830–1886 / 129
   I Had Been Hungry All the Years
   Wild Nights—Wild Nights!
   I Saw No Way
   After Great Pain
   Thoughts

A Letter to Mrs. J. G. Holland
A Letter to Susan Dickinson Gilbert
Myrtle Fillmore, Ohio, 1845–1931 / 135
  God Does Not Punish
  Other Teachings
Frontier Women on the Overland Trail, United States, 1840–1870 / 137
  A Page from the Diary of Catherine Haun
Sarada Devi, India, 1853–1920 / 139
  Teachings on Daily Spiritual Life
Concepción Cabrera de Armida (Conchita), Mexico, 1862–1937 / 141
  From *Her Diary*
Osage Chant, Native America, Oral Tradition / 143
  Planting Chant
Gemma Galgani, Italy, 1878–1903 / 144
  Mystical Burning
  How I See Our Souls in God
Elizabeth of the Trinity, France, 1880–1906 / 146
  O My Beloved Star
Eliza Calvert Hall, Kentucky, Nineteenth Century / 147
  Piecin' a Quilt's like Livin' a Life

VOICES OF OUR TIMES

Irina Ratushinskaia, Russia, Twentieth Century / 151
  The Babushki's Trousseau
Mary Mercedes Lane, California, 1871–1965 / 152
  Electronic Communications
Sidonie-Gabrielle Colette, France, 1873–1954 / 154
  Letter Concerning Her Pink Cactus
Evelyn Underhill, England, 1875–1941 / 155
  The Goal of the Mystical Journey
The Mother, France, 1878–1973 / 157
  A Dream
Isadora Duncan, California, 1878–1927 / 159
  I Live in My Body

Virginia Woolf, England, 1882–1941 / 161
    From *Mrs. Dalloway*
    From *A Room of One's Own*
    From *To the Lighthouse*
Georgia O'Keeffe, Wisconsin, 1887–1986 / 163
    About Painting Desert Bones
    On the Wideness and Wonder of the World
    On Saying What She Wanted To
    From *A Letter to Anita Pollitzer, January 1916*
    From *A Letter to Anita, September 1916*
    From *A Letter to Anita, October 1916*
    From *A Letter to Anita, 1929*
Anna Akhmatova, Russia, 1889–1966 / 167
    Selections
Gabriela Mistral, Chile, 1889–1957 / 169
    From *"Prayer"*
    The Powerful Against the Poor, 1928
    From *"Those Who Do Not Dance"*
Anita Scott Coleman, New Mexico, 1890–1960 / 171
    No. 60 in Ward 400
Anandamayi Ma, India, 1896–1982 / 173
    Sayings and Advice
Satomi Myodo, Japan, 1896–1978 / 176
    A Liberating Experience
Maria Valtorta, Italy, 1897–1961 / 178
    A Vision of Mary
    God Speaks to Mary During Creation
Dorothy Day, New York, 1897–1980 / 179
    Voluntary Poverty
    Jail
Elsa Gidlow, England, 1898–1986 / 183
    From *"Chains of Fire"*
Irina Tweedie, Russia, 1907–1999 / 183
    Circulation of Light in the Body
    This Is a Promise, and I Will Keep It

Simone Weil, France, 1909–1943 / 187
  From *Waiting for God*
  Divine Love in the Midst of Affliction
Mae V. Cowdery, Pennsylvania, 1909–1953 / 190
  A Dream of Love
Mother Teresa, Albania, 1910–1997 / 192
  Be a Candle
  Who Are the Poor?
Sivananda Radha, Germany, 1911–1995 / 194
  Why Practice Yoga?
Mahalia Jackson, Louisiana, 1911–1972 / 195
  From *Movin' On Up*
Clare Buckland, 1914– , and Diana Douglas, 1960– , Canada / 196
  Conscious Dying
Mary Caroline Richards, Oregon, 1916–1999 / 199
  Seeing with the Inner Eye
  How Can We Teach Love?
Twylah Nitsch, New York, 1920– / 202
  Digging a Hole Big Enough to Sit In
Ayya Khema, Germany, 1923– / 203
  From *Be an Island*
Carmen Bernos de Gasztold, France, c. 1925–?/ 205
  Prayer of the Cat
  Prayer of the Bee
  Prayer of the Butterfly
Leila Hadley, New York, 1925– / 207
  From *A Journey with Elsa Cloud*
José Hobday, Texas, 1928– / 209
  A "Beggar's" Gift: A Low-Budget Affair
Dorothy Walters, Oklahoma, 1928– / 211
  Why
  The Runaway
  Waiting
  A Kundalini Awakening

Marion Woodman, Canada, 1928– / 214
    Dancers: You Are Priests and Priestesses
    The Crone
Joanna Macy, California, 1929– / 216
    From *World as Lover, World as Self*
Ursula K. LeGuin, California, 1929– / 217
    Owl, Coyote, Soul
Thea O'Brien, Canada, 1930– / 219
    The Delight of Old Age
Anne Baring, England, 1931– / 220
    The Black Madonna
    Travels That Kindle Spirit
    Where Should I Turn for Guidance?
Toni Morrison, Ohio, 1931– / 223
    From *Beloved*
    A Wedding Sermon of the Reverend Senior Pulliam
    From *Her Nobel Lecture, December 7, 1993*
Audre Lorde, New York, 1934–1992 / 226
    The Erotic as Sacred
Jane Goodall, England, 1934– / 227
    Selections on Working with Chimpanzees
Mary Oliver, Ohio, 1935– / 230
    Wild Geese
Lucille Clifton, New York, 1936– / 231
    Holy Night
Sylvia Boorstein, New York, 1936– / 232
    Right Effort: "Remember, Be Happy"
Pema Chödrön, New Mexico, 1936– / 233
    From *Start Where You Are*
    From *When Things Fall Apart*
Chan Khong, Vietnam, 1938– / 236
    In the War Zone
Madeleine L'Engle, New York, Contemporary / 238
    From *"Mary Speaks"*
    Caring, One Person at a Time
    From *A Circle of Quiet*

Elizabeth S. Strahan, California, 1940– / 240
  Women of That Certain Age
Joan Chittister, Pennsylvania, Contemporary / 242
  A Time to Laugh
Sharon Olds, California, 1942– / 244
  New Mother
Julia Vinograd, California, 1943– / 245
  Ballad of Columbine High School Killings
Marilyn Krysl, Kansas, 1943– / 246
  Grandmother
Alice Walker, Georgia, 1944– / 247
  From *The Color Purple*
  From *The Universe Responds*
  From *The Temple of My Familiar*
Naomi Ruth Lowinsky, California, 1944– / 250
  Initiate (After H. D.)
Annie Dillard, Pennsylvania, 1945– / 251
  This Is Where the People Come Out
  Teaching a Stone to Talk
  Like a Hole in the Earth's Crust
Rachel Naomi Remen, MD, New York, Contemporary / 253
  A Room with a View
  The Recovery of the Sacred: Some Thoughts on Medical Reform
Michelle Lynn Ryan, California, 1945– / 256
  Midnight of the Soul (Fana Annihilation)
  Mountolive—The Apostate, Catacombs, 300 A.D.
  From *"Unde Malum?"*
Diana Eck, Montana, 1945– / 258
  Encountering God in Other Traditions
Christiane Northrup, MD, Maine, Contemporary / 260
  A One-Size-Fits-All Prescription
Regina Sara Ryan, New York, 1945– / 262
  The Way of Waiting
  The Way of the Warrior
Cynthia Bourgeault, Canada, 1945– / 264
  The Mystical Union of Two Souls

Carol Flinders, Oregon, 1945– / 266
    Our Daughters, Our Selves
Lauren Artress, Ohio, 1945– / 268
    From *Walking a Sacred Path*
Linda Hogan, Chickasaw People, 1947– / 270
    The Sweat Lodge
Luisah Teish, Louisiana, 1948– / 271
    Ancestor Reverence
Starhawk, California, Contemporary / 273
    Power-Over and Power-from-Within
Carolyn Myss, Illinois, Contemporary / 275
    On Healing
Kathleen Norris, South Dakota, 1950– / 276
    From *Dakota*
    Making Silence
    Feasting with the Benedictine Sisters
Nita Penfold, New York, 1950– / 279
    *The Woman with the Wild-Grown Hair Relaxes
        After Another Long Day*
Karen McCarthy Brown, New York, Contemporary / 281
    From *Mama Lola: A Vodou Priestess in Brooklyn*
Amy Tan, California, 1952– / 283
    From *The Joy Luck Club*
Fran Peavey, United States, Contemporary / 284
    The Chimpanzee at Stanford
Dominique Mazeaud, United States, Contemporary / 285
    The Great Cleansing of the Rio Grande
Tirzah Firestone, United States, 1954– / 287
    From *With Roots in Heaven*
Gurumayi Chidvilasananda, India, 1955– / 289
    Wake Up!
Adriana Diaz, California, 1955– / 292
    Tantric Tango
Louise Erdrich, North Dakota, 1955– / 294
    From *The Last Report on the Miracles at Little No Horse*
Nancy Diamante Bonazzoli, Massachusetts, 1957– / 296
    Lying with the Beloved

Marjorie Crocombe, Cook Islands, Contemporary / 297
  From *"The Healer"*
Sharon Lebell, California, 1957– / 300
  Conduct Yourself with Dignity
  Self-Mastery Is the Target That the Divine Will Wishes Us to Aim At
  Treasure Your Mind, Cherish Your Reason, Hold to Your Purpose
Eva Wong, Hong Kong, Contemporary / 301
  Taoist Chant and Dance
Maria Cristina Gonzalez, Texas, 1957– / 303
  The Nurturing of the Desert Mother: Ariditas
Paula Kane Robinson Arai, United States, Contemporary / 305
  To Become like a Plum Blossom (Not as Easy as It Sounds)
Lori Arviso Alvord, MD, New Mexico, 1959– / 307
  A Navajo Medicine Man Blesses the ICU
Rigoberta Menchú, Guatemala, 1959– / 308
  From *I, Rigoberta Menchú, an Indian Woman in Guatemala*
Oriah Mountain Dreamer, Canada, 1960– / 311
  The Invitation
Jackie Joyner-Kersee, Illinois, 1962– / 312
  Being an Athlete Is a Kind of Grace
Tracy Cochran, New York, Contemporary / 314
  Alexandra's First Retreat
  From *"Playing with God: A Child's Response to Religion"*
Toni Boehm, United States, Contemporary / 316
  Diagnosis
Malia Dominica Wong, Hawaii, 1964– / 318
  Recipes for Anyone Hungry on the Spiritual Path
Joan Duncan Oliver, Kentucky, Contemporary / 321
  Moving with Spirit
  The Spirit of Exercise
Tara Grabowsky, MD, Mexico, 1970– / 322
  Fury and Love
Julia Butterfly Hill, Arkansas, 1975– / 325
  The Storm
Miranda Shaw, United States, Contemporary / 327
  From *Passionate Enlightenment*
  Wild, Wise, Passionate: Dakinis in America

Sara Sviri, England, Contemporary / 329
     Black Light
     Khidr, the "Green Man"
Rashani, Birthplace Unknown, Contemporary / 331
     There Is a Brokenness
Koei Hoshino, Japan, Contemporary / 332
     The Zen Art of Cooking
Mercy Amba Oduyoye, Ghana, Contemporary / 334
     Woman with Beads
Clarissa Pinkola Estés, United States, Contemporary / 336
     Father Earth

INDEX OF AUTHORS AND SOURCES / 339
INDEX OF TITLES / 342
FOR FURTHER READING / 347
PERMISSIONS AND ACKNOWLEDGMENTS / 350
ABOUT THE EDITOR / 358

FOREWORD

I feel blessed and honored to be given a chance to write a foreword to Mary Ford-Grabowsky's glorious, subversive, pioneering anthology of women's sacred voices. In reading and rereading it, I feel as if long-vanished and suppressed parts of my own soul are being restored to it, as if sacred sounds and ranges of my own voice are being handed back to it, to nourish, strengthen, embolden, and inspire its song. I know already that *Sacred Voices* will be a permanent adventure, one whose significance will only grow with the years and with my own receptivity to the messages from the Sacred Feminine these wise, wild, vibrant voices are transmitting to us all.

I have known in my depths for a long time that the most profound reason for the contemporary holocaust of nature and of the psyche that we are all suffering from is the millennia-long degradation of the feminine and of the feminine as sacred. I have known this with deep pain and longing and in my own way tried to arrange all my life and thought and action to be inspired at ever-deeper levels by the Mother, to be initiated divinely by Her, as far as I could be, into the sanctity of all created life and of all relationships.

I have known also that the universe is the child of an endlessly fertile marriage between the "Father" and "Mother" aspects of God, between the Transcendence and the Immanence, the pure Light and the Matter emanated from it.

The obstacle that all of us meet when we try to meet the Mother in all Her power and glory, so that both the Feminine and Masculine aspects of the Divine marriage can be real to us and in us, is simply that, for thousands of years, our consciousness has been deprived of any access to Her—although she has never been and could never be absent from us and from Her cosmos. The Bride in us has been imprisoned in a dark cellar with black tape over Her mouth, and the keys either lost or thrown away.

How can there be a true marriage without a Bride restored to her full dignity, with all the nuances of her voice hallowed and revered just as sacredly as the voice of the Bridegroom?

Now in this wonderful anthology, the black tape over the Bride's mouth has been removed, and I can hear Her speaking in a vast variety of Her voices—as nun, as victim soul, as woman traveler, as teacher, as doctor, as ravaged woman of the world, as mystic poet, as sacred prostitute, as hedonist, as satirist, as agonized subversive, as moralist and iconoclast. All the forbidden voices of the One voice are here allowed to play in their holy intensity and in their mysterious interconnection.

So as I read and love and celebrate and allow myself to be elated and harangued and calmed and made wilder by the voices in this glorious book, my inner Bride becomes more and more transparent, more and more majestic, and more and more down-home, fuller in her transcendent glory and in her no-nonsense, sober, immanent truth, and the marriage within me as a male and as someone who aspires to the sacred androgyny that is the birth of the Father-Mother becomes more and more vivid and mysterious.

It is this vividness and this mystery that this magnificent anthology makes available to us all, male or female, gay or straight. We are immeasurably enriched, suddenly seated, as if by Divine magic, at the feast of the marriage, whose celebratory joy announces a restored nature, transfigured institutions, the birth of tantric love, a healed psyche, the intermeshing and intermingling in perfect communion of the sacred voices of the Father and—now, here, and forever—the sacred voices of the Mother.

ANDREW HARVEY

SPECIAL ACKNOWLEDGMENTS

$\mathcal{A}$xel L. Grabowsky, my beloved, for the soaring spirit, love of learning, consummate research skills, and peaceful mind he brought to this book and brings to daily life.

Tara Grabowsky, for the incomparable reward of being her mother; for the joy of watching her unfold through all the years; for the beauty of her contribution to this book.

Tom Grady, a wonderful agent, editor, writer, and a beacon of light in the world. I feel blessed to know him.

John Loudon of HarperSanFrancisco, a brilliant editor to whom I am deeply indebted for a wealth of insights and ideas.

Kris Ashley, for the pleasure of working with her, and for her huge contribution to this book: my warmest thanks.

Kathi Goldmark, whose amazing talents and strong spirit of helpfulness have made all the difference: my deepest possible gratitude.

Priscilla Stuckey, with boundless admiration and gratitude for her copyediting; she is better than the best.

Jim Warner, a consummate artist, for gracing this book with a beautiful cover.

Lisa Zuniga, the perfect production editor, who has mastered the art of grace under pressure.

Lauren Artress, for permission to reprint excerpts from *Walking a Sacred Path*, and for her enormous contribution to church and society.

Anne Baring, for her kind permission to reprint from *The Myth of the Goddess* and *The One Work*.

Toni Boehm, for permission to reprint from *The Spiritual Intrepreneur* and for her wide-reaching leadership.

Tracy Cochran, for permission to reprint deep and delightful excerpts from her publications in *Parabola* and *The Best Spiritual Writing, 1999.*

Adriana Diaz, for illumining insights into sacred dance, and for the joy of her friendship.

Diana Douglas and Clare Buckland, for sharing their sacred story.

Margaret Fermoyle Flagg, for conversations about God from the time we were seventeen and fell in love with Pascal.

Carol Flinders, for gracious permission to reprint from her wonderful book *At the Root of This Longing.*

Austin Ford Sr., my twin, for inspirited, deeply caring support and endless helpfulness.

Austin Ford Jr., my nephew, a brilliant thinker, whose disarming charm is a gift I treasure.

Helen Ford, without whose loving support and encouragement this book would not exist.

Tory Ford, my beloved niece, for the caring, intelligence, and knowledge she poured into a list of suggestions for this book (all of which I used).

Matthew Fox, for his brilliant elucidation of creation-centered theology and for his support of my work since 1983 and especially of this book; I am infinitely grateful.

Nancy Freedom, a great yoga teacher and librarian: my deepest gratitude for invaluable research help.

Barbara Gibson, who brought so much culture, learning, intelligence, and passion to this book as my research assistant that no words are big enough to hold my gratitude.

Maria Cristina Gonzalez, for her gorgeous, unique spirituality of *ariditas.*

Leila Hadley, for so kindly allowing me to reprint enchanting material from *Journey with Elsa Cloud.*

Eryk Hanut, cherished friend, brilliant writer, huge soul; with a heart full of love and gratitude for all the encouragement, time, and inspiration he contributed to this book.

Andrew Harvey, "a flute that the Christ's breath moves through." I cherish and thank him with all my heart.

Jane Hirshfield, *inspiratrice,* for her poetry, translations, and beautiful book, *Women in Praise of the Sacred.*

Janabai, dearest friend on the path, for her teachings and surrender.

Llewellen Vaughan Lee of the Golden Sufi Center in Inverness, California, for the gift of beautiful books: Sara Sviri's, Irina Tweedie's, and his own.

Naomi Ruth Lowinsky, for the gift of deeply illuminating words.

Sr. Mary Juan Mahan, for a lifetime of inspiration.

Betty McAfee, for bringing the gifts of a filmmaker, writer, and poet to the task of editing, and providing more help than she knows.

Joan Duncan Oliver, for permission to reprint excerpts from her beautiful book *Contemplative Living*.

Michelle Ryan, Sufi mystic, poet, and friend, the only person I have ever known to be genuinely called to life alone. To her, my most loving, admiring, respectful gratitude.

Regina Sara Ryan, for permission to reprint wonderful material from her book *The Woman Awake: Feminine Wisdom for Spiritual Life*.

Debby Sloan, who gave me books about Unity and showed me through her own generosity what daily practice of spiritual teachings accomplishes.

Sr. Malia Dominica Wong, for the beauty of her writing and her soul.

My friends from the Women's Spirituality Group in Princeton, New Jersey, my first initiators in the Sacred Feminine: Violet Franks, Bineke Oort, Darlene Prestbo, Hazel Staats-Westover.

The generous people who helped me with research at the Graduate Theological Union in Berkeley, California; the University of California at Berkeley; Stanford University in Palo Alto, California; Harvard Divinity School in Cambridge, Massachusetts; Princeton University and Princeton Theological Seminary in Princeton, New Jersey.

All the men of radiant, strong, soaring spirits through whom I revere the Sacred Masculine: my grandfathers, father, twin brother, nephew, son-in-law, male teachers, priests, ministers, rabbis, writers, artists, friends in a lifetime of love and respect.

This book began when I was seventeen, a college freshman majoring in theology. One morning that fall I was in a French lit class taught by Sister Juan, a tall and lanky, hilariously funny, warm and brilliant nun who was also the housemother in our dorm. She mentioned that when she came across a quote she loved, she copied it onto a bit of paper and taped it inside her closet door. I soon had covered not only the door but all the walls of my closet with strips of white paper the size of Band-Aids, each with an inspiring message from readings that semester.

Quite a few years later, I was a college teacher, Axel's wife, and Tara's mother, moving for the third time. Peeling the third crop of little messages from the inside of *all* the closet doors and *all* the walls of *all* the closets, I noticed for the first time that most of my citations were from men. I was too busy to give it much thought, and went on packing. Then during our fourth move when I was harvesting a fourth crop, this time on state-of-the-art yellow Post-Its, I noticed it again and began seriously wondering why I almost never copied down any quotes from women. But it was only during our fifth move, packing up yet another harvest of beautiful words— this time on hot pink, green, and lavender, as well as yellow, Post-Its—that it really struck me.

I carefully read each message before placing it in the old box that had traveled with us from Boston to Mexico; Mexico to Bonn, Germany; Bonn back to Boston; Boston to Princeton; and now in 1995 would journey from Princeton to the San Francisco Bay. There was a line I loved from St. Francis of Assisi: "Praise be to you, my Lord, for Brother Son, who is beautiful and glorious and gives us the light of day." There was one of Pascal's great *pensees*: "The heart has its reasons that reason will never understand." A verse from Ibn al-Arabi: "Listen Beloved! I am the reality of the world." There were sublime teachings from Jesus, like the Beatitudes; and from the Buddha, especially on the cessation of suffering. Bernard of Clairvaux was there, on mystical love. Several selections from Camus. One each from Beethoven ("O, deliver me from these heavy depths"); Henri Bergson ("Behind every joke lies a tragedy"), and Kierkegaard ("To will one thing"). Plus hundreds and hundreds of others.

All of them had to do with some common denominator I couldn't name. Was it religion? Theology? Philosophy? Ethics? No, the key to the whole collection was experience of the sacred. It was men-who-knew-the-Divine that had been nurturing, guiding, inspiring, sustaining me all these years, filling my life with grace. The Divine Masculine, men's sacred voices—from all over the world, East and West, North and South—had been inspiring me on the best days of my life and encouraging me on the worst.

Among the Post-Its were three from women mystics. Only three: Teresa of Avila, Emily Dickinson, and Simone Weil. The discovery hit me in the stomach.

How could I have ignored the sacred wisdom of my own sex? The wisdom of my mother, grandmothers, all my aunts, my daughter, my niece, my sister-in-law, my friends, the luminosity of half the human family? A broad movement of women's spirituality had grown up all around me and I hadn't heard a word. Yes, I was abroad—three years in Mexico, three years in Germany—and I was busy, but women's spirituality was flourishing all over Latin America and Europe. I was puzzled. Something was prompting me to filter it out, some long acceptance or passivity or submission to cultural norms had deafened me to women's wisdom. Why was I ignoring not only other women's voices but the Divine Feminine in myself? I felt like I was missing half of my soul.

A powerful memory came up of attending a women's spirituality group five years earlier, in 1990, in Princeton, New Jersey, and how shocked I was when, during the most sacred part of the ritual, the women had whispered, talked, joked, and laughed. I had been horrified at their "irreverence," at what seemed like disrespect and superficiality. Even when the ritual was completed and we were sitting on the floor around the altar, now transformed into a coffee table, and were chatting and "feasting" on wine and cheese, purple grapes, fresh-baked breads and homemade cakes, even then I felt uncomfortable.

I had never seen women go anywhere near an altar, let alone eat at one. Since earliest childhood, my soul was steeped in the hushed solemnity and grandeur of high Christian masses and sacramental rites designed in the Middle Ages by men for men—deeply religious men who were not quite sure that women (and animals) had souls and therefore omitted from their liturgies all consideration of women's needs, gifts, wisdom, and love.

Looking back at that holy ritual created-by-women-for-women, I suddenly "got" it! I finally understood how important and freeing that evening was. The Sacred Feminine was being allowed to flame out without constraints on that beautiful altar-made-by-women-for-women, with its tiny flickering flames, shiny stones soaking in oil, white shells, and sweet fragrances of flowers and incense. I felt the fire of Divine immanence leaping out from the vibrant spirits of happy women—and from the plants and tables and chairs and walls and Otis, the wiry gray cat who alternated between his usual feistiness and cuddling up in our laps. The very room where we were celebrating was a shrine. A woman's shrine. How warm and intimate it had felt to pray, dance, chant, laugh, feast with other women, to connect with our eyes and words and hands, to be close to that altar blazing in holy light. Women's most cherished values were being allowed expression: spontaneity, flexibility, connectedness, the spirit of love and joy. Here women were free to be themselves, shedding patriarchal constraints and soul-crushing stereotypes, doing what women love to do, being what women love to be. Women's rituals were providing a desperately needed, antipuritanical correction to father religions so ignorant of woman's soul.

From that moment on, from that one flash of insight in 1995, I promised myself I would start collecting sacred messages from women. Like an archaeologist digging into holy ground, I would go searching and preserve what I found for the rest of my life, to know my past as a woman and feel whole. How perfectly poet Mary Oliver captured the moment:

> One day you finally knew
> what you had to do, and began.

Now it is 2001. The era of sacred Post-Its has long since melted away. My closet doors and walls look naked without them. I need more space on my hard drive, and thirty-seven disks back up writings and bios from hundreds and hundreds of women mystics, contemplatives, healers, rabbis, singers, dancers, artists, nurses, physicians, teachers, homemakers, workers for the poor, founders of movements and communities. I now know that women's sacred voices resound like a trumpet call through all the centuries, across every country and culture in the world, and today more than ever are making a glorious sound in praise of reality, life, Goddess/God.

Getting to know these voices has been an initiation into the unknown Feminine in myself and has brought me, unexpectedly and sometimes in spite of myself, into a new place of dormant power, of sacred feminine energy in myself. I no longer avoid the Feminine, I no longer avoid the "other half" of my soul that I was taught to see as inferior. I now understand that women's holiness reveals the Mother side of God, the Divine Mother whom billions of Hindus and indigenous peoples have known for untold millennia. Now "She" is as real to me as "He." As Julian of Norwich said:

As surely as God is our Father, just as surely is She our Mother.

In 1997 I participated in a moving initiation ritual for three twelve-year-old girls (see Luisah Teish, 271). One of the most impressive parts came at the end, when the radiant initiates suddenly picked up baskets overflowing with small packages they had been preparing for weeks and then ran out among the three hundred people present to give each of us a gift. Inside was a colored eggshell with earth and seeds in it (which I planted and treasure to this day).

With that wonderful event in mind, I want to complete my initiation into the Feminine with the gift of this book. I hope you will be as enriched as I have been by the "Voices from History" in Part I, by the "Voices from Our Times" in Part II, and especially by the stories in the introductions.

My years of expeditions into the deepest library floors and the dustiest stacks uncovered jewels of information, anecdotes, and revelations about the motivation and lifestyles of the 172 women brought together here. I have placed many of these biographical details in the introductions because they came to mean almost more to me than the writings. I was amazed at the courage they reveal. I had no idea of the monumental strength, the perseverance, the warrior behavior that appears continuously across time. I had expected the spiritual beauty and tenderness, the love and quiet wisdom, but not the towering, tested, truly holy strength. The stories made all the difference in the way to understand woman's soul, to put the two pieces together and experience at firsthand how vastly different the truth is from a stereotype.

I think of Perpetua (see page 26), Agape (page 30), Margery Kempe (page 96), Chan Khong (page 236), Julia Butterfly Hill (page 325), and so many more, whether heroines of the great, or heroines of the everyday. What they did matches what they said; what they said matches what they believed.

You will also find the writers' dates and birthplaces—insofar as we have knowledge of them—either the country in which they were born or, in the case of Americans, the state.

My initiation in the Divine Feminine is complete, and a new era of my journey is coming into view. It is time to raise once again that priceless question Mary Oliver poses for every stage of our lives:

> What is it you plan to do
> with your one wild and precious life?

MARY FORD-GRABOWSKY
SAN FRANCISCO
JULY 4, 2001

PART 1

VOICES OF
HISTORY

ANONYMOUS HYMN
IN PRAISE OF INANNA

MESOPOTAMIA, SECOND OR THIRD MILLENNIUM B.C.E.

Inanna rests at the very foundation of global civilization as the archetype of the Sacred Feminine. The Great Mother Goddess of ancient Sumea, she was known in Babylonia as Ishtar. Fragments of hymns and prayers to Inanna Ishtar have endured for five thousand years, and perhaps longer. Images discovered in the verses are echoed in every century of history and throughout the entire world in the biblical figures of Eve, Sophia, and Mary the mother of Jesus; the Gnostic Great Mother; the Shekhinah in the Jewish Kabbalah, and indigenous, Hindu, and Buddhist goddesses.

This powerful chant sings the praises of Inanna in her role as Queen of Heaven, a title that Mary the mother of Jesus would inherit some two or three thousand years later.

~⌐

SHE MADE THE NIGHT COME FORTH
LIKE THE MOONLIGHT

She made the night come forth like the moonlight,
She made the morning come forth like the sun.
On her sacred bed the sweet night came to an end,
All the lands and the black-haired people were assembling—
Who had slept on the roofs, who had slept on the walls—
Chanting prayers they approached her, to bring her their words,
Then did she study their words, knowing those with evil intent,
Against them rendering judgment, while
Looking with kind eyes on the truthful,
Blessing them.

Inanna, I sing your praise.

A PRIESTESS OF INANNA

SUMEA, C. 2000 B.C.E.

Almost nothing is known of the author of this rapturous poem, a celebra-
tion of sacred sexuality rites. Her poem dramatizes the ancient Sumerian
myth of Inanna and Dumuzi, whose ecstatic sexual union caused the earth
to bloom. Every year in ancient Sumer at the new year, a priestess of
Inanna and the ruling king would consummate sexual union to sustain the
political and cultural flowering of Sumer. The author of the poem may have
been a priestess named Kubatum, whose name was engraved on a necklace
given to her by "Shu-Sin," the Bridegroom of the poem. Archaeologists exca-
vated the necklace at a temple site in Sumer. A curious element of the poem,
the Bride's invocation of her parents, may symbolize the perpetuation of life
from generation to generation.

BRIDEGROOM, BELOVED OF MY HEART

Bridegroom, beloved of my heart,
Your pleasure is my pleasure, honey sweet;
Lion, beloved of my heart,
Your pleasure is my pleasure, honey sweet.

You have won my soul, I stand now trembling before you,
Bridegroom, carry me now to the bed.
You have won my soul, I stand now trembling before you,
Lion, carry me now to the bed.

Bridegroom, let me give you my caresses,
My sweet one, wash me with honey—
In the bed that is filled with honey,
Let us enjoy our love.
Lion, let me give you my caresses,
My sweet one, wash me with honey.

Bridegroom, now we have taken our pleasure,
Tell my mother, she will give you sweets,

Tell my father, he will give you gifts.

Your spirit—do I not know how to please it?
Bridegroom, sleep in our house till dawn.
Your heart—do I not know how to warm it?
Lion, sleep in our house till dawn.

Because you love me,
Lion, give me your caresses—
My husband and guardian, my spirit magician,
My Shu-Sin who gladdens the Wind-God's heart—
Give me your caresses, because you love me.

The place sweet as honey, put in your sweetness—
Like flour into the measure, squeeze in your sweetness—
Like pounding dry flour into the cup to be measured,
Pound in, pound in your sweetness—

These words I sing for Inanna.

TRANSLATED BY JANE HIRSHFIELD

HASHEPSOWE
EGYPT, RULED 1503–1482 B.C.E.

The formidable Hashepsowe was the only one of the five queens of ancient Egypt who ruled in her own right. The daughter of Pharaoh Tuthmosis I, she was said to be chosen to rule by the god Amun-Re, her birth midwifed by four goddesses. Hashepsowe was proud of her own achievements and immortalized herself in writings full of hyperbole, according to the custom of Egyptian kings. While Egypt accorded more dignity and respect to women than any other ancient civilization, there was no real approval for a woman to rule alone, and, predictably, Hashepsowe's power was contested by her younger half-brother. She responded by taking for herself the titles of a king and putting on the linen kilt, pectoral, and double crown of a male pharaoh. This iron-willed woman prevailed over all opposition and ruled successfully for over twenty years.

Considerable information about Hashepsowe has been transmitted to us through many histories of ancient Egypt, a brief biography, sacred inscriptions on tombs and monuments erected by her subjects, and writings she caused to be carved on her own monuments and in her great funerary temple at Deir el Bahri. (Reconstructed after three thousand years of neglect, the temple is a tourist attraction regarded by many as the most beautiful temple in Egypt today.) One inscription notes that Hashepsowe controlled all Egypt, and "all Egypt bowed the head to her." On one of her typically ambitious constructions, a giant obelisk, which weighs one thousand tons, in the Karnak temple east of the Nile, she left an inscription boasting how in only seven months the massive column was quarried, transported, plated in pure gold, and erected.

The selections here come from various inscriptions written by Pharaoh Hashepsowe.

~୨

HAIL, KING . . . FEMALE SUN!

What was within her was godlike and godlike was everything she did. She had the spirit of a god. Her Majesty became a beautiful maiden, blossoming out. At that moment, the goddess Uto applauded her loveliness. Her beauty was divine. She was a woman of distinction; her bearing was dignified.

O my mother Nut, stretch yourself over me, place me among the imperishable stars, that I live eternally like you.

And you who after long years shall see these monuments, who shall speak of what I have done, you will say "we do not know how they can have made a whole monument of gold as if it were an ordinary task." To gild them, I have given gold measured by the bushel, as though it were sacks of grain. Never had the two lands [of Egypt] seen the like. When you shall hear this, do not say that this is boastful. Say "How like her this was!"

ANONYMOUS LOVE SONG

EGYPT, BETWEEN 1300 AND 1100 B.C.E.

This lovely poem was transmitted to us without any information about the author, who is generally considered female.

~⁀

MY HAND IS IN YOUR HAND

The voice of the swallow is singing and says,
"The land has brightened—
What road do you walk?"
You shall not, little bird, trouble me!
I have found my beloved in his bed.
And my heart gladdened all the more
When he said to me:
"I will not go far away
My hand is in your hand."

SAPPHO

LESBOS, GREECE, SEVENTH CENTURY B.C.E.

Sappho was the leader and teacher of a group of young women poets on the Greek island of Lesbos, where she was born. The first woman poet in the Western tradition, she wrote about the sacredness of sexuality and sensuality on the path to reunion with the Divine. Her works were presumably destroyed with the burning of the great library at Alexandria, but fragments quoted by other writers have endured as well as one complete poem, her "Ode to Aphrodite." Plato wrote of her:

> *Some say nine muses—but count again.*
> *Behold the tenth: Sappho of Lesbos.*

The Greek people referred to her as "the poetess" and imprinted her por-
trait on a coin. We know little of her life, except that she married and had a
daughter named Kleis to whom she wrote poems.

~)

THANK YOU, MY DEAR

Thank you, my dear,

You came, and you did
well to come: I needed
you. You have made

love blaze up in
my breast—bless you!
Bless you as often

as the hours have
been endless to me
while you were gone.

TRANSLATED BY
MARY BERNARD

LEAVE CRETE

Leave Crete,
Aphrodite,
and come to this
sacred place
encircled by apple trees,
fragrant with offered smoke.

Here, cold springs
sing softly
amid the branches;
the ground is shady with roses;

from trembling young leaves,
a deep drowsiness pours.

In the meadow,
horses are cropping
the wildflowers of spring,
scented fennel
blows on the breeze.

In this place,
Lady of Cyprus, pour
the nectar that honors you
into our cups,
gold, and raised up for drinking.

TRANSLATED BY
JANE HIRSHFIELD

PATACARA

INDIA, SIXTH OR FIFTH CENTURY B.C.E.

Born to well-to-do parents who arranged their children's marriages, Patacara was horrified at her family's selection for her and ran away with her lover, one of the family's servants. Some years later when she was expecting her second child, she set off with her first child on a strenuous journey to her parents' home. By the time her husband caught up with them, they were in a raging storm. While he was collecting wood for a fire, a poisonous snake bit him, inflicting a fatal wound. The shock of his sudden death brought on Patacara's labor, and she delivered her baby in the forest with only her infant at her side. Not long afterward she set out again for her parents' home, and, as she tried to cross a flooded river, both of her children drowned. When she reached her parents' home, only to learn they were dead, she lost her mind.

Wandering aimlessly around the countryside, her clothes in tatters, she came upon the Buddha, who looked at her disheveled state and said to her, "Sister, recover your presence of mind," which she did. Patacara took up the study of the Four Noble Truths and Eightfold Path of Buddhist practice and eventually requested ordination as a nun, becoming, like her follower

Canda (see below), a member of the first Buddhist community of women.
Her writing appears, as do theirs, in the Therigatha, *the collection of*
enlightenment poems composed by the first Buddhist nuns.

~♪

I'VE DONE WHAT I WAS TAUGHT

I've done what I was told.
I followed my teacher's advice.
Without laziness or pride.
Why haven't I found emptiness?

I bathed and saw the water
trickle down the hill.
I meditated, focused my mind,
As though training a powerful horse.

Then I took an oil lamp
to my tiny room,
sat down on my wooden cot,
took out a needle
and pushed the wick way down.

When the room went dark,
I was freed.

CANDA

INDIA, SIXTH OR FIFTH CENTURY B.C.E.

Canda is one of the first of the five hundred women (more or less) to be
admitted to the Buddhist community, which originally accepted only men.
It was largely because of the persuasive powers of Pajapati, the aunt who
raised the Buddha after his mother died in the first week of his life, that
women were admitted and ordained as nuns. When Pajapati first approached
the Buddha with her request, he responded, "Enough, Pajapati! Don't set
your heart on women being allowed to do this." But under her pressure, he

relented, ordaining her as the first Buddhist nun, assuring her place in the history of the movement as the "Founding Mother" of Buddhism. Canda was typical of women who were cut off from society because of the loss of their families and who joined the community to find new meaning for their lives. After her parents, husband, and children succumbed to a plague epidemic, she happened to meet one of the foremost nuns at this time, Patacara (see p. 15), who had also lost her family through a series of tragedies and could provide exactly the guidance Canda needed. Canda advanced rapidly on the path to freedom. Her poem comes from the Therigatha, the collection composed by the first Buddhist women.

~9

I WAS LOST

I was lost,
my husband dead,
no children, no friends,
no relatives to shelter me.
I became a beggar
wandering with my bowl
for seven years
in heat and cold
from town to town.

I met a woman
with food and water,
a nun, I begged her
"Take me into homelessness."
It was Patacara.
Understanding,
she taught me
how to leave home,
she inspired me,
guided me to the ultimate.
No word was wasted.
I followed her advice.

Gone my obsessions,
I understand.

METTIKA

INDIA, SIXTH OR FIFTH CENTURY B.C.E.

Mettika was one of the earliest female followers of the Buddha. Her magnificent poem-prayer is a translation from the Therigatha, *a collection of seventy-three enlightenment poems written by the first Buddhist women. Like the first male monks, these Buddhist women committed themselves to a life of meditation in pursuit of enlightenment. The* Therigatha *was transmitted orally for about five hundred years before being recorded in the first century* B.C.E.

~)

PSALM

Though I be suffering and weak, and all
My youthful spring be gone, yet have I come
Leaning upon my staff, and clambered up
The mountain peak.
My cloak thrown off,
My little bowl o'erturned, so sit I here
Upon the rock. And o'er my spirit sweeps
The breath of liberty! 'Tis won. 'Tis won.
The triple lore!
The Buddha's will is done.

TRANSLATOR UNKNOWN

SUMANGALAMATA

INDIA, SIXTH OR FIFTH CENTURY B.C.E.

Sumangalamata, also known as Sumangala's mother, belonged to the first community of ordained Buddhist women, whose writings were collected in the Therigatha. *In the following poem, in a burst of happiness, she celebrates her joyful and promising new life. For she has abandoned household tasks that have become meaningless to her and gone off into the forest, where she will assuredly prepare meals again and wash more pots and pans but without drudgery, following the Buddha's teachings on her own path.*

~⁀

AT LAST FREE!

Free! At last free!
No longer tied to the kitchen,
Bound to my pots and pans!
No longer bound to a husband
who never looked at me.
Free of anger! Free of despair!
How glad I am
To sit at the foot of a tree,
Focusing my mind.
I am peaceful, I am free.

PRAXILLA
GREECE, C. 450 B.C.E.

Praxilla wrote lyric poetry prolifically, but few of her works—primarily fragments—have survived, probably because people of her era demeaned women's writing and, judging it unworthy of preservation, destroyed or discarded it. The beautiful lines below come from her poem "Adonis," which contains Adonis's response to the question posed to him by the Shades of the Underworld after his death: "What was the most beautiful thing you left behind?" These lines endured because Zenobius quoted them in his dictionary of proverbs to explain the maxim "Sillier than Praxilla's Adonis." Only a simpleton, he added, could put cucumbers in the same poem with the sun and moon. Praxilla lived in Sicyon, close to the southern coast of the Gulf of Corinth.

~⁀

CUCUMBERS, APPLES, AND PEARS

Most beautiful
Of all the things that I have left
Is the light of the sun;
next, gleaming stars
and the face of the moon.
Then cucumbers in the summer,
And apples and pears.

THE BOOK OF RUTH
PALESTINE, FIRST MILLENNIUM B.C.E.

The loving-kindness of the heroine of the book of Ruth has charmed Hebrew Scriptures readers for well over two thousand years. The book expresses a deeply moving stream of Hebrew thought that sees the Israelites as "a light to the nations" and "a blessing on the earth" (while other books of the Bible portray the Israelites as an inward-looking, warring tribe that forbids its men to marry outside the community). The book tells the story of Ruth, a foreigner from the land of the Moabites, and Naomi, her Jewish mother-in-law. When Ruth is widowed, she chooses to share the lot of her husband's people, accompanying her beloved mother-in-law to Judah and abandoning the comfort of her native land. In Judah, her loyalty to Naomi inspires the love of Boaz, whom Ruth marries. She will also be remembered as the great-grandmother of King David.

~✑

WHERE YOU GO WILL I GO

Entreat me not to leave you,
Nor to return from following after you.
For where you go will I go,
Where you dwell will I dwell.
Your people will be my people
And your God my God.
Where you die will I die also,

And there will I be buried.
May God do this to me and more
If death part me from you.

RUTH 1.16–17

JUDITH

PALESTINE, SECOND HALF OF THE SECOND CENTURY B.C.E.

In the book of Judith, from the apocryphal Hebrew Scriptures, a woman emerges as a wisdom figure, prophetic leader, and heroine who saves the Jewish people from massacre by a vastly superior army. Whether "Judith" represents a woman's voice or a portrayal of a woman's voice by a man, her story is vital to women's history, especially today, when many female revolutionary leaders in a number of countries are looking to her for inspiration and strength. Guatemala's Rigoberta Menchú (see p. 308), for example, and Sister Eufracina Brandigan in the Philippines see Judith as a model for fighting a "just war" despite inevitable violence.

Many passages in the book celebrate women's leadership, as when Judith acknowledges, "I am about to do something which will go down through all generations of our descendants" (Judith 8.32b). Or when the enemy admits they "admired the Israelites, judging them by her, and everyone said to his neighbor, 'Who can despise these people, who have women like this among them?'" (Judith 10.19b).

∼⟩

IN PRAISE OF JUDITH'S COURAGE

[Judith and her attendant go to the enemy camp, where she gains admittance to the quarters of the leader, Holofernes, by pretending to betray her people, and says to him: "God has sent me to accomplish with you things that will astonish the whole world." A few days later, after he has drunk too much wine and fallen asleep, Judith prays for resolve.]

She went up to the post at the end of the bed, above Holofernes' head, and took down his sword that hung there. She came close to his bed and took hold of the hair on his head, and said: "Give me

strength this day, O lord God of Israel!" And she struck his neck twice
with all her might, and severed his head from his body. Then
she...gave Holofernes' head to her maid, who put it in her food bag.

[The two escape to the Israelite camp, where no one had
expected them to return alive.]

And Uzziah said to her, "O daughter, you are blessed by the Most
High God above all women on earth! And blessed be the Lord God
who created the heavens and the earth, who has guided you to
strike down the leader of our enemy. Your hope will never depart
from the hearts of men, as they remember the power of God. May
God grant this be a perpetual honor for you, and may he visit you
with blessings, because you did not spare your own life when our
nation was brought low, but have avenged our ruin, walking in the
straight path before our God." And all the people said, "So be it, so
be it."...

[Achior] fell at Judith's feet and knelt before her and said: "Blessed
are you in every tent of Judah. In every nation those who hear your
name will be alarmed."

[Then the high priest and senators come to greet Judith and all
bless her.]

"You are the exaltation of Jerusalem! You are the great glory of
Jerusalem! You are the great pride of our nation. You have done all
this singlehanded; you have done great good for Israel, and God is
well pleased with it. May the Almighty Lord bless you forever." And
all the people answered, "So be it!"

JUDITH 11.16b; 13.6–10, 18–20;

14.7; 15.9c–10, RSV

ANONYMOUS LAMENT

MESOPOTAMIA, ANCIENT ORAL TRADITION, B.C.E.

*In this millennia-old chant, believed to have been written by a woman,
Tammuz is the lover of the Great Mother Goddess, Ishtar.*

LAMENT OF THE FLUTES FOR TAMMUZ

When he is no more a lament rises:
"O my beloved."

When he is no more, her lament rises:
"O my beloved."

Beneath the deep-rooted cedar tree, shady and silvery,
At Eanna, over mountains and hills, her lament rings out,
"O my beloved."

A world is rising to weep with her.
No longer does the grass grow green;
No longer does the grain grow tall;
No longer is there joy in the home.
She is a weary woman, a girl withered far too soon.
The river weeps for the willows that disappear;
Swamps weep for the lake and the fish that have gone;
Pastures weep for the flowers that have gone;
Fields weep for the missing herbs and grains;
Forests weep for the grasses that are parched;
Hills and valleys weep for the cypresses;
The vineyards weep for the dying vines;
The palace weeps for the life that is no more.

MARY THE MOTHER OF JESUS
PALESTINE, FIRST CENTURY C.E.

*One of the world's most treasured prayers, the Magnificat spoken by Mary
the mother of Jesus has been prayed for almost two thousand years. According
to the Gospel of Luke, it contains Mary's response to the angel who
announced to her that she was to be the mother of Jesus. In recent decades,
the prayer has been interpreted by liberation theologians, especially in Latin*

America, *as a message of hope to the poor. The Magnificat reflects the tradi-*
tion of Hannah's Prayer in the Hebrew Scriptures (1 Samuel 2.1–10).

~⁹

THE MAGNIFICAT

My soul magnifies the Lord,
and my spirit rejoices in God my Savior.
For he has regarded the low estate of his handmaiden;
For behold, henceforth all generations shall call me blessed;
For he who is mighty has done great things for me,
and holy is his name.
And his mercy is on those who fear him
from generation to generation.
He has shown strength with his arm,
he has scattered the proud in the imagination of their hearts,
He has put down the mighty from their thrones,
and exalted those of low degree;
He has filled the hungry with good things,
and the rich he has sent empty away.
He has helped his servant Israel,
in remembrance of his mercy,
as he spoke to our fathers,
to Abraham, and to his posterity forever.

LUKE 1.46–55, RSV

THE GOSPEL OF MARY
PALESTINE, FIRST CENTURY C.E.

Mary Magdalen came from Magdala on the western side of the Sea of
Galilee and was an especially important member of the Jesus movement in
the first half of the first century, loved and esteemed by Jesus. She has been
identified with an unnamed, repentant sinner, perhaps a prostitute, who is
mentioned in the Gospel of Luke (7.37–50). She is cited specifically as the
person from whom Jesus "cast out seven demons," perhaps a symbolic way
of saying he healed her of an unknown affliction, and she accompanied

Jesus and cared for him as he traveled, preached, and healed. Historians suppressed her incalculable significance as the fountainhead of a vast stream of Christian women's spirituality that included countless unknown desert mothers, abbesses, women leaders like Egeria (see p. 32), conscientious objectors, saints, deacons, and others.

The following excerpt from the extrabiblical Gospel of Mary exposes conflict about the place of women that had quickly broken out in the early church after the death of Jesus. The writer, most likely a man, imagines Mary Magdalen recounting a vision in which Jesus appears to her to impart new knowledge and to honor her. Andrew and Peter, perhaps envying her especially close friendship with Jesus, refuse to take her seriously until Levi comes to her defense acknowledging that "[Jesus] loved her more than us."

~〇

FROM THE GOSPEL OF MARY: THE SACREDNESS OF MARY MAGDALEN TO JESUS

When the Blessed One went away... [the disciples] grieved and mourned greatly, saying, "How shall we go to the Gentiles and preach the Gospel of the Kingdom of the Son of Man? If even he was not spared, how shall we be spared?"

Then Mary stood up and greeted all of her brothers and said to them, "Do not mourn or grieve or be irresolute, for his grace will be with you all and will defend you. Rather, let us praise His greatness, for He prepared us and taught us to be men." When Mary said this, they took heart, and they began to discuss the words of the Son of Man.

Peter said to Mary, "Sister, we know that the Savior loved you more than other women [cf. John 11.5, Luke 10.38–42]. Tell us the words of the Savior which you have heard in your vision since you know them and we do not."

Mary answered, saying, "What was hidden from you I will impart to you." And she began to say the following words to them. "I saw the Lord in a vision and I said to him, 'Lord, I saw you today in a vision.' He answered and said to me, 'Blessed are you since you did not waver at the sight of me.'" [Then Mary related what Jesus said to her.]

When she had said this, she was silent.... But Andrew answered, saying to the brothers, "Say what you think concerning what she said, I do not believe that the Savior said these things. For these ideas are not His teachings."

Then also Peter opposed her concerning these ideas and asked the brothers about the Savior: "Did he then speak secretly with a woman [cf. John 4.27], in preference to us, and not openly to all of us? Are we to turn back and listen to her? Did he prefer her to us?" Then Mary was sorrowful and said to Peter, "My brother Peter, what do you think? Do you think that I thought this up by myself in my heart? That I am lying about the Savior?"

Levi answered and said to Peter, "Peter, you are always angry. You are contending against the woman just like our adversaries. But if the Savior made her worthy, who are you to reject her? Surely the Savior knew her very well [cf. Luke 10.38–42]. For this reason he loved her more than us [cf. John 11.15], and we ought to be ashamed and put on the Perfect Man and proclaim the gospel as He commanded us."... When Levi had said this, they began to go out to preach the gospel of Christ.

PERPETUA

CARTHAGE (TUNISIA, NORTH AFRICA), C. 182–202 OR 203

Perpetua's diary is one of the most gripping and moving documents in the history of women's spiritual literature. A monument to courage born of conviction, to woman's towering power of commitment to beliefs she holds sacred, the diary recounts the last days of a woman only twenty years old, a leader among her fellow Christians, a new mother who is nursing her baby, who refuses to participate in the annual sacrifice to the Roman gods required of every Roman citizen. Perpetua insists she would rather die than betray her Christian beliefs by worshiping pagan gods and is subsequently arrested by Roman authorities, along with her teenage servant, Felicitas (who is pregnant and gives birth to her baby in prison). Both Perpetua and Felicitas are sentenced to die for their faith by public combat in the arena with wild animals.

Perpetua's journal is a mirror of growing self-confidence and trust in the Divine, a living portrait of a young woman whose courage parallels Martin Luther's when, at the risk of death, he spoke the historic words:

> *Here I stand.*
> *I cannot do otherwise.*
> *So help me God.*
> *Amen.*

Thirteen hundred years before Luther, Perpetua spoke similar words when she too was confronting death:

> *I cannot be called*
> *Anything else than what I am.*

Little is known about Perpetua except that she came from a close-knit family of well-to-do provincials in North Africa and converted to Christianity as a teenager. Her diary is the first known text written by a woman in Christian history. Poignantly struggling to cope with her fears of the violent death ahead of her and her anguished guilt over leaving her baby, she describes a series of chaotic confrontations with her father, beside himself at the prospect of her death. He begs her to renounce her faith and escape execution—if not for her own sake, then for his or her baby's.

As death approaches, Perpetua has a powerful series of dreams that rapidly transform her adolescent religious fervor into mature courage and commitment, reassuring her that her beliefs are true. In the final dream she sees herself as a man, perhaps a symbol of the psychic integration forced by the imminent end of her life, and she goes with dignity and grace to a death her conscience will not let her flee.

~⁹

FROM PERPETUA'S
DIARY

When I was held by the police authorities, my father came to see me, trying—because of his love for me—to dissuade me from my resolution. "Father," I said, picking up a vase or pitcher or whatever it was, "Do you see this?" "I do," he said. "Can it be called anything else than what it is?" I asked. And he said, "No." "So I, too, cannot be called anything else than what I am: a Christian." Infuriated by that, my father rushed at me as though he were going to rip out my eyes. He only managed to annoy me. Then he left, overwhelmed by his own fiendish arguments.

My father stayed away for a few days, and I thanked the Lord. I felt relieved over his absence. During these days, [Felicitas and I] were baptized, and I felt the Spirit instruct me to not ask for anything from the baptismal waters except strength to endure the physical suffering ahead. A few days after that, we were imprisoned. I was terrified because never before had I seen anything like the darkness. What a horrible day! The heat was unbearable, it was terribly crowded, and we received rough treatment from the soldiers. My situation was worsened because of my anxiety for my baby.

But two kind deacons, Tertius and Pomponius, who were taking care of our immediate needs, gave money so that we might be transferred for a few hours to a better part of the prison, to refresh ourselves a little. We left the dark dungeon and all went about our own business. I nursed my child, who was already weak from hunger. I spoke to my mother about my anxiety for the infant, tried to console my brother, and asked them to take care of my son. I suffered terribly because I sensed the agony that I was causing them.

These are the kinds of trials I had to endure for several days. Then I was granted the privilege of having my baby with me in prison for the remainder of my stay. With my concern and anxiety for the infant relieved, my strength returned. The prison suddenly became my palace, and I preferred to be there than any other place in the world.

Then my brother came to visit and said to me, "Dear sister, you have such a good reputation, you could ask for a dream that would tell you if you will be . . . released." I knew I could speak with the Lord, because I had experienced great blessings already, so I confidently promised my brother to do so. . . . That night I prayed for a dream. [And I saw a bronze ladder reaching up to heaven, with a dragon at its base. I prayed in the name of the Lord, and the dragon crouched. Stepping on its head as my first step, I climbed to the top. A gray-haired man surrounded by thousands of white-robed people said, "Welcome, my child," to which all answered "Amen."]

I immediately told my brother about the vision, and we both realized that we were going to suffer and die. From then on we gave up all hope of anything in this world.

A few days later, it was rumored that our case was about to be heard. My father, totally beside himself, came from the city to see me, still determined to weaken my faith. He said:

Daughter, have mercy on my gray head. Have mercy on your father, if I have the honor of being called such by you. With these two hands I have guided you into the prime of your life. I have always favored you over your brothers. Do not leave me in this disgrace. Think of your brothers. Think of your mother and your aunt. Think of your son who will die without you. Stop this stubbornness before you kill all of us. None of us will ever again be free to speak if anything happens to you.

These were the kinds of things my father said to me out of his love. He was kissing my hands and threw himself at my feet. There were tears in his eyes, and he began to call me not "daughter" but "woman." I was very upset and tried to comfort him. . . .

One day as we were eating we were suddenly rushed off to a hearing. We arrived at the forum and the news spread quickly throughout the area near the forum and a huge crowd gathered. We went up to the prisoners' platform. All the others confessed when they were questioned. When my turn came, my father appeared with my son. Dragging me from the step, he begged: "Have pity on your son!"

Hilarion, the governor . . . also said: "Have pity on your father's gray head! Have pity on your infant son! Offer sacrifice for the emperor's welfare!"

But I answered, "I cannot." . . .

Then the sentence was passed. All of us were condemned to the beasts. . . .

Since I was still nursing my child who was ordinarily in the cell with me, I quickly sent the deacon Pomponius to my father's house to ask for the baby, but my father refused to give him up. Then God saw to it that my child no longer needed my nursing, nor were my breasts inflamed. After that, I was no longer tortured by anxiety about my child or by pain in my breasts....

[In the arena, Perpetua was quickly knocked down by the charge of a wild animal. Dazed but not yet mortally wounded, she replaced a hairpin that had fallen out, brushed off her skirt, and stood up to face the next blow. She eventually died from the thrust of a gladiator's sword.]

A COURT RECORD
SALONIKI (GREECE), 304

From Saloniki comes this astonishing testimony to women's courage, an official court record of the trial and sentencing of seven women who chose to face death rather than betray their convictions. The event took place at the beginning of the fourth century when the Roman emperor Maximian, appointed by Diocletian as his co-emperor, had ordered Christians on pain of death to offer sacrifice to the Roman gods. We do not know if the writing comes from a court stenographer or from a grief-stricken friend who witnessed the wild unfolding of a story that was by any accounts dramatic, passionate, searing with anger and terror. These few women—five of them only teenagers, the others perhaps in their twenties—are determined to fight for their lives and for their convictions, but they are forced to choose between the two. As the dramatic intensity crescendos, the judge Dulcitius almost begs them to recant so that he can spare them

The text has enormous significance as a rare historical record of conscientious objection on the part of women. Agape, Chione, Irene, Agatha, Cassia, Philippa, and Eutychia did not want to die. They had fled to the wilderness in the hope of saving their lives. They wanted to hide their sacred scriptures—in disobedience of Diocletian's edict of 303 demanding the surrender of Christian books to Roman authorities—and they wanted to live in peace as a community of consecrated women devoted to the spiritual life. Instead they were arrested and brought to trial before the Roman pre-

*fect Dulcitius, a trial that is reminiscent of Jesus' trial before the Roman
procurator Pontius Pilate three centuries earlier.*

~◠

THE TRIAL AND SENTENCING OF AGAPE,
CHIONE, IRENE, AND FOUR OF THEIR FRIENDS

The Roman Prefect Dulcitius: You may read the charges.

Court Official [reading a letter]: "To you, my lord, greetings from Cas-
sander, beneficiarius. This is to inform you Sir, that these seven
women, Agatha, Agape, Irene, Chione, Cassia, Philippa, and Eutychia refuse to eat sacrificial food, and so I have referred them to Your
Genius."

Dulcitius: What is this insanity? You refuse to obey the orders of our
most religious emperors and Caesars? [turning to Agatha] When you
came to the sacrifices, Agatha, why did you not perform the cult
practices like other people?

Agatha: Because I am a Christian!

Dulcitius: Do you still remain of the same mind today?

Agatha: Yes!

Dulcitius: What do you say, Agape?

Agape: I believe in the Living God. And I refuse to destroy my conscience!

Dulcitius: What do you say, Irene? Why did you disobey the command
of our lords the emperors and Caesars?

Irene: Because of my hope in God.

Dulcitius: What do you say, Chione?

Chione: I believe in the Living God, and I refuse to sacrifice to false
gods.

Dulcitius: How about you, Cassia?

Cassia: I wish to save my soul.

Dulcitius: Are you willing to partake of the sacrificial meat?

Cassia: I am not!

Dulcitius: And what say you, Philippa?

Philippa: I say the same.

Dulcitius: What do you mean, "the same"?

Philippa: I mean I would rather die than partake of it!

Eutychia: I say the same, I would rather die!

Dulcitius [longing to spare the young women's lives, hoping they will give in]: What say you now, Agape? Will you perform your duty in honor of our lords the emperors and Caesars?

Agape: Not even Satan's power can move my reason; it is invincible.

Dulcitius: What say you, Chione?

Chione: No one can change my mind.

Dulcitius: Have you in your possession any writings, parchments, or books of the impious Christians?

Chione: We do not, Sir.

Dulcitius [trying another tack, yet hoping to let them go free]: Who was it who gave you this idea to defy the law?

Chione: The Living God.

Dulcitius [despairing of their determination]: It is clear that you are all liable for the crime of treason against our lords the emperors and Caesars. And seeing as you have persisted in this folly for a long time, in spite of strong warnings and so many decrees, sanctioned by stern threats, and have despised the commands of our lords the emperors and Caesars, remaining in this impious name of Christian, and seeing that even today when you were ordered by the soldiers to deny your belief and signify this in writing, you refused—therefore you shall receive the punishment appropriate for you.

[reading from a sheet] Whereas Agape and Chione have acted with malicious intent against the divine decree of our Augusti and Caesars, and whereas they adhere to the worthless and obsolete worship of the Christians which is hateful to all religious men, I sentence them to be burned to death. Agatha, Irene, Cassia, Philippa, and Eutychia, because of their youth are to be put in prison in the meanwhile.

[In March and April of 304, all seven women were executed.]

EGERIA

WESTERN EUROPE, LATE FOURTH TO EARLY FIFTH CENTURY

We know almost nothing about Egeria except what can be surmised from the journal she left of her travels between 404 and 417. This enchanting text tells the story of a highly independent and adventurous woman who loved life and enjoyed herself thoroughly doing what few women in the fifth century had the funds or freedom to do: she traveled. In contrast to most of the premodern women in this book who never left their own villages— Hildegard journeyed beyond the Bingen area for the first time in her sixties; Teresa of Avila took working trips in Spain; Lalleshwari wandered locally in India—Egeria voyaged far beyond her country of origin. Her travels took her all the way to and through the Middle East—on foot, in wooden-wheeled wagons, by ferry, in sailboats, and on horseback.

Evidently Egeria was well educated since she was able to write, sending a steady stream of letters about her adventures to "sisters" at home whose identity remains unknown, perhaps a community of devout women in western Europe. She may have held a place of leadership in the church, since she was well received everywhere she went—by bishops, monks, nuns, and a famous deaconess, Marthana, who headed local communities of women in the Middle East.

Egeria's manuscript was lost for some fifteen hundred years.

∼◞

JOURNEY TO JERUSALEM

We had a very pleasant experience on the day we arrived at the stopover of Arabia because it happened to be Epiphany, and the community there was keeping a vigil in the church. We were put up for two days by the bishop, a holy man, in the truest sense a man of God, whom I have known since the time I first visited the Thebaid. He comes from the monastery here; the monks raised him from early childhood on, so he is very learned in the scriptures and leads an exemplary life.

At this point, we sent back the Roman soldiers who had come with us under Roman jurisdiction, escorting us this entire time through the dangerous areas. There was no need to impose on the soldiers any longer, since we planned to take the public highway that goes to Egypt and which runs from the Thebaid to Pelusium, passing through the city of Arabia.

We journeyed through the whole land of Goshen, curving along apparently boundless vineyards which produce both wine and balsam wood, and among orchards and farmlands and many excellent gardens along the banks of the Nile. We passed by many estates also, which once belonged to the children of Israel. For two full days, we made our way from Arabia across the land of Goshen. How can I describe it? I think that the land of Goshen is the most beautiful territory I have ever seen.

Next we arrived at Tanis, where Moses was born, the very same city which used to be Pharaoh's capital. As I mentioned above, I already knew this area from my trip from Alexandria to the Thebaid, but I wanted to learn more about the places where the children of Israel crossed. We traversed the land from Rameses to Mount Sinai, the holy mountain of God.... Making our way by each of the stopovers in Egypt along the road we had traveled before, I reached the borders of Palestine and from there went on to Jerusalem....

Each time that we reached a place we wished to visit, we would follow customary ritual. First we would say a prayer, then read a passage from the Scriptures, then sing an appropriate psalm, concluding with a another prayer....

We hurried on to reach Mount Nebo with a local presbyter from that area, Livias, who was serving as our guide. We had asked him to join us after the last stopover because he was much more familiar with the area than we were. He asked if we would like to see the place where water flowed from a rock when the children of Israel were wandering in the desert, and Moses wanted to assuage their thirst. Of course we eagerly agreed to go there and thus, at the presbyter's directions, turned off the road at the sixth mile, after which we arrived at a small church at the foot of a mountain near Nebo. Very holy monks live in a monastery there who are called ascetics.

These holy monks received us most graciously, offering us their hospitality according to their custom. They invited us to pray with them, then they took us to a rock that is found between the church and the monks' cells, where a great stream of water flows that is very beautiful and limpid and has a most delicious taste. We commented on the quality and taste of the water and the monks explained, "The water that you are drinking is the very same water that Moses gave to quench the thirst of the children of Israel when they were wandering in the desert." Then again we conducted a ritual in our customary manner. First the monks read from a book of Moses, then we prayed and recited an appropriate psalm.

Next we left for Mount Nebo with some of the clerics, and those who were able to climb the mountain, which was very high, kindly offered to accompany us on our climb. The lower level of the mountain could be ascended by riding donkeys, but the rest was so steep that one had to leave the donkeys and go on foot, which we did.

We came to the little church of Mount Nebo and once inside, I noticed a curious place, slightly elevated, near the pulpit. It was about the size of a tomb, and I asked the holy men what it was. "This is where Moses was placed by the angels," they explained, "for as the Scripture says, 'No human being shall know his tomb'" [cf. Deuteronomy 34.6]. It is known for certain that angels buried Moses. . . . The monks who live there today were taught that by older monks, who were taught by monks of the previous generation, and in that way the tradition was transmitted by men in monastic life.

Again we prayed in our usual way, and when we were leaving the church, the presbyters and the monks familiar with this site invited us to stop just outside the front doors on the summit of the mountain. From there we enjoyed a vast view of the places that are written about in the books of Moses. Not far below us, we could see Livias, on this side of the Jordan, and we could see the spot where the River Jordan enters the Dead Sea. We could even see . . . Jericho in the distance, across from the Jordan. That shows you how high the place was where we were standing! We were able to see most of Palestine, "the promised land," as well as the whole land of Jordan [cf. Deuteronomy]. . . .

On the third day after I departed from there, I arrived at Selucia of Isauria and called on the bishop, another truly holy man who was raised by monks. There was a beautiful church there that I visited, then decided to go on for another mile and a half to spend the night near the memorial to Thecla [who, according to legend, was miraculously saved from Roman efforts to execute her]. There is a very beautiful church there and seemingly endless monastic dwellings for men and women.

I found there my beloved friend, Marthana, a most holy deaconess whom I had gotten to know in Jerusalem when she was visiting there to spend some time in prayer. She leads one of the communities of celibate monks, and everyone in the East testifies to the holiness of her life. How can I ever express to you what joy it was for her and for me when we saw each other! But let me return to my topic, my visit to Thecla's shrine.

A vast protective wall extends around the entire church and monastery for defense against the Isaurians, who are known to rob. Without the wall surrounding the monastery, they would probably attack the monastery and steal what is there. I prayed with others at the shrine and the reading was from the Acts of Thecla. I gave thanks to God, for all my desires had been fulfilled.

I spent two days visiting with the monks and celibates—both women and men. It is from this sacred place that I am writing to you today, my sisters, my light, with all affection. I will now go on to Asia to pray in the name of our God at the shrine of the holy apostle, John. If after this I am still in the body, and if I discover new places or anything else happens to me, I will write to you, or I will tell you about everything when I return and will be once again in the presence of your affection.

My sisters, my holy light, remember me, whether I am in the body or out of it.

HYPATIA

EGYPT, D. 415

One of the most amazing women of all time, still unknown to most people, Hypatia was like a female Plato. A dazzling luminary in the intellectual, mystical, political, and social life of Alexandria, the third-largest city in the Roman Empire; a genius famous all over the Roman Empire for the "holy wisdom" in her work in philosophy, mathematics, and astronomy; an author "filled with God" who wrote prolifically in these three fields; a teacher nearly worshiped by her students for the "divine spirit" in her words; and a woman beloved by everyone for the "holiness that flowed from her lips," Hypatia exuded an "interior radiance" that her contemporaries saw in no one else. The sheer brilliance of her intellect and goodness felt in her presence drew the best and most uplifted youth to her circle, where "the divine guide" taught them what human beings most need to know: the highest ethical standards, love of studying and thought, contemplation of the Divine.

It is said that in Hypatia "the spirit of Plato lived in the body of Aphrodite." A number of men proposed marriage, but she chose to remain a lifelong celibate, remaining at home and earning through her own merits her place of influence in the patriarchal, hierarchical, elitist world of Alexandrian society. She lived with her father, Theon, a philosopher who, like many of the fathers of the women in Sacred Voices, had educated her. Not only pagans studied with Hypatia but also Christians, most of whom rose to top positions in the ecclesiastical and imperial power structures of Alexandria and the greater Roman Empire, thus steadily advancing her influence in state and church.

Hypatia always lived moderately, dressing simply in the tribon, the philosopher's white robe, driving her own chariot around the city, refusing to be driven by slaves. Showered with adulation and civic honors, however, she inevitably incurred the envy of a few, most notably the unpopular Bishop Cyril, a great theologian but small-minded man who had already driven out the Jews and crushed the adherents of "pagan" religion by destroying their temples, holy objects, and art. (One "pagan" leader remarked that while "the physical object was destroyed, the spirit dwelling in the statue departed to heaven.")

Suddenly, without warning, in the year 415, Hypatia was dragged from her chariot by a mob of Christian fanatics and brutally murdered. One of women's most sacred voices in all history was permanently stilled, all of her writings destroyed, each brilliant commentary on philosophy, mathematics, and astronomy irrevocably lost for all time. Her death marks one of the most evil pages in church history, hastening the end of classical culture in the West and the extinction of woman's light for well over half a millennium.

We have no words directly from Hypatia, but a number of poets, playwrights, and novelists have written about her ever since she died, among them the nineteenth-century French poet Leconte de Lisle, whose verses may come as close as anything we have to Hypatia's own words. In the following verse from de Lisle's poem, Hypatia responds with loving composure

and eloquence to Bishop Cyril's declaration: "Your gods are reduced to dust
at the feet of the victorious Christ."

~⁹

SUCH ARE MY GODS!

You're mistaken, Cyril. They live in my heart.
Not as you see them—clad in transient forms,
Subject to human passions even in heaven,
Worshipped by the rabble and worthy of scorn—
But as sublime minds have seen them
In the starry expanse that has no dwellings:
Forces of the universe, interior virtues,
Harmonious union of earth and heaven
That delights the mind and the ear and the eye,
That offers an attainable ideal to all wise women and men
And a visible splendour to the beauty of the soul.
Such are my Gods!

TRANSLATED BY LECONTE DE LISLE

ANONYMOUS LAMENT OF MARY
SYRIA, SIXTH CENTURY

During the past two millennia, artists of every form and school imaginable
have tried to express the archetypal sorrow of Mary the mother of Jesus at
the crucifixion of her son—among them the unsurpassable Michelangelo
with his exquisite Pietà. *This beautiful lament, cherished for over fourteen*
hundred years, expresses poignantly the harrowing grief of a mother who
outlives her child.

~⁹

LAMENT OF MARY FOR HER SON

I am overwhelmed, O my son,
I am overwhelmed by love
And I cannot endure

That I should be in the chamber
And you on the wood of a cross
I in the house
And you in the tomb.

YAMATOHIME
JAPAN, SEVENTH CENTURY

Empress Yamatohime served as imperial regent after the death of her husband, Emperor Tenji, in 671.

~~

OTHERS MAY FORGET YOU

Others may forget you, but not I.
I am haunted by your beautiful ghost.

LADY KASA
JAPAN, EIGHTH CENTURY

We have little information about Lady Kasa except that she lived in the eighth century and was the lover of Yakamochi, whose dates are 718–785. General Yakamochi came from a noted political family and became a senior counselor of state. His father, the grand counselor of state, wrote a famous series of poems in praise of sake.

It is speculated that Lady Kasa was related to the Monk Manzei, who was a poet, or to the family of Kasa Kanamura, who also wrote poetry.

~~

I DREAMED I HELD A SWORD

I dreamed I held
A sword along my side.
What did it mean?
It meant you will soon be here.

RABIA AL-ADAWIYYA
PERSIA (IRAQ), 717–801

One of Sufism's most revered and beloved poet-saints, Rabia was born to poor parents who died of hunger when she was a very young child, resulting in homelessness and permanent separation from her three siblings. She was found wandering on the streets of Basra, begging for food, by a criminal who seized her and sold her into slavery. Her master eventually freed her, awed by her holiness and by the light he saw shining from her face when she prayed.

Rabia pursued a life of solitary prayer in the desert, later taking up residence in a tiny house at the edge of Basra. Someone, perhaps a student, wrote that he saw nothing in the entire house but "a pitcher with a chipped spout which she used for bathing, a brick which she used as a pillow, and a reed mat on which she prayed." As her twelfth-century biographer, Attar, wrote, "She was set apart in the seclusion of holiness." She needed nothing because she had everything, and she refused to marry, even when a suitor promised her wealth. She replied that material riches bring only anxiety and sadness, while the life of surrender brings peace. She wrote to him:

> *It does not please me that you would be my slave and that all you possess should be mine, or that you should distract me from God for a single moment. Renunciation means peace, while desire brings sorrow. Curb your desires and control yourself and do not let others control you. As for me, God can give me all that you offer and more.*

~ゝ

STARS ARE SHINING

O my Lord, stars are shining
And the eyes of men are closed.
Kings have shut their doors
And every lover is alone with his beloved.
Here I am alone with you.

A DREAM

I said a few prayers of praise and fell asleep just before dawn. I dreamed of a tree of indescribable beauty and great height. Growing on it were three kinds of fruit unlike any fruit known in this world. The size of a girl's breast, each shone like a moon or a sun against the green surface of the tree.

Awestruck, I looked at the marvelous tree and asked, "Whence comes this tree?"

The answer came, "It grows from your prayers of praise."

As I wondered about this saying, I walked around the tree and noticed that some of its golden fruit was lying on the ground. "Shouldn't this fruit be back on the tree?" I asked.

And the voice replied: "This fruit was growing on the tree, but when you were saying your prayer of praise, you wondered if the dough had risen, and at that moment, it fell."

YOU ARE SUFFICIENT

O my Lord,
Whatever you have apportioned to me of worldly things
Give it all to my enemies.
And whatever you have apportioned to me in the world to come,
Give that to my friends.
For you are sufficient for me.

WITHOUT YOU

Without You, O my life, O my love,
I would never have wandered
Across these endless countries,
How many gifts and graces You have given me!
How many favors You have fed me from your hand!

I look for your love in all directions
then suddenly its blessing burns in me.
O captain of my heart—
Radiant eye of longing in my breast—
I will never be free of You as long as I live.
Only be satisfied with me,
Life of my heart,
And I am satisfied.

TRANSLATED BY ANDREW HARVEY

FROM HER BIOGRAPHY

I entered Rabia's presence, and I saw the light shining on her face.

MY JOY

My Joy—
My Longing—
My Sanctuary—
My Friend—
My Food for the Journey—
My Final End—
You are my Spirit and my Hope.
You are my Yearning.
You are all my Good.

TEACHINGS ON PRAYER

One day Rabia was seen running with fire in one hand and water in
the other. They asked her why she was doing this and where she
was going. She replied, "I am running to light a fire in Heaven and
to pour water on the flames of Hell, so that both veils to the Face
disappear forever."

Rabia was once asked, "How did you attain that which you have attained?"

"By often praying:

'I take refuge in you, O God, from everything that distracts me from You, and from every obstacle that prevents me from reaching you.'"

The source of my suffering and loneliness is deep in my heart.
This is a disease no doctor can cure.
Only Union with the Friend can cure it.

TRANSLATED BY ANDREW HARVEY

MANDARAVA OF ZAHOR
INDIA, EIGHTH CENTURY

Venerated in her time as a dakini, *or goddess, Mandarava was a princess who, like Clare of Assisi and many other women in this book, renounced her privileged status to ennoble life for others. Padmasambhava, the foremost Buddhist teacher of her century, so respected Mandarava that he credited her with his ability to carry out enlightened activities in the world, even her traveling from India to Tibet to spread his message. In the fullest sense a prophet and a bodhisattva, she gave her life to helping countless women and men grow toward the goal of enlightenment. She and Yeshe Tsogyal are often depicted in Buddhist art with Padmasambhava as his two principle consorts.*

Padmasambhava so greatly revered Mandarava that he wrote a book about her life and remarkable accomplishments. The passage printed here comes from an ancient Tibetan copy found at the Library of Congress in Washington, D.C., and translated in 1998 by Lama Chonam and Sangye Khandro under the title The Lives and Liberation of Princess Mandarava, The Indian Consort of Padmasambhava. *Written well over a thousand years before Kahlil Gibran published his world-famous book* The Prophet, *Padmasambhava's portrayal of Mandarava's leave-taking from her disciples*

at death evokes the same sorrow as the Prophet's departure from his follow-
ers—with the difference, however, that here the prophet is a woman.

~♪

THE LEAVE-TAKING

[H]er disciples made individual queries and received complete
instructions until they were fully satisfied. Then a young girl from
Zahor came forward and respectfully made this request: "E ma!
Daughter of the gods, guide of sentient beings! By passing on to
the sphere of truth rather than remaining among us as the protector of beings, what could your enlightened awareness be consider-
ing? Is it really possible that you could just leave us here without a
protector? Wisdom *Dakini,* precious as our hearts, how can you not
remain here to teach the sacred *Dharma* to your disciples? How
can you now consider passing to the place beyond sorrow? Is it
possible for your loving-kindness and compassion to abandon those
with weak minds, those full of negative karma? Venerable mother,
Dakini Mandarava, if you do not stay here to show the path to sentient beings, what will you accomplish by going instead to a place
of great bliss? Is it really possible for you to leave us here in this
dark place without eyes to see? For myself and all living beings, you
are the only mother, the only guru! How can you not stay here
among us in these difficult times? How can you consider dissolving
into the sphere of truth? How can you leave us like a mother leaving her only child? O *Dakini* consort, lamp for the Buddha's teachings, how can you consider passing to the paradises of great bliss
without remaining here to uphold the teachings on explanation and
accomplishment through your enlightened activity? Who will lead
beings upon the path away from the place of darkness? Alas, alas!
O mother, please remain here with us!"

The girl's words caused everyone present to begin lamenting
aloud. This compelled the *Dakini* to speak: "Listen to me, assembly of faithful disciples! No one in the world is permanent. Though
a rainbow appears clear and stationary in the sky, it vanishes in an
instant. Even though a girl like me appears youthful and full of life,
I am powerless to remain when the time has come for me to go else-

where in order to help other beings. Though the flowers of summer bloom with a brilliant luster, this beautiful sight will quickly vanish, as soon as the season changes. Though this girl has health and energy beyond measure, she cannot control the time of her departure when it comes to helping others. . . .

"Listen, my devoted disciples gathered here. Maintain my last testament carefully within your hearts. Without ever wasting this precious human birth, polish it with *Dharma* and cherish it as the true course through which all wishes are fulfilled! . . . Be diligent in *Dharma* and you will find everlasting bliss! . . . Meditate unceasingly on emptiness and compassion and become fully endowed with the ability to accomplish the great purpose of benefitting others."

RAYHANA
TODAY'S IRAQ?, EIGHTH TO NINTH CENTURY

Some twelve hundred years ago, after writing this prayer, apparently her favorite prayer, Rayhana embroidered it on the front of her dress over her breast. Her archetypal feminine gesture has been echoed through the centuries by women who sew their favorite scriptural passages on their dresses or shoes to remain mindful of the teachings they love.

Otherwise, little is known about the woman called "Rayhana the Madwoman." The sixteenth-century Sufi hagiographer, Abd al-Munawi, mentions her along with thirty-four other women in his book, Shining Stars of the Biographies of the Masters of Sufism.

~_9_

YOU ARE MY LONGING

O my Friend,
You are my lover, my longing, all my joy.
My soul knows how to love only you.
My yearning, my longing burns only for you,
To see your face I would sacrifice
every delight In the Garden of Paradise.

DHUODANA

SEPTIMANIA (SOUTH OF FRANCE), 803–843

During Advent of 842, the aristocratic Dhuodana was forcibly separated from her two children by her husband, who took the boys and abandoned their mother in the castle. Dhuodana coped with the extreme isolation and despair by creatively refining her writing skills and putting her fine education to use: she wrote a book for her sixteen-year-old son, William, and his infant brother. How she acquired her learning is a mystery; perhaps upper-class Carolingian women had more freedom to study than the rest of ninth-century women (who were deliberately kept ignorant). But her literacy saved her from total powerlessness, enabling her to transform a lonely Christmas season into an inspirited era of creativity. The result was an eloquent book that would never die: a "manual of conduct" for William, for him to share in later years with his little brother, "whose name," Dhuodana laments, "I do not even know." A treasury of spiritual, moral, motherly, and courtly guidance, the book imparts with maternal tenderness the intellectual, social, and spiritual values that Dhuodana was prevented from teaching her boys in person—"unlike most women in the world," she notes indignantly, "who are able to live with and enjoy their children."

Dhuodana had married Bernard of Septimania in a regal ceremony in the imperial chapel of Aachen in 824, giving birth to William in 826 and to her second son some fourteen or fifteen years later. Bernard isolated her in the castle while he fought political battles, heartlessly sending William to the court of Charles the Bald for political purposes and taking her other son away from her in infancy to an unknown location where she would never see him again.

Throughout the eleven substantial chapters of her manual, she repeatedly urges William to read and to own many books and to always pray and believe in God. Like Christine de Pisan (see p. 94), she counsels him to work for peace instead of perpetuating wars.

Dhuodana died in 843, a year after completing the book.

~⁀

FROM A MANUAL FOR WILLIAM

Here Begins the Manual of Dhuodana Which She Sent to Her Son, William.

While most women in the world are able to live with and enjoy their children, I, Dhuodana, find myself living far away from you, my dear son William. Filled with anguish because of this and with strong desire to be of help to you, I send you this little manual, which I have written for your perusal and education. I am over-joyed knowing that although I am absent in body, this little book will recall to you as you read it the things you are required to do for my sake, as well as your son....

When you have begun to consider who or what God is, when you are unable to understand,...you will know, through this very inability to know, that God is God. The very one, as a certain poet said, who "commanded and they were created," who spoke and all was fashioned—heaven and earth, the underwater depths, the orbs of the sun and the moon.

To be sure, if the heavens and the earth were stretched out through the air like a parchment, and if all the gulfs of the seas turned into ink, and if all of the inhabitants of the earth born from the begin-ning up until now were scribes,...they would not be able to write down the greatness, the breadth, the height, the sublimity and pro-fundity of the Creator, or to express the divinity, wisdom, holiness, and loving-kindness of the One-Who-is-Called-God. Since God is so great that no one can comprehend his essence, I beg you to have awe of him and to love him with all your heart, all your mind, and all your understanding, and to praise God in everything you do, remembering that he is good and his mercy endures for all days....

I also advise you, O my handsome and beloved William, that amid the mundane cares of this world you not neglect to acquire many books, so that you may learn from the learned something greater and better than is written here concerning your Creator. Study the teachings of the holy doctors. Pray to God, cherish him, love him—and he will be a Protector, Leader, Friend and Fatherland for you: "the Way the Truth and the Life," and will bring you abundant prosperity in the world and will guide your conflicts with enemies toward peace....

Read these words which I send you—read, understand, and put them into practice. And when your little brother, whose name I do not know, has received the grace of Christ in baptism, do not be reluctant to instruct, support and love him, challenging him always from the good to the better. When he is old enough to speak well and to read, show him this bound copy of the book which I have prepared and in which I have written your name. Urge him to read it, for he is your own flesh and your brother. I, your mother, urge you both as though you were able to respond to me right now, that you raise up your hearts, at least from time to time, above the burdens and cares of daily life. Fix your sights on the One who lives eternally, who is called God. May the all-powerful one make you, along with your father, happy and joyous at this moment. May you succeed in everything you do....

What more can I say? Your admonisher, Dhuodana, is always with you, my son, and if I am absent someday because of death, which must occur, you will have this little book of moral guidance as a memorial. And you will be able to see me in it like a reflection in a mirror, reading and praying in mind and body, and you will have a record in writing of the duties that you must perform for me. Son, you will have other teachers, who will teach you other matters of greater usefulness, but not in the same circumstances, and not with a soul burning in their breasts as I, your mother, have, O first-born son....

My son, honor and befriend those by whom you wish to be befriended. Love, visit and respect all, so that you may be worthy of reciprocal honor and respect. As a certain learned man...said elucidating Psalm 41, "As the deer have this habit: When several of them wish to cross a sea or a broad river of swirling waters, they place their horned heads one after another on the back of their companions, holding up each other's heads, so that by getting a little rest, they can make a quicker crossing. They have received such intelligence and wisdom that, when they see the first to be tiring, they exchange places ... letting the second be first and so on, each upholding and comforting the others. By changing place, each has an experience of the compassion of brotherly love. Taking care that the head with the horns be held up, they do not become submerged in the water.

The meaning that is hidden here is not concealed from the learned: it is immediately clear to their eyes. In the upholding of one another, and in the exchange of place, you see the love which is to be fostered by all in the human race, both to the powerful and to the weak....

Consult this little book frequently, and always, my noble son, be strong and brave in Christ.

This book was begun in the second year of the death of the emperor, Louis, on the 30th of November, St. Andrew's Day, the beginning of Advent. By the grace of God, it is concluded on the 2nd of February, the Feast of the Purification....

Reader, pray for Dhuodana....

UMM ABDALLAH
TIRMIDH (CENTRAL ASIA), NINTH CENTURY

All that we know of this amazing mystic whom scholars call "Umm Abdallah" comes from an autobiography written by her husband that is probably unparalleled in world literature. In his manuscript, which may be the first such document preserved in Islamic history, Abu Abdallah, whose full name is Abu Abdallah Muhammed ibn Ali al-Hakim at-Tirmidhi, reports how his divine calling to be a spiritual guide unfolded through the dreams of his wife. He had engaged in a spiritual quest for some time without a teacher when his wife began to have numinous dreams about his destiny and her own, bringing the two into a marital relationship of rare mutuality, beauty, and loving respect.

As Muslims, Umm Abdallah and her husband regarded dreams as the direct word of God, auspicious messages or teachings spoken in the soul during sleep to impart purpose and direction. At first, both partners interpreted the dreams as a revelation of his path of mystical development and the impact his teaching would have on the world. Soon they realized that God was acting in her soul as powerfully as in his, and Abu Abdallah included in his autobiography painstaking descriptions of his wife's dreams and concluded the book with careful accounts of her mystical experiences.

Here are two of the mystical dreams of Umm Abdallah, each rich in life's holiest symbols and archetypes, a field of diamonds yet to be mined, each a mirror of faith and a window on the integration process in the human psyche: the Sacred Feminine united for once with the Sacred Masculine—within the soul of each partner, between their two souls, and in relationship to God. Their graced relationship holds great implications for marriage and partners of all kinds today.

~ 9

THE SECOND DREAM

I saw a big pool in a place unknown to me. The water in the pool was as pure as spring water. On the surface of the pool there appeared bunches of grapes, clear white grapes. I and my two sisters were sitting by the pool, picking up grapes from these bunches and eating them, while our legs were dangling upon the surface of the water. . . .

I said to my youngest sister, here we are, . . . eating from these grapes, but who has given them to us? [Then a man in white clothes who was carrying herbs came towards us and said], I am one of the angels. . . . We roam the earth . . . and we place these fragrant herbs on the hearts of sincere worshippers so that by them they can carry out acts of worship. And this myrtle [a symbol of healing], we place upon the hearts of the just. . . .

Tell [your husband], don't you wish that you could have these two? And he pointed to the myrtle and the herbs. Then he said, God can raise the piety of the pious to such a stage that they will need no piety. Yet God commanded them to have piety so that they will come to know this.

Tell him: Purify your house! I said, I have small children, and I cannot keep my house completely pure. He said, I don't mean from urine. What I mean is this—and he pointed to his tongue. I said, And why don't you tell him so yourself?...Then he moved the hand that was holding the myrtle and said: Because this is as yet remote from him.

Then he plucked out of the bunch that he was holding some of the myrtle and handed it to me. I said, shall I keep it for myself or shall I give it to him? He laughed, and his teeth shone like pearls. He said, this is for you, and as for these that I am holding, I myself shall take them to him. This is between the two of you, because you are both at the same place together....

THE THIRD DREAM

[I] was in the open hall of our house.... There were several couches there, upholstered with brocade. One of the couches stood next to the family mosque.... I saw a tree growing by the side of this couch, facing the mosque. It grew up to a man's height, and it looked very dry, like a withered piece of wood.... Now from the bottom of the trunk new branches emerged, about five or six, and they were all green and moist. When these branches reached the middle of the tree it started stretching and extending upwards to about three times a man's height, and so did the branches too. Then from amidst the branches there appeared bunches of grapes. I heard myself saying: "This tree is mine!" No one from here to the end of the world has a tree like this!

I came closer to the tree and...looked at the trunk and saw that it had grown out of a rock, a big rock. By the side of this rock I saw another big rock which had a hollow, like a pool. From the trunk of the tree a brook emerged and its water, which was pure, flowed into the hollow of the rock and gathered there.

...I heard a voice calling to me from the bottom of the tree: Can you pledge to protect this tree so that no hand would touch it? Then this tree is yours. Its roots have stood in sand and soil; many hands have touched it, and its fruit became worthless, then rotted and dried up. But now we have placed the rock around it, and we have nominated a bird over it, to watch over the fruit of this tree. Look!

I looked, and saw a green bird, the size of a pigeon. It perched on one of the branches, not on the green moist ones which grew up from the bottom of the trunk, but on a dry one.... The bird hopped upwards, climbing from branch to branch; whenever it perched on a dry branch, which looked like a dry peg, it became green and moist, and bunches of grapes hung down from it. The voice said: If you protect this tree faithfully the bird will reach the top of the tree and the whole tree will become green; if not, the bird will stay here in the middle. I said: I will. Indeed I will protect it! ...

The bird flew to the top of the tree, branch after branch, and the whole tree became green. When it reached the top of the tree I exclaimed with amazement: *la ilaha illa 'llah* ("There is no god but God"). Where are all the people? Can't they see the tree and come nearer? And the bird answered from the top of the tree: *la ilaha illa 'llah!* I wanted to pick a tender grape from the tree, but a voice said to me: No! Not until it has ripened! And I woke up.

BHIKṢUNĪ LAKṢMĪ
KASHMIR, TENTH OR ELEVENTH CENTURY

It is said that when Princess Laksmi learned that lambs and other animals that she loved were slaughtered to feed people, she renounced the world and, against her parent's protests, became a nun. Ordained, she mastered Tantric teachings and the art of logical debate, becoming a teacher in her own right who debated with the best male scholars of her era, usually winning, and was appointed abbess of a monastery. Some years later she fell ill with leprosy and was driven into the forest to die. We are not sure why her community turned against her, but perhaps, as one variant of the story has it, because of a miscarriage. Taking refuge in a cave, Laksmi prayed to the Bodhisattva of Compassion, Avalokitesvara, who appeared to her in a resplendent white vision with a miraculous purifying drink that removed her symptoms. Avalokitesvara then revealed to her a sacred fasting practice, instructing Laksmi to teach it not just to favored individuals but to every-

one everywhere, laypeople as well as monks and nuns. The fast that Laksmi introduced marked a milestone in the history of Buddhism. Before her, fasting was not fostered since the Buddha, before he reached enlightenment, had nearly died from a fast. Laksmi wrote an instructional manual describing how the person fasting performs a visualization of oneself as Avalokitesvara with a thousand arms. Additional instructions were carefully transmitted orally, and the fast is still practiced today in all branches of Tibetan Buddhism. One undertakes the fast during the sixth month of the year, or at other times, abstaining totally from eating or drinking for two to four days. Laypeople have the option of shaving the head and going barefoot to experience monastic austerities. Prayers, meditation, bows, prostrations, and mantras accompany the fast, and a chant written by Laksmi, part of which appears below, is repeated for hours while prostrations are performed in praise of Avalokitesvara. The fast closes with a feast.

∼〇

FROM THE CHANT TO ACCOMPANY
HER FASTING PRACTICE

Your face glows
with full moon radiance;
your eyes are exquisite,
tapered like lotus petals
snowy white as a conch shell;
you hold glistening sacred beads,
immaculate pearls. . . .
Eternal source of bliss,
you cure illness, old age, and death.

ANONYMOUS LOVE SONG
SPAIN, C. 1042

The earliest extant writing in the Spanish language is a four-line lyric traditionally attributed to an unidentified woman expressing her love. It is a kharja, the final lines of a Hebrew or Arabic poem from medieval Spain.

∼〇

SO MUCH LOVING

So much loving, so much loving,
My lover, so much loving;
Healthy eyes grow dim,
Give me pain.

CHRISTINA OF MARKYATE

ENGLAND, C. 1096—C. 1166

Christina's mother, a wealthy noblewoman named Beatrice, underwent a mystical experience during her first pregnancy that persuaded her that her child had a sacred calling and destiny. She had been looking out a window toward the Monastery of Our Lady in the distance when she saw a white dove fly from the monastery directly toward her and through her window onto her arms. The dove remained with her for seven days, sometimes nestling into the wide sleeve of her long medieval gown, sometimes resting contentedly on her lap, letting her pat and love it like a pet. Beatrice interpreted this extraordinary experience as an outpouring of the Holy Spirit on her child and a calling to great things.

Mystical history is replete with stories of animal interventions that awaken divine awareness and effect personal transformation. Sometimes a problem is gracefully resolved, sometimes a person taps into springs of fresh courage to hold to beliefs and desires. Such was the case with the baby born to Beatrice, a daughter named Theodora, who later took the name Christina. Ironically, the more Christina grew and deepened in the very calling foreseen by her mother, the more her mother resisted the calling. While Christina wanted to remain unmarried and celibate, her parents wanted her to marry a nobleman, perhaps to increase the family's wealth. Christina fought fiercely for power over her own body and her personal relationship with the Divine, but her parents were relentless in their determination for her to marry, going to unbelievable extremes, as related below. The monastery where Christina eventually sought and found support is dedicated to "Our Lady," a title given to Mary the mother of Jesus, to Inanna-Ishtar, and to the Gnostic Goddess or Great Mother in many other eras of history. In the passage that follows, from her biography, Christina's parents trick her into a marriage, but she uses all her intelligence, skills, and cleverness to get her own way, eventually winning the right to choose the lifestyle she feels called to.

~

YOU CANNOT MAKE ME FORGET

The more her parents became aware of her perseverance in her attitude, the more they tried to break down her resistance, first by flattery and cajoling, then by reprimands and admonishments, sometimes by lavish gifts and promises, even by threats and punishments. And though everyone united against her—all her friends and relatives—her father Autti surpassed them all in his efforts to block her purposes, while he himself was surpassed by Christina's mother, as we will see later on.

They devised many methods to persuade her but without the result they sought, then finally came up with this scheme, which they carried out: On one hand, they placed her under stern and unyielding guard, preventing any monk, nun or person of faith from having any association with her. On the other hand, they liberally invited to their home people given to joking and jesting, arrogance, bragging and worldly amusements, even those who communicate evil to corrupt good behavior. Moreover, they prevented her from going to the monastery of Our Lady, because it became obvious that every time she paid a visit there she came back more confirmed and strengthened than ever in her resolution. This was the hardest deprivation for Christina to bear, and to those who forbade her she said with great passion, "You may deny me access to the monastery of my beloved Lady, but you cannot wrench the memory from my heart." Her parents then forbade her to go to the chapel which she loved the most, blocking her access to that place. While at the same time taking her with them against her will to great banquets where various sumptuous foods were served with choice meats and drinks of many kinds, where the singers' seductive melodies were accompanied by the alluring tones of the zither and the harp. They were hoping that by hearing these sounds, her determination might be weakened. . . .

Their ruses failed at every turn, however, only serving to strengthen and highlight their daughter's unconquerable wisdom. When they saw that they had been outwitted in all this, they devised yet another plan. [They forced her to marry a man of their choosing, but Christina refused to live with him.] So, one night they secretly gave her husband entrance to her bedroom, expecting that he would find her asleep and, catching her by surprise, might overpower her and take her against her will. But by Providence, to which she had given her life, she was found wide awake and dressed, and she welcomed the young man as if he had been her brother. Sitting down on her bed with him, she strongly encouraged him to live a [celibate] life, telling him stories about the saints as examples.... "Do not be hurt that I have declined your embraces," she said. "Here is a plan. So that your friends cannot say that you have been rejected by me, I will go home with you and live with you for some time, making it seem that we are husband and wife, but in reality we will live as celibates in the presence of God.".... After most of the night had passed with conversation like this, the young man left.

[Christina's parents chided him for being outwitted and made further efforts to overpower her, but eventually she escaped, making her way to the monastery and later to the life of solitary prayer that she had always sought.]

HELOISE
FRANCE, C. 1100–1163

The wild and tragic love affair of Heloise and Abelard has flourished in romantic writings, songs, myths, and art for well over a thousand years, yet the spiritual dimension in Heloise's letters to Abelard is rarely discussed. A woman of striking beauty and intellect, Heloise was raised by an uncle who fostered her love of learning by hiring as her tutor one of the most brilliant philosophers of the era, Peter Abelard, who, then in his thirties, was famous for brilliance and handsome good looks. The two fell passionately in love and entered into a fiery affair that inspired Abelard to compose romantic songs that soon all Paris was singing. When Heloise's undoubtedly envious uncle learned of the affair and found out that she was pregnant, he had

Abelard attacked in his bedroom and castrated. Now ostracized, their repu-
tations and careers destroyed, the two separated. Heloise hid in a convent to
give birth to their baby (Peter Astrolabe), while Abelard entered a
monastery. After the child's birth, Abelard had Heloise installed as abbess of
another monastery, and they saw little of each other for the rest of their
lives. A reluctant nun at first, Heloise eventually settled into convent life,
rebelling against women having to follow a "Rule" or way of life designed by
men for men, and she succeeded in establishing an innovative lifestyle
appropriate for women. The following letter was written not long after the
end of the affair and their entrance into separate monasteries, when Heloise
was still deeply in love with Abelard but his feelings for her had died.

~

FROM A LETTER TO ABELARD

To her lord and father, her husband, or rather brother; from his servant and daughter, his wife, or rather his sister; to Abelard, from
Heloise:

...You know, beloved, as the whole world knows, how much I
have lost in you, how at one wretched stroke of fortune that
supreme act of flagrant treachery robbed me of my very self in rob-
bing me of you, and how my sorrow for my loss is nothing com-
pared with what I feel for the manner in which I lost you. Surely
the greater the cause for grief the greater the need for the help of
consolation, and this no one can bring but you; you are the sole
cause of my sorrow, and you alone can grant me the grace of consolation.... God knows I never sought anything in you except yourself; I wanted simply you, nothing of yours. I looked for no marriage
bond, no marriage portion, and it was not my own pleasures and
wishes I sought to gratify, as you well know, but yours. The name of
wife may seem more sacred or more binding, but sweeter for me
will always be the word mistress, or, if you will permit me, that of
concubine or whore.... God is my witness that if Augustus,
emperor of the whole world, thought fit to honor me with marriage
and conferred all the earth on me to possess forever, it would be
dearer and more honorable to me to be called not his empress but
your whore....

What king or philosopher could match your fame? What district, town, or village did not long to see you? When you appeared in public, who did not hurry to catch a glimpse of you, or crane his neck and strain his eyes to follow your departure? Every wife, every young girl, desired you in absence and was on fire in your presence; queens and great ladies envied me my joys and my bed.

You had beside, I admit, two special gifts whereby to win at once the heart of any woman—your gifts for composing verse and song, in which we know other philosophers have rarely been successful. This was for you no more than a diversion, a recreation from the labors of your philosophic work, but you left many love songs and verses which won wide popularity for the charm of your words and tunes and kept your name continually on everyone's lips. The beauty of the airs ensured that even the unlettered did not forget you; more than anything this made women sigh for love of you. And as most of these songs told of our love, they soon made me widely known and roused the envy of many women against me. For your manhood was adorned by every grace of mind and body, and among the women who envied me then, could there be one now who does not feel compelled by my misfortune to sympathize with my loss of such joys? Who is there who was once my enemy, whether man or woman, who is not moved now by the compassion which is my due?

Wholly guilty though I am, I am also, as you know, wholly innocent. It is not the deed but the intention of the doer that makes the crime, and justice should weigh not what was done but the spirit in which it was done. What my intention toward you has always been, you alone who have known it can judge.

HILDEGARD OF BINGEN
GERMANY, 1098–1179

This great woman, a mystical genius illumined with wisdom, a prophet inflamed with faith, a huge soul blazing with Living Light, single-handedly unleashed a broad river of Christian women's spirituality that had been trickling along for over a thousand male-dominated years. Only the holy work of unknown desert mothers, anonymous abbesses, deacons, nuns, and leaders like Egeria (see p. 32) prevented women's spirituality from being completely submerged before Hildegard arose in the twelfth century and gave new birth to the Sacred Feminine. Stronger in spirit than the strongest—but not until she was in her forties—Hildegard emerged because she heeded the voice of God commanding her to write and speak and use her gifts. Little by little she released her voice until she was being heard and listened to all over Europe.

She became profoundly involved not only in church leadership and reform but also in the sociopolitical realities of her day, battling for forty years on behalf of causes she believed just. Even in the last summer of her life, her eighty-second year, with failing health, she travelled all the way to Mainz, about eighty miles one way, to do battle with a bishop who had ordered her to exhume a man buried on her property. She won her fight with the hierarchy but returned home exhausted and not long after died.

Hildegard's parents, the count and countess of Bermersheim, handed her over when she was only five to be raised as a nun by her aunt, Jutta, an anchorite living in a two-room cell attached to the male Benedictine monastery of Disibodenberg. Perhaps they gave her up because she was the family's tenth child (who was often tithed to the church in the Middle Ages) or because she was "different," subject to visions, a little odd. Whatever the cause, Hildegard revealed in her theological trilogy, Scivias, *how devastating the abandonment was for her, arguing angrily for a child's right to choose her own vocation at an appropriate age.*

If inner tensions resulting from the abandonment helped impel Hildegard toward her sublime mystical realization and passionate involvement in her era, then abandonment was a gift of God. For she became abbess of two monasteries and made a significant contribution to history in thirteen distinct areas of human endeavor: theology (writing five volumes); mysticism (recording visions and revelations); iconography (inspiring paintings of fifty of her visions); biography (penning two hagiographic books); music (composing seventy-seven songs), medicine (writing two medical textbooks), pharmacology (recording hundreds of natural medicines and remedies); natural science (writing a textbook); drama (creating the first morality play of the Middle Ages, Ordo Virtutum*); history (writing the history of the diocese of Mainz); preaching (sparkling sermons with fresh images and ideas); administration (of her monasteries and extensive properties bequeathed to*

EDWIN O. SMITH HIGH SCHOOL
LIBRARY MEDIA CENTER
1235 STORRS RD., STORRS, CT 06268

her); and the epistolary genre (a vast correspondence with people from all walks of life including three popes and the emperor, Barbarossa). In addition, she invented a secret language (perhaps only for fun).

Yet Hildegard's greatest gift to life, preserved for eight centuries and flourishing today, was her rediscovery—in the Bible, in nature, and in her own soul and experience—of the Sacred Feminine. Long suppressed, long derided, feared, and split off from human consciousness, the Sacred Feminine made itself known to Hildegard in blindingly beautiful visions of Love, Faith, Wisdom, Justice, Truth, and Peace allegorized as women, often dressed in white robes with jewels shining in the colors of the chakras (seven bodily energy centers central to Eastern religions). Sacred Feminine imagery appears in every one of her books.

~୨

A VISION OF THE
SACRED FEMININE

I saw a form like a lovely maiden, her face glowing with such radiance that I could not long look at her. Her garment was whiter than snow and more shining than stars, and her shoes were made of the purest gold. In her right hand she held the sun and the moon, which she tenderly embraced. On her breast was an ivory tablet and on it the form of a man, the color of sapphire blue. All creation called this maiden "Lady." And she spoke to the form that appeared on her breast these words: "... I bore you from the womb before the morning star." [Psalm 109.3]

VISION OF THE SHADOW OF
THE LIVING LIGHT

I saw a marvelous and majestic immeasurability. With such a fierce shine I could only behold it indirectly, as if in a mirror. I knew that within it was every manner of sweet blossoming, of fragrant aroma and lovely scent. I knew in it endless delight.

A VISION OF THE LIVING LIGHT

[At mass one day, the consecration was about to take place and the priest had just pronounced the words *Sanctus, sanctus, sanctus, Dominus Deus Sabaoth:* "Holy, holy holy, Lord God of Hosts."]

Suddenly the heavens opened wide. A fiery brilliance of incalculable clarity descended over the offering, streaming completely through it with its Light; just as the sun illumines whatever its rays transpierce.

ANTIPHON FOR DIVINE WISDOM

Sophia!
you of the whirling wings.
circling encompassing
energy of God:

you quicken the world in your clasp.
One wing soars in heaven
one wing sweeps the earth
and the third flies all around us.

Praise to Sophia!
Let all the earth praise her!
TRANSLATED BY BARBARA NEWMAN

FROM ANTIPHON FOR THE ANGELS

Inspirited Light!
At the furthest reaches of the Presence
Your longing burns in dark hiddenness.

O angels,
insatiably gazing into the face of God.

FROM ANTIPHON FOR THE HOLY SPIRIT

The Spirit of God
Is a Life-giving Life,
Root of the world-tree
Breezes in its boughs.

This Spirit heals sin,
pouring balm
over all the world's wounds.

She is Radiant-Life,
All-awakening
All-reviving
Alluring all praise.

I, GOD, AM IN YOUR MIDST

I, God, am in your midst.
Whoever knows me
Can never fall,
    Not in the heights
    Nor in the depths,
    Nor in the breadths.
For I am love,
Which the vast expanses of evil
Can never still.

SUN BU-ER
CHINA, 1124–?

Popularly known as "one of the seven immortals," Sun Bu-er became the greatest woman teacher of Taoism in China. Both she and her husband earned reputations as completely realized beings, although she first raised three children and undertook full-time spiritual practice only at the age of fifty-one. Her short poems offer a rich field for interpretation in Western religions as well as Eastern, reminding Westerners that the Divine is both now and not yet—fully in the "here and now" and yet ahead—while expressing primary Taoist-Buddhist insights. As Jane Hirshfield has noted, the poem that appears here "speaks of the relationship between effort and the realization already everywhere present."

~⁀

CUT BRAMBLES LONG ENOUGH

Cut brambles long enough,
Sprout after sprout,
And the lotus will bloom
Of its own accord:
Already waiting in the clearing,
The single image of light.
The day you see this,
That day you will become it.

TRANSLATED BY
JANE HIRSHFIELD

MAHADEVI
INDIA, TWELFTH CENTURY

When she was very young Mahadevi was given the honorific title Akka, meaning elder sister, in recognition of her high spiritual attainment. She was born to a happily married couple from a humble background who practiced the Saivite religion, one of the innumerable streams of Indian Hinduism, and she was initiated into the Virasaiva community at the age of ten. When a local prince proposed marriage to Mahadevi, her parents begged her to accept, fearing reprisals if she rejected him, but she indignantly refused on the grounds that he was a Jain and did not share her faith. Incensed, the prince sent ministers to her parents threatening them with death if they failed to arrange the marriage. Remembering the adage "You shall protect the devotees of Saiva at any cost," Mahadevi reluctantly resolved to marry the prince—on the condition that she be allowed to continue her spiritual practice, worshiping Saiva as many hours a day as she wished, continuing to keep company with her teacher and other members of her community. The prince agreed to her terms, and the marriage took place.

Miserably unhappy nevertheless, with aversion to her husband only increasing, Mahadevi decided to leave him, facing whatever it would take to be alone with her "white jasmine Lord," who alone could satisfy her heart. She set out into the countryside in the direction of the holy mountain, Srisaila, casting off her clothes, like Lalleshwari (see p. 87), and pouring her feelings into vachanas, brief rhythmic prose writings, a form of religious expression popular with devotees in her time.

Mahadevi's parents came in search of her, begging her to come home with them, but she refused and remained for the rest of her short life outdoors, becoming one of the era's brightest stars. Harihara, who recorded the story of her life, says that when she died, brilliant light shone all around her.

~૭

THE WHOLE FOREST IS YOU

The whole forest is you,
All the trees of the forest
The birds and the animals
Moving among the trees.

O white jasmine Lord.

I WEAR THE MORNING LIGHT

I wear the morning light
of my white jasmine Lord
Without shame.
What do I have to hide
Under robes of silk
and jewels?

I AM WATCHING ALL THE ROADS

I am watching all the roads,
I am thirsting for your love.

O my beloved.

CLARE OF ASSISI
ITALY, 1194–1253

The two mystical saints of Assisi, Clare and Francis, represent the West's first organized protest against obscene wealth and materialism. Before them, many mystics born into the nobility had renounced their titles and luxurious lifestyle to embrace a life of rigorous spiritual discipline, where property was communal rather than personal. But Clare and Francis moved a giant step further by bringing radical, personal, and communal poverty to the forefront of religious life. It is said that when Francis was invited to dine with the Pope, he silently protested the sumptuous papal banquet. Accepting only a small amount of food, he carried it to the grand fireplace, where he sprinkled a handful of ashes over it. Then he returned to his place at the table while gluttonous prelates feasted greedily on over-rich foods.

Clare also ate little, and wore and repeatedly patched the same cloak for the forty years of her enclosure. It hangs today in her basilica in Assisi.

Francis and Clare met when he was about twenty-seven and she was eighteen. She heard him preach on the streets of Avila and, captivated by the beauty of his message, was determined to join il poverello, "the little poor one." She cut off her long hair, donned the coarse brown robe he and his followers wore, and tried to join them as they wandered and preached. But Francis insisted she be enclosed, and she acquiesced. Clare became the beloved abbess of San Damiano, guiding a large and happy community of women for over forty years in the practice of poverty, simplicity, joy, and peace. Her movement spread rapidly, and Clare found herself the spiritual mother of twenty-two other houses of "Poor Clares" in Europe and the East. Her own mother and two sisters joined her community at San Damiano.

Clare collaborated with Francis in writing a "Rule" (or "Way") for daily life in Poor Clare communities. Because her commitment to radical poverty required strenuous fasting, strict enclosure, a demanding schedule of prayer, meditation, and manual labor, her Way differed substantially from any prior rule for religious women. The local bishop and later the Pope attempted to impose a milder Rule on the women, but Clare defied their usually unchallenged authority by rejecting their versions, which treated the women like unreliable children and potential temptresses. She insisted that the Way express her own desires. In 1253—like Hildegard of Bingen, who died at eighty-two after winning her last great siege with the Bishop of Mainz— when Clare was on her deathbed, she won her historic battle for women's rights. Approval of her Way—the first Rule written by a woman, the first nonhierarchical Rule in Christianity—arrived from Pope Innocent IV two days before she died. Her sisters saw her kiss the sacred document.

GO FORWARD SECURELY

What you hold, may you always hold. What you do, may you always do, and never abandon. But with swift pace, light step, and unswerving feet, go forward securely, joyfully, and lightly, on wisdom's path. Believing nothing, agreeing with nothing, which would dissuade you from your resolution. Or which would place a stumbling block for you on the way. So that you may offer your promises to the Most High God, in the pursuit of the sacred goals to which the Spirit has summoned you.

CONTEMPLATION

Place your mind before the mirror of eternity! Place your soul in the brilliance of glory! Place your heart in the heart of the Divine! And transform your entire being into the image of the godhead itself through contemplation.

FROM THE "WAY" OF SAINT CLARE

Chapter II. How a candidate for our life is to be received by us.

1. When a woman comes to us with the desire to embrace this life, the Abbess must seek the consent of all the sisters, and if the majority agree, she may interview her.
2. And if she finds the candidate appropriate, she will question her about the Christian faith and sacraments.
3. If she believes all these things and promises to observe the sacraments until the end, and if she is unmarried or her husband has already entered religious life, . . . and if she has no impediment to living our life, such as advanced age or some mental or physical weakness, let the nature of our life be carefully explained to her.
4. If she then seems suited, let her go out and sell all that she has and give it to the poor. . . .
5. After that, her hair must be cut off and her secular dress set aside. She is to be given three tunics and a mantle.
6. Thereafter, she may never go outside the monastery except for a useful, reasonable, evident, and approved purpose. . . . [Editor's note: Many sisters went out daily to work.]
7. When the year of probation is over, let her take a vow of obedience, promising to observe forever our form of poverty. [Editor's note: Obeying the requirements of poverty receives far more emphasis than obeying people deemed superior.]
8. During the period of probation, no one is to receive the veil.
9. The sisters may have small cloaks for convenience in serving and working.
10. Indeed, the Abbess should provide them with clothing wisely, according to the needs of each person and place, the seasons and climate. . . . Sisters who work outside the monastery may wear shoes.

BEATRICE OF NAZARETH

BRABANT (NETHERLANDS AND BELGIUM), C. 1200–1268

Beatrice is one of those rare individuals remembered through the ages for the beauty of her friendships. As a Cistercian sister, she was well acquainted with the guidance of the twelfth-century Cistercian monk Aelred of Rievaulx, in his magnificent book, On Spiritual Friendship. *Aelred influenced generations of Cistercians to trust in the intimacy of consecrated friendship, moving many of them to write lines like the following, which comes from Matthew of Rievaulx:*

> The winter will lose its cold, as the
> snow will be without whiteness,
> the night without darkness, the
> heavens without stars, the day without light,
> the flower will lose its beauty, all fountains their water,
> the sea its fish,
> the tree its birds, the forests its beasts, the earth its harvest—
> All these will pass before anyone breaks the bonds of our love,
> And before I cease caring for you in my heart.

An artist and scholar, Beatrice received an exceptional education in the seven liberal arts, first with the Beguines (celibate women dedicated to a communal life, prayer, and service without religious vows), and later with the nuns at the Cistercian convent of Florival, where she took her vows. She had begun to write poetry and prose during her years in the Beguinage, and her gifts flourished in the cultured environment of Cistercian women. Here she learned also the arts of calligraphy and manuscript illumination, perhaps to copy or translate books for the community to study.

~つ

A WATERFALL OF INEFFABLE DELIGHT

It happens sometimes that a sweet and joyful love is awakened in the heart and swells like a great wave through the soul by itself without any effort at all on our part. One is so powerfully moved by love, so passionately drawn up into love, so strongly taken by love, so tenderly embraced and utterly mastered by love that she surrenders herself entirely to its power. In this embrace the soul experiences directly the radiance of the Divine, a wonderful bliss, pure freedom, ecstatic sweetness, complete overpowering by love, a waterfall of ineffable delight. She feels that all her senses are sacred and she is so totally engulfed by love and so deeply immersed in love that she is one with love, and will never cease to be love. For the beauty of love has clothed her, the power of love has submerged her, the holiness of love has consumed her, the greatness of love has so sublimely drawn her into herself that she will always love and do nothing but acts of love.

VISION OF THE WORLD AS A WHEEL

[She writes about herself in the third person.]

After she had been prioress for a long time, Beatrice heard a nun reading a passage from Bernard of Clairvaux in which he says that there are many who accept suffering for Christ's sake, but few who love themselves perfectly for Christ. These words stayed with her and for two days she pondered them. But she was unable to discover the meaning, wondering how self-love could be more important than experiencing suffering as Christ did in his passion. Since anyone naturally loves himself—"no one hates their own flesh" (Ephesians 5.29)—the addition "for Christ's sake" seemed to give special significance to the words....

When meditation failed to give her the deepest meaning of the words, she prayed for illumination... and the grace of divine love brought what she was seeking, as well as the secrets of many divine mysteries.

Raised aloft into ecstasy, she envisioned beneath her feet the whole machine of the world as if it were a wheel. She saw herself placed above it, her inner eyes contemplating the incomprehensible Essence of Divinity, as though magnetized, while the innermost point of her intelligence looked on the eternal and true God....

In this union, she became "One spirit with God" (1 Corinthians 6.17), realizing that she had touched that... freedom of spirit and

glory for which she was created. As if her spirit had been transferred entirely within the Divine spirit, she understood that for a
short while she was one with God.

Coming back to herself, she remembered this contemplation and
delighted in it without ever experiencing it again. Comforted by the
indescribable sweetness, peaceful, as though resting in the arms of
the beloved, she understood the words of Bernard. Less by intelligence than by experience she became aware through the purified
eye of the spirit that she loved herself perfectly for Christ's sake....

MECHTHILD OF MAGDEBURG
GERMANY, C. 1212–1282

*Mechthild of Magdeburg was a mystic and a Beguine, a member of a
sacred women's movement in the thirteenth century. The Beguines gathered
together to create a mutually supportive lifestyle based on prayer and
work—apart from hierarchical jurisdiction (or so they hoped) and without
pronouncing religious vows. They lived in cottages, communal houses,
apartment complexes, or row houses, according to the number of women in
each community. By the end of the thirteenth century, many Beguignages
had become self-sustaining walled medieval cities where large populations
of women of all ages found a meaningful life educating one another and
serving the poor. One of the largest is said to have housed fourteen thousand
women and included a cathedral and hospital.*

*Mechthild exercised formative influence on the thinking of the West's
great Zen-like mystic, Meister Eckhart, who served as chaplain at her
Beguignage and must have known her well. Her vastly beautiful cosmic
and symbolic vision suggests that she knew the work of Hildegard of Bingen
and probably introduced it to Eckhart. In her early sixties, Mechthild left
the Beguines—presumably under pressure from the Inquisition, which
never approved of the independent-minded Beguines and surely disap-
proved of her lifelong attack on church corruption. Apparently seeking
refuge, she entered the famous convent of Helfta, where the arts and love of
learning were flourishing under the enlightened leadership of abbess
Gertrude the Great (see p. 76), and she was welcomed with reverence. After
her death, Mechthild's mystical poems were collected in a lyrical*

masterpiece entitled The Flowing Light of the Godhead. *She may have been the "Matelda" mentioned by Dante in* The Divine Comedy.

THAT PRAYER HAS THE GREATEST POWER

That prayer has the greatest power
Which you make with all your might.
It makes a bitter heart grow sweet,
A sad heart merry,
A poor heart rich,
A foolish heart wise,
A timid heart brave,
A sick heart well,
A blind heart full of sight,
A cold heart passionate.
It draws the great God down to the little heart,
It drives the thirsty soul up to the fullness of God.
It brings two lovers together,
God and the soul,
In a wondrous place where they speak much of love.

I CANNOT DANCE, O LORD

I cannot dance, O Lord,
Unless You lead me.
If You wish me to leap joyfully,
First You must dance and sing—

Then I will leap into Love—
And from Love into Knowledge,
And from Knowledge into Fulfillment,
A harvest of sweet fulfillment beyond human sense.
There I will stay with you, circling
and circling
forevermore.

WOULD YOU KNOW
MY MEANING?

Would you know my meaning?
Lie down in the Fire
See and taste the flowing
Godhead through your being;
Feel the Holy Spirit
Moving and compelling
You within the flowing Fire and Light of God.

LORD, YOU ARE MY LOVER

Lord, you are my lover,
my longing,
my flowing stream.
You are my sun and universe.
And I am a mirror of your love.

LORD, NOW I AM NAKED

Lord, now I am naked,
and you are still.
Our interchange of eternal love,
the love that can never die,
now brings a blessed stillness
welcome to us both.
He gives himself to her,
she gives herself to him.
What happens now
The soul understands,
so I am comforted.
When two lovers come together secretly
they must part without saying goodbye.
Dear friend, I have written down for you

my way of love.
May God impart it to you in your heart.

MUKTABAI

INDIA, THIRTEENTH CENTURY

*Muktabai is one of India's most sublime women mystics, a wandering
ecstatic who achieved a high spiritual realization, much like Mirabai (see
p. 101), and whose extant poems abound in spiritual and philosophical
learning. Although little information about her life has surfaced to date, she
apparently endured extreme hardship, having been abandoned by her parents. Like Rabia, who was orphaned, she and her sisters and brothers survived by begging in the streets.*

~⁹

WHERE THE EYES
SEE NOTHING

I live where the eyes see nothing
where the night has gone, and I am free.
Loss and gain cannot trouble me.
The Divine One lives in my soul.

Mukta says:
My Lord is my heart's only home.

FIRE IN MY MIND

Mukta's Lord
Has no shape or coloring
But my eyes saw his face.
Like fire in my mind.
I knew
The secret hidden
Deep in the soul.

ANGELA OF FOLIGNO
ITALY, 1248–1309

Until recently, few people outside Foligno, a tiny Italian town near Assisi, had heard of its most famous resident, Angela, "the nightingale of the ineffable." Born to a wealthy family, she lived feverishly and extravagantly without any interest in spirituality until she was almost forty. By then widowed, she underwent a mystical experience that led her to give all her wealth to the poor, join a woman's devotional community, the third-order Franciscans, and begin the hazardous task of caring for lepers. Apparently indifferent to the high rate of contagion associated with leprosy, she threw herself into her work and into the life of prayer with equal passion and, like saints all over the world exposed to deadly diseases with apparent immunity, she never caught the dreaded disease. (The Dalai Lama has suggested in our own time that "spirituality is the immune system of the body.") Angela advanced rapidly along the mystic way, oscillating between lofty mystical experience and extreme ordeals, her fame increasing in direct proportion to her holiness. She came to the attention of a Franciscan, Arnold, who recorded her visions and teachings, and by the end of the seventeenth century her major writing, The Book of Divine Consolation, *had achieved genuine literary standing and the status of a mystical classic. As reliance on science rose in the modern era, however, and interest in mysticism waned, she faded into near oblivion for three centuries. Today, with a mystical renaissance at high tide, her great spirit is rising again, this time all over the world. In the following section from* The Book of Divine Consolation *Angela protests that she only "stammers" because no words can convey the magnificence of what she has seen.*

~୨

AN EXPERIENCE OF ONENESS

The Eighth Vision: the clearest possible experience of the presence of the Holy, empowerment to live according to my deepest desires and goals, great joy.

During Lent my spirit was so lifted up that I felt myself become one with God in a much greater and more powerful way than usual. I thought I was right in the center of God. The blessings I received were very unusual, over and over again huge gifts of delight and joy that are truly indescribable. All this was so far beyond anything that had happened to me before that I truly felt a Divine change take place in my soul, which I could not describe or explain if I were a saint or an angel or any other kind of creature on earth. This change was so profound that not even the wisest angel or woman or man could fully understand it, and that is why I feel that it would be blasphemy for me to try.

Here I was, lured away from everything that used to give me delight, such as meditation on the humanity of Christ and on his companions whom God had loved from all eternity and sent to him out of love. Similarly I was pulled away from meditations that gave me happiness; I could not do my meditations on suffering and poverty, which used to give me peace. Also I was drawn out of that sacred darkness where I had found such deep joy. And finally I was led out of every spiritual state that I had ever experienced—and I cannot understand it at all. I only know that now I do not have those things. . . .

There are two ways in which the Divine is experienced by the soul. In the first way, the Divine is known intimately, and we have consciousness of this presence, and it is in everything, in every creature that has being. As much in demons as in angels; in hell as in heaven; in adultery and murder; in all work and all things, whether beautiful or ill-favored. When I am in this state of oneness with God, I feel as much joy when I see a bad angel or an evil behavior as when I see a good angel or good behavior. And this is how the Divine presence comes most often into my soul, and with it comes illumination and profound truth and grace. It is such a sacred state that it is impossible for me to offend anyone in any way.

And this experience of enlightenment brings many other blessings into the soul. For example when I become aware that the Divine presence is with me, I receive so much wisdom and such bliss that it is like a consolation from God for the sorrow of life.

Now as I have said, God appears to the soul in another and more special way, very different from the foregoing, which similarly brings joy, but this is a different kind of joy. For in this instance, the entire soul is drawn into God so that many Divine things occur in it—with much greater grace and an indescribable depth of joy and enlightenment. This presence of God is the blessing of eternal life....

Because my soul has so often been uplifted to know Divine secrets, I understand why the scriptures were written, what they appear to affirm or deny, what is easy and what is difficult, and why some people get absolutely nothing out of them, and why people who do understand the scriptures are healed by them. I have an advantage here, for after learning the secrets of God, I can speak at least these words with certainty.

And I can truly say that if every spiritual joy, every Divine bless-ing, every heavenly delight that was ever in this world were given to me, if all the saints who have ever lived since the beginning of the world came to teach me and give me all their wisdom, if all good and evil were converted into only good spiritual joy, so that I could become a perfect person, I would not, even then, even to gain all that, give away or exchange, not for the space of the twinkling of an eye, that joy which I now have in the ineffable presence of God.

GERTRUDE THE GREAT
GERMANY, 1265–1301

Gertrude the Great was abbess of the women's Cistercian monastery of Helfta at the height of its glory, when both Mechthild of Magdeburg (see p. 70), and Mechthild of Hackeborn, also a great Christian mystic, were members of the community. Under her leadership, Helfta became a distin-guished center of learning and the arts, almost a women's equivalent of the eminent School of Saint-Viktor in twelfth-century France. The monastery included a large library as well as a scriptorium where manuscripts were copied and illustrated, and a number of the nuns wrote theological and didactic works or accounts of their mystical lives. Gertrude and both Mechthilds won fame, and all three are being rediscovered in our time.

From the age of five, when Gertrude was entrusted to the care of nuns who nurtured her prodigious intelligence as diligently as her spirit, she revealed

driving intellectual curiosity. In her twenties she berated herself for enjoying
intellectual pursuits more than spiritual practices, but intense visionary
experiences ensued, motivating her to pursue an impassioned practice of
prayer that led, at the age of twenty-eight, to the stigmata, mysterious bodily
wounds resembling those of the crucified Christ. Her heart mysticism echoes
the romantic language of courtly love and the minnesingers *popular in the*
thirteenth century, but for her that language revealed and concealed an
infinity of Divine love. Like the author of the Song of Songs, Gertrude *resorts*
to bridal mysticism to convey her experience of the ineffable.

~)

DIVINE BIRTH
IN THE SOUL

On a holy night,
With sweet dew falling on all the world,
My soul in the courtyard totally exposed
Prepared for the mystical birth,
as a star produces a ray.
In this night of tender love
We met.
And I saw come into being before me
the Divine Child.

THROUGH A DESERT
WITHOUT A PATH

O sweetness of my life,
Only love of my soul,
You led me through a desert without a path
Over arid land,
To this green valley,
To praise your love.

I FIND ALL MY JOY IN YOU

I find all my joy in you,
like a friend
who invites a beloved friend
to a garden
to breathe together
exotic air and sweet fragrances
to delight in lovely flowers
to hear an exquisite concert
and feast on luscious,
delicious fruit.

MARGUERITE PORETE

FRANCE, C. 1277–1310

Like the extraordinary Mechthild of Magdeburg, Marguerite Porete was a Beguine, and like Joan of Arc, she was burned at the stake by church officials. Because she was also known as Margarita of Hannonia (or Hainaut), it is believed that she was born in the south of Flanders in an area now part of France and Belgium.

Marguerite first came to the attention of church authorities between 1296 and 1306 when theologians judged her book, The Mirror of Simple Souls, *as contrary to church teachings and it was publicly burned. Like Matthew Fox in our time, she was officially silenced—forbidden to either write or speak about her "dangerous" ideas. Marguerite chose to ignore the church's condemnation, however, and boldly continued her work, which led to imprisonment in Paris for a year and a half on orders to recant. While she was in prison, the papal inquisitor sent out chapters of her book for examination by canon lawyers, who found her guilty of doctrinal errors. But even with death at the hands of the Inquisition plainly in sight, she refused to renounce her beliefs. Thus she was condemned to death and burned at the stake in Paris in 1310, only thirty-three years old.*

Little else is known of her life. Records of her trial for heresy indicate that her so-called errors were similar to those for which other Beguines were condemned: She refused to take religious vows or acknowledge the church's absolute authority in matters of faith and morals. Ironically, it was the teaching most desperately needed in the centuries since she lived—her idea of mystical love—that led to the charges of heresy and to the atrocities committed against her.

In the following, from The Mirror of Simple Souls, *Marguerite's ideas are so relevant that she could be writing for twenty-first-century readers.*

~

THE EMPTY MIRROR

You who will read in this book, if you want to understand it deeply, think about it before you speak about it, for it is difficult to understand. You must be your real self, neither more nor less, unconcerned with appearances. If you want to treasure spiritual knowledge, you must have the modesty of a mother.

Theologians and other clerics: You will not understand it at all— so learned are your minds—if you do not proceed humbly, with love and trust, the only forces in your soul that can lead you where Reason cannot go.

Reason itself will show you later in this book that love and trust give Reason life and that she cannot live free of them, for they empower the soul far more than Reason ever could. This is why Reason must be humbled—and humbled all sciences which are founded in Reason alone.

Place all your trust in science illumined by faith and love. And then you will understand this book, written in the love that gives life to the soul.

How ambitious was the soul who wrote this book! For it isn't possible to put into words a thing so precious, so beautiful that it can't even be thought, nor spoken, nor done. It is as if I'd wanted to pour the whole sea into an eye, or carry the world on the point of a reed, or use a candle to illumine the sun. It is impossible.

When I tried to express the ineffable, I only encumbered myself, wasting words. But a sacred elation took hold of me and lifted me up high, toward the highest summit of love; toward perfect love.

Where the soul finds peace in nothingness, in the empty mirror,
without words or thoughts, or needing to do anything.

THE SOUL SPEAKS TO THE BELOVED

Beloved, what do you want of me?
I hold all that ever was, that is, and ever can exist,
I am filled with the all.
Take of me all you please—
If you want all of myself, I'll not say no.

HADEWIJCH
FLANDERS (BELGIUM), C. 1250–?

*Like Mechthild of Magdeburg and Marguerite Porete, Hadewijch entered a
Beguignage to live in community with women dedicated to spirituality and
helping the poor without taking the religious vows professed by nuns. Ecstatic, passionate, visionary, and tumultuously emotional, her early poetry
and letters, especially, express an experience of "holy madness" that is virtually traumatic and threatens her health. Love overtakes her and then disap-
pears as quickly as it comes, leaving her shaken but irrevocably connected
to her Divine Beloved.*

*Hadewijch's later writings are more Zen-like in their language and influ-
enced such great Rhineland mystics as the Dominican Meister Eckhart. Her
language of "nothingness," of spiritual emptying, seems so unlike the exuber-
ant language of her youth that some scholars attribute the later works to
another woman with the same name. But most likely the Buddhist flavor
reflects the mature spiritual realization of the same woman. Hadewijch's work
was lost until the nineteenth century, when scholars came across it in two
small volumes among some medieval manuscripts in a Brussels attic. Each
volume seemed to have been recorded in different handwriting, leading in
part to the theory that there were two writers, but, again, it is more likely
that two people copied earlier and later manuscripts of a single writer.*

GOD BE WITH YOU, DEAR FRIEND

God be with you, dear friend, and give you
True knowledge of the ways of Love.
May God enable you to understand
What the bride says in the Songs of Songs:
I am my Beloved's and he is mine.
If you let Love completely conquer you,
You will completely conquer Love.
I hope this will be your experience.

IF I DESIRE SOMETHING

If I desire something, I know it not,
For in a boundless unknowing
I have lost my very self.
In His mouth I am engulfed,
In a bottomless abyss;
Never could I come out of it.

As quoted by
Jan van Ruysbroek, 1293–1381
Translated by Sheila Hughes

LOVE HAS SUBJUGATED ME

Love has subjugated me
To me this is no surprise,
For she is strong and I am weak.
She makes me
Unfree of myself,
Continually against my will.
She does with me what she wishes;
Nothing of myself remains to me;

Formerly I was rich.
Now I am poor: everything is lost in love.

TRANSLATED BY
MOTHER COLUMBA HART, OSB

THE MIND CAN NEVER UNDERSTAND

The mind can never understand how Love,
By Love sees all the way to the Beloved's depths,
Sees how freely Love lives in everything.
When your soul has come to this freedom
You will no longer fear life or death.
Your soul wants the whole of Love,
And nothing else.

IRENE EULOGIA

CONSTANTINOPLE, 1291–1355

Irene Eulogia Choumnaina Palaiologina was a woman of phenomenal individuality and personality, healthily proud and self-confident, almost as well educated as the men in the imperial family to which she belonged. At the death of her husband, John Palaiologos (the despotic son of Emperor Andronikos II), when she was only sixteen, she retired to a convent for the rest of her life, perhaps voluntarily, perhaps forced, and pronounced Christian vows of celibacy (generally adhered to in her time) and poverty and obedience (not strictly observed in her time). While losing the opportunity to reign as empress, she retained both her wealth and title, spending part of her fortune to palatially rebuild the monastery and retain her social ties. Influential at every level of Byzantine society—the court, the intelligentsia, the Greek Orthodox Church—Irene apparently enjoyed enclosure and the paradoxical freedom it gave her to develop her gifts.

We know Irene and much about Christian Byzantium because of a rare and priceless fourteenth-century manuscript containing eight letters she wrote to her spiritual guide in the year 1332 and fourteen he wrote to her. Rediscovered by scholars in the 1950s in the Library of the Escorial in

Madrid, the intimate, highly personal correspondence contrasts sharply with monastic spiritual writing of the era, disclosing fascinating details about everyday life and about her relationships with her four adored "fathers": her biological father (a prominent intellectual who had founded a monastery), her father-in-law (the emperor), her first spiritual guide (the Metropolitan Theoleptus of Philadelphia, who "tonsured" and "initiated" her), and the young anchorite whom she addresses as "Holy Father" in the letters below.

Grieving inconsolably over the recent deaths not only of her biological father but also of her husband, and feeling abandoned by God, Irene implores this charismatic anchorite (probably the hesychast monk Ignatios) to become her spiritual guide. Famous for uncommon holiness, brilliance, and the collecting of fine books and poetry, he alone inspires her. He is unwilling, however, to leave his hermitage more than once or twice a year, lest glamorous city temptations lead him astray, and he refuses to come to her monastery to counsel her. But Irene insists unrelentingly on her desperate need for connection to a holy soul who can help keep her centered on life in Christ, and he eventually relents. The relationship evolves into that of two good friends, he counseling her to work on her arrogance, she thanking him with gifts such as writing paper, both sharing the other's books, ideas, and wisdom.

~ 9

A THIRTEENTH-CENTURY SEARCH
FOR SPIRITUAL GUIDANCE

[From Irene's third letter to her spiritual father.]

As for the causes of my sorrow, they were the following: the fact that a man was born filled with blessings—wisdom, knowledge, eloquence and what is more important, virtue—and he races through time and time hurries him off, stealing away the glory which is his due. All this because of his virtue and because he does not care to show off, there being no one who desires and seeks out the good.

As I was turning these thoughts around in my mind, I said to myself with many tears: Where is your spirit, my lord and father-in-law, the mighty and holy emperor? You were born a philosopher and loved virtue and learning and goodness and the monks.

And you, my most wise father, who gave me life? Here [in the anchorite Ignatios] is the friend you were seeking! Here is the kind of monk in whose company you delighted! O what a loss you suffered [in not knowing him], both you, my father, and you, Your Holiness, . . . holy Father!

[From Irene's seventh letter to her spiritual father.]

Anything else that has happened to me up to now I might think of as an obstacle to my spiritual labor set up by the enemy and I might bear it.

But I cannot bear [being rejected] by you: I find it to mean that God has openly abandoned me. . . . That is why I have come to feel desperate and absolutely dazed. For such is the property of our mind: when it is aware of submission, it is restrained by it as if by a bridle, but when it is released from the yoke and set free, it is immediately susceptible to capture by wild beasts. Thus ever since my mind has been released from the yoke of spiritual submission [at the death of Theoleptus], it has been caught by the wild beasts and become a prisoner and gone under. But now, stirred by God, my soul found full assurance in you. I breathed again: I found peace and recovered. I beg you, therefore, for the sake of Christ, . . . do not let me go under again.

CATHERINE OF SIENA
ITALY, 1347–1380

Catherine was born to a prominent bourgeois family engaged in Siena's prosperous dye industry, the twenty-fourth child of twenty-five. She grew up in a large stone house, which may still be visited today, made of the characteristic stone that gives Siena its rosy glow. Catherine's own room has been preserved intact, as empty as it was when she lived there, her head resting at night on a stone "pillow." On the walls of an adjacent room, joyful frescoes recall holy moments in the young saint's life.

Catherine underwent her first mystical experience at the age of seven and put on a veil, vowing that she would remain single to devote herself to the spiritual life and care of others. Although both of her parents observed at first hand her illumination and precocious visionary gifts, they pressured her to marry, until, at eighteen, in defiance of their wishes, she cut off her long hair, making herself—according to medieval standards—unfit for marriage. Convinced of her resolve, they relented and allowed her to have her own room, a luxury in such a large family. She retreated to the little room for three years, abandoning herself to a fervent mystical life of raptures, ecstasies, illuminations, and travails. At the age of twenty-one, she abruptly emerged from her solitude to involve herself in the chaotic politics of her era and activism on behalf of the poor. Barely escaping assassination on one occasion while counseling princes to stop a civil war, she threw herself into church reform and, already revered as a saint, was selected to attempt to return the Avignon papacy to Rome. Catherine traveled to Avignon, and because of her reputation for the highest kind of mystical attainment, including the stigmata (wounds resembling Christ's), was granted audiences with the pope, Gregory XI. She pleaded her case persuasively, and Gregory did in fact return to Rome.

Since she was essentially illiterate, her disciples wrote down what she said during mystical states, some four hundred letters that she dictated, and a mystical classic entitled The Dialogue. *Like Simone Weil (see p. 187), Catherine died at the age of thirty-three after three years of "fasting" undoubtedly induced by "holy anorexia," or anorexia made sacred by love.*

~〇

A SOUL RISES UP

A soul rises up,
Restless with tremendous desire
To praise and serve Divine purposes on earth.
For three years she has dwelled alone
in the cell of self-knowledge
in search of true Knowledge of God.
Her Knowledge was followed by Love,
And now loving,
She wants to live in Truth.

A PRAYER OF PRAISE

I was enclosed, O eternal God, within the orchard of your breast, like a child in her mother's womb. You drew me out of your holy Self like a flower, petaled with all the powers of the soul. And into each power, You poured the whole plant, so I too would birth sacred fruit for Your beautiful world. So I would give back to you holy fruit like you gave to me. And you would remain in my soul, filling me over and over again with Your blessings of life. In You my soul now dwells—like the fish in the sea—and the sea in the fish.

PRAYING IN THE SPIRIT

I remember when you told me how you prayed in the Spirit, lifted high above yourself. You heard the voice of God say: "Open the eye of your mind and look within. There you will see the Beauty and Dignity of women and men. And beyond the Beauty, look at the Love, the Love they wear like a bride and groom. I will say, if you ask me, that through this Love they are one with me. Through this sacred love, they are another me."

THE BRIDGE:
GOD SPEAKS TO THE SOUL

Look at the bridge of my beloved, Christ, and understand its greatness, because it connects the heavens to the earth. It is the connection I have created between myself and humankind. The heights of the Divine and the depths of the earth are one in humankind. I made the bridge and paved and re-paved the way for your journey—in order that you would be happy.

ON CORRUPTION IN THE
FOURTEENTH-CENTURY CHURCH

You must despise the clergy's sins and try through your prayers to clothe them in clean garments of prayer and holy love, washing away their evils with your sorrow. Lift them up to God with great sadness and desire, so that God will clothe them in charity. For it is not the Divine will that they should administer the Sun to the people out of their own dark states.... God has appointed them to be angels and suns on earth, and when they are less than that, you must pray for them. But never judge anyone.

LALLESHWARI
KASHMIR, FOURTEENTH CENTURY

Lalleshwari, "the mystical poetess of Kashmir," is as well known and beloved today as she was six hundred years ago in the majestic countryside of her birth. Each generation has carefully preserved her poems and songs. As Richard Carnac Temple notes in the preface to his book, The Words of Lalla the Prophetess, *"The sayings of Lal touch the Kashmiri's ear as well as the chords of [their] hearts and are freely quoted as maxims in conversations, having molded the national mind and set up a national ideal."*

Like Gurumayi Chidvilasananda in our century (see p. 289), Lalleshwari taught the exalted ideas and spiritual practices of Kashmir Saivism, a Hindu theology dating from the eighth century whose adherents believe in the oneness of the soul with Saiva. Spawned in a land of snowcapped mountains that appear to touch the sky, Kashmir Saivism throughout the centuries has birthed many sages, saints, and philosophers, enticing pilgrim seekers from all over the world to withdraw from daily life for at least a while to pray there and experience the lofty sense of self that Kashmir stimulates.

At the age of twelve, Lalla was forced into a bitterly unhappy marriage with an inappropriate husband who was apparently indifferent to the harsh treatment she received from his mother. Since in Hindu custom then the mother-in-law had authority over the daughter-in-law, Lalla had no recourse but to run away and take up the wandering life of an aspiring yogini. She met Siddhanath, a teacher of Kashmir Saivism who initiated her and whom, it is said, she soon surpassed in learning, philosophical argument, and wisdom. Legend relates that she attained the supreme state of an avadhut, one who transcends ego centeredness and lives in the Self. Like Mahadevi, her twelfth-century predecessor, Lalla cast off her clothing, leaving only her long hair to cover her as she went about, dancing and singing her rapturous poems to the Divine Beloved, ignoring the derision her nakedness often elicited. As the homes of twelfth-century France once rang out with Abelard's love songs for Heloise (see p. 56), so the houses of four-teenth-century Kashmir resounded with Lalla's songs. Many of them have been recently translated by Coleman Barks and others.

~)

WILD LONGING

Wild longing in my eyes,
I searched everywhere,
whole days and nights.
Until the Truthful One
found me,

Right here in my own house.

WHY LALLA STOPPED
WEARING CLOTHES

Lalla says:

I dress in the holy air,
Wear nothing but sky.
What dress is more beautiful?
What clothing sets free?

LIVE IN THE SOUL!

My teacher told me:
Live in the soul!
Then I learned
to sing and dance.

GO BEYOND EXPERIENCE

Why cool the flames, Yogi?
Do you want to stop the tide?
Why do you want to walk upside down
in the sky?
Why do you milk a bull?

Lalla says,
Let go of your juggler's tricks!

MOONLIGHT FULL
OF KNOWLEDGE

My teacher told me
Truths that blistered my heart.
Flocks of consciousness lost
From the shepherd beyond recall.

I couldn't bear it,
Then moonlight full of knowledge rose.
Naran stopped playing games.

O, Naran, you are all that Lalla sees.

HIDDEN IN MY BODY

My work,
my thoughts
and words.

That was worship
in my body.

CUTTING THROUGH
THE SIX FORESTS

Cutting my way through six dense forests
I came upon the moon.
Breathing and breathing,
My heart roasting in the fire of love,
I fixed my gaze on him.

GENTLY, GENTLY,
I TRAINED MY MIND

Gently, gently, I trained my mind
To let go of thoughts
Suspend processes.
A breezeless peace
Then a flickering lamp
Shining brighter and steadier
Illumined who I am,
Lighting distant caverns in my soul.
I saw him, I seized him,
and would not let him go.

TRANSLATOR UNKNOWN

JULIAN OF NORWICH

ENGLAND, 1342–C. 1423

Julian's spirituality of the motherhood of God has made her one of the most popular mystics of our time, as she was in the fourteenth century. In a daring departure from the dominant language of her era, she portrays the three masculine persons of the Christian Trinity (Father, Son, and Spirit) as a nursing mother overflowing with kindness and love.

Little is known about Julian, not even her real name. Apparently she took her spiritual name from the church of St. Julian in Conisford, where she lived for much of her life as an anchoress in a two-room cell attached to the church. From one window she could look into the church, hear the divine office, and receive the sacraments, and from another she could counsel villagers and pilgrims who sought her wisdom. On May 13, 1373, when she was seriously ill and thought to be dying, she had a profound experience of the Divine presence, which unfolded in sixteen visions, or "revelations." She pondered the revelations for twenty years before describing and discussing them in her book, Showings, *one of England's most profound medieval writings.*

There is a movement in the Roman Catholic Church today to make Julian the third female Doctor of the Church (the other two are Teresa of Avila and Catherine of Siena).

～◯

THE HAZELNUT

> God showed me in my palm
> a little thing round as a ball,
> about the size of a hazelnut.
> I looked at it with the eye of understanding
> and asked myself:
> "What is this thing?"
> And I was answered:
> "It is everything that is."
> I wondered how it survived
> since it seemed so little,
> as though it could disintegrate in a second

into nothingness.
The answer came:
"It exists and always will exist,
because God loves it."
Just so does everything have being
because of God's love.

TRANSLATOR UNKNOWN

BE A GARDENER

Be a gardener
Dig and ditch
Toil and sweat,
And turn the earth upside down
And seek the deepness
And water the plants in time.
Continue this work
And make sweet floods to run
And noble and abundant fruits
To spring.
Take this food and drink
And carry it to God
As your true worship.

TRANSLATOR UNKNOWN

OUR SENSUALITY

I understood that our sensuality is grounded in Nature, in Compassion, and Grace. This enables us to receive gifts that lead us to everlasting life. For I saw that in our sensuality God is. For God is never out of the soul.

GOD IS OUR MOTHER

As truly as God is our Father, so truly is God our Mother, and that is revealed in everything. . . .

The mother can give her child to suck of her milk, but our precious Mother Jesus can feed us with himself, and does, most courteously and most tenderly, with the blessed sacraments, which is the precious food of true life; and with all the sweet sacraments he sustains us mercifully and most graciously. . . .

The mother can lay her child tenderly on her breast, but our tender mother Jesus can lead us easily into his blessed breast through his sweet open side and show us there part of the Godhead and celestial joys—with inner certainty of endless bliss. And that he revealed [to me] in the tenth revelation, giving us the same understanding in these sweet words which he says: "See how I love you.". . .

This fair and lovely word "mother" is so sweet and so kind in itself that it cannot be truly said of anyone or to anyone except of him and to him who is the true mother of life and of all things. To the property of motherhood belong nature, love, wisdom, and knowledge, and this is God. For though it may be so that our bodily bringing to birth is only little, humble, and simple in comparison with our spiritual bringing to birth, still it is he [our Mother] who does it in the creatures by whom it is done. The kind, loving mother who knows and sees the need of her child guards it very tenderly, as the nature and condition of motherhood will have. And always as the child grows in age and in stature, she acts differently, but she does not change her love. And when it is even older, she allows it to be chastised to destroy its faults, so the child will receive virtues and grace. This work, with everything which is lovely and good, our Lord performs in those by whom it is done. So he is our Mother in nature by the operation of grace in the lower part, for love of the higher part.

FROM *SHOWINGS*

ALL SHALL BE WELL

All shall be well.
And all shall be well.
All manner of thing shall be well.

CHRISTINE DE PISAN
ITALY, 1365–C. 1429

Christine de Pisan is Europe's earliest known professional woman writer, and few medieval documents are more masterful or astonishing than her Book of the City of Ladies *and its sequel,* The Treasure of the City of Ladies. *Both titles allude to St. Augustine's* City of God. *Christine writes about women's strengths, such as compassion, faith, wisdom, love of justice, and peacemaking, as a counterpoint to the long tradition of misogynist medieval literature denouncing women as sinners and temptresses. Greatly respected and admired in her time by men and women alike, she convinced society that women were not after all without souls but had values, convictions, intelligence, knowledge, and communication skills to contribute to life.*

Christine was born in Venice but moved to France in early childhood when her father was called to the court of King Charles V as court physician and astrologer. The family's status climbed steadily, and at fifteen she married a young nobleman, Etienne de Castel. In 1380, however, her fortune met with sudden reversal when the king died and her father was demoted. Within a few years, her father and also her husband died, leaving her at twenty-five a widow with a mother and three children to support, and this in an era that offered virtually no professional opportunities for women.

Christine turned to writing to try to earn a living, and—against all odds—succeeded, first as a lyric poet, soon as a prolific authority on women's role in society. Ingeniously, she simply filled a huge gap in European society by assuming a moral and spiritual leadership role rarely attempted in prior history except by nuns. Before long she had become the authoritative center of a virtual movement among upper-class women, inspiring them to turn away from materialism, consumerism, and frivolity to take part consciously and morally in society.

Christine's biography of Charles V and writings on the art of govern-ment, public affairs, education, and related matters also met with success, and she won the respect of men as well as women. Throughout her career, a succession of wealthy and influential patrons supported her, and some com-missioned artists to make sumptuously illustrated copies of her manuscripts, many of which have been preserved in European museums.

Christine's books were forgotten as mores changed, but she has earned a second reading in our time because of her courage, independence, and abil-ity to shape public opinion, and for the trailblazing accomplishment of giving medieval women a voice—a voice tempered by the requirement of honoring others.

~〇

HOW A WISE WOMAN, IN THE YEAR 1405, WORKS FOR PEACE

If a neighboring or foreign prince is preparing to start a war for some reason, perhaps against her husband, or if her husband wants to start a war, the wise woman will reflect on this mindfully. She will consider the great evil and infinite cruelty, destruction, slaugh-ter, all the terrible outcomes of war. She will ponder carefully and deeply how she might intervene to prevent this war. Knowing what a delicate matter this is, she will want to work mindfully, first call-ing on God, praying for Divine assistance, then counseling the par-ties involved, doing whatever she can to find a peaceful solution.

Or perhaps one of the princes of the kingdom or one of the barons or knights or powerful subjects commits some crime, and a neighboring power wants to make war on him...and she sees that if he is warred against or taken prisoner and punished, great evils can befall the country. Such cases have been seen in France and in other lands.... Indeed it happened not long ago that my lord Robert d'Artois, in a dispute with the king, greatly injured the king-dom of France to the benefit of England.

The wise woman will meditate on these things and, feeling com-passion and dreading loss of life, will work for peace. She will counsel everyone involved, her husband and his council, to think through the consequences of war before undertaking any action, pondering it in the light of the evil that could come about. She will say that deep deliberation is needed, as engaging in war is no small matter, and it would be far better to think of some appropriate way to reach agreement. She will not hesitate an instant, but (preserving her honor of course and that of her husband) will speak or have someone else speak to the ones who have committed the misdeed. She will reprimand them for it severely, saying that what they did was gravely wrong, and that the prince is quite rightly offended and quite understandably wants to avenge himself. She, however, who always wants the blessing of peace, should they be willing to atone for their wrong or to make appropriate amends, will gladly go to great trouble if need be to bring about peace between them and her husband.

With words like these, the wise woman will always serve to the best of her ability as the means to peace, even as good Queen Blanche, mother of St. Louis, did with her many efforts to bring about peace between the king and the barons—with the count of Champagne and others. This work is properly the duty of the wise queen and princess: to be the means to peace and harmony. Women must attend to the business of peace, because men are instinctually more bold and hot-headed. . . .

O, God, what great blessings have been brought about in the world by noble women making peace between enemies. . . . The Scriptures are full of such examples. . . . Blessed is the land where such a woman lives. . . . She is like a goddess in whom one can trust and hope.

MARGERY KEMPE
ENGLAND, 1373–1439

The author of the first known autobiography in the English language, Margery Kempe married at twenty and, after the birth of the first of her fourteen children, lost her mind. A vision of Christ helped her to recover, and she began wandering around Europe speaking about her mystical experience and teaching a spirituality of the everyday sacred. Her teachings centered on woman's experience, from bliss to anguish, especially in marriage and motherhood, and the near-impossibility of a woman's finding her voice and speaking her truth. Margery's this-worldly focus and a habit of sobbing in public brought her to the attention of churchmen, who condemned her as either insane or evil. Her book was discovered in 1934 after being lost for some five centuries but was not taken seriously until recently. Today more and more critics agree with author Joan Goulianos's interpretation of the book as "a rare medieval work, a work in which a woman had described pregnancy, post-partum depression, her relations with her husband, her travels, her humiliations, her triumphs, even her times of madness."

In the following selection from The Book of Margery Kempe, *Margery bravely holds her own against crudely intimidating authorities who want to kill her—in the barbaric tradition of the murdered Perpetua, Agape, Chione, Marguerite Porete, Joan of Arc, and innumerable other women and men who have died for exercising good leadership. Happily, Margery did not receive a death sentence, but she was banished to another diocese. Below, the archbishop's heartless meeting with Margery—whom he places so cruelly and needlessly in chains, only to intimidate her and frighten others— contrasts vividly with the tender compassion of anchoress Julian of Norwich, who welcomes a visit from Margery.*

～♪

THE ARCHBISHOP PUTS HER IN CHAINS

The poor creature was brought into the Archbishop's Chapel and many members of the archbishop's staff appeared who despised her and accused her of being a prostitute and a heretic. Some of them swore oaths that she should be burned. And she found the courage to accuse them in return: "Sirs," she said, "I fear that it is you who shall burn—in hell—since you do not keep the commandments of God." Then they slunk away, evidently ashamed. And Margery prayed fervently within herself.

...At last the Archbishop came into the chapel with his clerics and he said fiercely to her: "Why are you dressed in white? Are you a virgin?" Getting down on her knees before him, she answered, "No, I am not a virgin. I am a wife." He commanded his men to bring a pair of chains and said she should be chained because she was a heretic. And she said, "I am not a heretic, and you will not be able to prove me such." Then the Archbishop went away and left her standing all alone for a long time. She prayed for God's help against her enemies, and she trembled so much out of fear that she wished she could put her hands in her sleeves to hide her shaking.

Eventually the Archbishop came back to the chapel with many good clerics, including a doctor of divinity who had questioned her previously and a monk who had preached against her.... The Archbishop took his throne and his clerics sat according to their rank. The whole time that people were gathering and the Archbishop was taking his seat, Margery was at the back praying for help. She prayed so fervently and for so long that she dissolved into tears and then began to cry so loudly that everyone was amazed.

When she stopped crying she came forward and fell on her knees before the Archbishop who asked her fiercely: "Why do you weep this way, woman?" She responded, "Sir, someday you will wish you had wept as bitterly as I." Then the Archbishop questioned her on the Articles of Faith and she answered well, accurately and easily. So he could not find fault with her and said to the clerics, "She knows her faith well enough. What do you want me to do with her?" They answered, "We know that she knows the Articles of Faith, but we do not want her to live here, since the people trust her and she may lead them astray."

Then the Archbishop said to her, "I have heard evil things about you. I have been told that you are a very wicked woman." And she replied, "Sir, I have been told that you are a very wicked man. And if you are in fact as wicked as people say, you will have to change your ways or you will never reach heaven."...

The Archbishop said, "Lay your hand on the book before me and swear that you will go out of my diocese." "No, sir, give me permission to go back to York to say goodbye to my friends." He said she could stay for a day or two, and she replied that she could not leave that quickly.... "You must swear that you will not teach or provoke the people of this diocese." "No, sir, I will not so swear. I will speak of God when and where I want... for the all-powerful God does not forbid us to speak of him. And the Gospel states that when a woman heard Jesus preach, she went up to him and said out loud for all to hear, 'Blessed is the womb that gave you birth and the breasts that nursed you.' And Jesus replied to her, 'Blessed are those who hear the word of God and keep it.' Therefore, Sir, it is my opinion that the Gospel gives me permission to speak about God."

...A high-ranking cleric brought out a book and cited the passage where St. Paul says that a woman shall not preach. She answered that by saying, "Sir, I do not preach. [St. Paul says that women should not preach in church.] I have no pulpit.... I speak in good words to people, and that I shall do as long as I live."

CATHERINE OF GENOA
ITALY, 1447–1510

A lover and a doer, a profound thinker as well as a saint and philanthropist who used her spiritual genius in the service of poor and ill women, Catherine of Genoa wrote about the experience of "purification," of awakening to the soul's shadow elements, in order to know Pure Love. For her, awakening is like polishing an empty mirror, revealing only pure light.

The fifth child born to the noble Fieschi family of Genoa, Catherine wanted from early childhood on to become a nun and at thirteen applied to the Augustinians, who refused her admission because of her youth. Three years later, her family forced her for financial and political advantages to marry an unreliable man whom she did not love, Giuliano Adorno. Lonely and unhappy in the marriage, she buried herself in social life.

At thirty-six, during a Lenten confession, she had a sudden, overwhelming experience of "Pure Love" and came away crying out, "No more sins! No more sins!" At that moment she suddenly saw her Self in the presence of Infinite Reality and understood (as Evelyn Underhill wrote in her book Mysticism*) that all her life she had been measuring her candlelight by other candles and now for the first time was out in the open air, seeing the sun.*

This instantaneous illumination never left. It released phenomenal energy and commitment, and from that moment on Catherine devoted herself to contemplation and caring for the poor and the sick, a life ideally balanced between the inner and the outer. A glowing soul whose ecstasies never abated, she administered a women's hospital and established an open-air infirmary during the plague of 1493, being credited with many healings.

COMMITMENT

Lord, I give myself to you. I do not know where I am going. I do not know what to do. I offer this prayer to you. I place myself in your hands. For I know You are the holy one, the only one who can care for me and guide me in the right way. I ask for Your Pure Love, to extinguish my selfishness. Busy me so much in the care of the sick and the poor that I will have no more time to waste in trivialities.

TRANSPARENCY

When God sees the soul less transparent than it was at its origins, He tugs at it with a glance, lures it, and binds it to Himself with a fiery love that by itself could annihilate an immortal thing. This way the soul is so transformed that it knows nothing other than God. He continues to draw the soul into this fiery love until it is wholly restored to that state of transparency in which it was born. Divine energies sear and purify the soul until it becomes like gold that has melted in the refiner's fire, all dross having fallen away. When the gold has come to the point of 24 carats, it cannot be further purified. This is what happens in the fire of God's love.

THREE TEACHINGS

These sacred things I speak about work within me in secret—and with great power.

Fight yourself, and you need have no other foe.

If you want to know Pure Love, stay with the knowledge of your Self. There you will learn all that you need to know.

MIRABAI

INDIA, 1498–C. 1550

India's most beloved woman poet-saint, a sage who inspired Gandhi, a composer of mystical songs still sung in India today, Mirabai was a Rajput princess who, like Clare of Assisi and so many other women in this book, abandoned her noble birth and luxurious palace life for the fuller life of mystical love. As the poet Ramprasad once asked, "Who can keep a blazing fire tied in a cotton cloth?"

Mirabai received some education at the court of her grandfather and married the prince of Mewar, but she eventually left her family to become an ascetic mendicant, singing and dancing rapturous prayers to the Divine Beloved. "I weighed all on the scales," she explains, "and then I gave my body, my life, things like that."

Like the measureless stream of women and men throughout history who have worshiped black gods and goddesses, Mirabai knew her Beloved Krishna as "the Dark One," the Lord of night beauty and mystery. She associates "him" with the moon's phases and the cosmic darknesses, concealing unfathomable secrets she longs to understand while revealing all that she needs to know. Like the Black Christs in Lucca, Italy, and all over the world, Mirabai's dark Lord is more androgynous than masculine, hinting at the Divine Marriage of the Sacred Feminine and Sacred Masculine within her soul. Stormy oscillations of bliss and pain mark every stage of her journey to, in, and with the Dark One, who arrives unexpectedly to fill her whole soul with ecstasy, only to leave abruptly, tossing her into despair. But she ultimately learns what all genuine mystics discover: that the Beloved arrives without ever leaving.

For all Mirabai's unconventional struggles to separate herself from class and family duties, she never completely escaped their social pressures. But when her mother insisted she learn the etiquette of a typical royal household and throw herself into wifely duties, Mira replied,

> *O Mother, I am married. I married the Dark One in a dream. I wore a glowing red and yellow veil, and henna was beautifully applied to my hands. My Beloved [Krishna] played the flute for me on the banks of the river Yamuna, as he has since my very childhood. I can't give up my love for him. I can't. It is eternal.*

When the man she was forced to marry eventually died, Mira bluntly refused to adopt the settled conduct of a princely widow, and when her powerful father-in-law demanded that she become sati—throw herself on her husband's funeral pyre and die with him—she answered him definitively:

> Mira is dyed in Hari's color [Krishna's love].
> She has set aside all other colors.
> I will sing.
> I will not become sati!
> My heart loves only Hari.
> The relation of eldest daughter-in-law exists no more!

Charged with ruining the family's honor through her defiance, Mira was persecuted by her in-laws for most of her remaining years. Toward the end of her life, probably supported by her brothers, she moved to the Ranachora temple and ashram at Dvarka, singing her illuminated songs to Hari.

~୨

WHY MIRA CAN'T GO BACK

> Mira is dyed in the colors of the Dark One,
> She has washed out all other hues.
> Making love with the Dark One, fasting,
> those are my jewels and wealth.
> Meditation beads and forehead streaks,
> those are my scarves and robes.
> They are enough. My teacher taught me.
> Approve me or disapprove me;
> I praise the Dark One day and night.
> My path is ecstasy.
> I don't harm. I don't steal. I don't strike anyone.
> What crime can you charge me with?
> I have danced in the forest with Hari,
> and now you want me to ride an ass.

O FRIENDS, I AM MAD

O friends, I am mad
With love.

Impossible to sleep
Since he left me.
My mattress a bed of thorns.

The heart that knows this knife
Knows the meaning of pain,
Like a jeweler
Who understands the essence of the pearl.

Mira cries out: O Hari,
Only you can heal this pain.

THE DARK ONE IS HERE INSIDE

The Dark One is here inside.
Never leaving, He never arrives.
Mira says:
I gaze at the road day and night.

THE CITY SEEKS ITS LORD

The city seeks
Its lord
Dark of hue
As a night
Its moon.

TRANSLATED BY
SHAMA FUTEHALLY

I PUT BELLS ON MY ANKLES

I put bells on my ankles
And danced.
The people said
Mira is mad!
My mother-in-law declared
I ruined the family's reputation.
The king sent a cup of poison
And I drank it with a smile.

I have offered my body and mind
To Hari
And drink the nectar of holy sight.

TRANSLATOR UNKNOWN

O FRIEND, UNDERSTAND

O friend, understand
The body
Is like the sea,
Hiding treasures
All its own.

TRANSLATOR
UNKNOWN

TERESA OF AVILA
SPAIN, 1515–1582

Everyone's favorite saint—an ecstatic mystic; the founder of seventeen monasteries for women; the beloved friend of St. John of the Cross; a witty, vivacious, pretty, clever, fiercely independent, and delightful woman— Teresa of Avila was loved by men and women equally. She prayed, worked, and lived passionately despite heavy opposition from conservatives within her own Carmelite order. Criticized for the voluptuous way she devoured her meals, she replied with the absolute confidence of one who has earned self-knowledge through strenuous inner discipline: "When praying, pray! When eating partridge, eat partridge!" Of less friendly accusers, such as the neurotic priests of the Inquisition who watched her every move and had the power to burn her at the stake, she wrote, "Without doubt I fear those who have such great fear of the devil more than I could ever fear the devil himself."

The turning point in her life from spiritual immaturity to true intimacy with the Divine occurred when she made the difficult decision to stop socializing in the parlors of her convent, especially with one particular man, and to commit herself wholeheartedly to the life of prayer. When she wrenched herself away from "frivolities," immersing herself in prayer, her spirit caught fire, and like her famous image of the silkworm, who emerges from its cocoon as a beautiful butterfly, she was reborn with the authority of a great leader.

She remarked of her lifelong raptures (immortalized in Bernini's world-famous statue Teresa of Jesus in Ecstasy) *that such transporting communion with God's love can result in healing: "Very often one who was before sickly and full of pain comes forth healthy and even with new strength: for it is something great that is given to the soul in rapture."*

Dismayed with the laxity and excessively comfortable lifestyle of the Carmelite order in sixteenth-century Spain, she initiated a bold reform to reduce socializing and restore the ancient Carmelite ideal of poverty and deep prayer. Her tireless work for reform provoked death threats from the extreme right and rage from laypeople living near her convents, who feared having to share their food and resources with the nuns. Teresa used wily self-belittlement in her books to keep her ecclesiastical enemies at bay, but there was no compromise in her determination to reform the Carmelite order. During her forties and fifties, she canvassed Spain in crude carts with wooden wheels (long before paved roads existed) to inspire and reinspire personally the women who joined her communities. She wrote magnificent books on prayer, such as the immortal Interior Castle, *and she became (with Catherine of Siena) one of only two women Doctors of the Church.*

One evening when Teresa was sixty-three, after a long day of hard traveling, she arrived at her destination apologizing for being so tired that she was going to have to go to bed, although it was only about six o'clock. The next day, it was apparent her life was drawing to a close, and within weeks

she spoke her last words: "My Lord, it is time to move on. Well, then may
your will be done. O my Lord and my Spouse, the hour that I have longed
for has come. It is time for us to meet one another."

~૭

TWO FOUNTAINS, TWO WAYS OF PRAYER

Let us imagine we see two fountains with basins which fill with
water. I can find no simile more appropriate than water by which to
explain spiritual things.... I love this element so much that I have
studied it more attentively than many other things. The Creator,
who is so great, so wise, has doubtless hidden secrets in all created
things, and we can benefit from knowing them (as those say who
understand such matters). Indeed, I believe that in each smallest
creature, though it be but a tiny ant, are more wonders than we can
comprehend.

These two basins are filled in different ways; one with water
flowing from a distance into it through many pipes and waterworks;
while the other is built near the source of the spring itself and fills
quite noiselessly. If the fountain is plentiful—as is the one we
speak of—after the basin is full the water overflows in a great
stream which flows continually. No machinery is needed here, nor
does the water run through aqueducts.

Such is the difference between the two kinds of prayer. The
water running through the aqueducts resembles devotion, which is
obtained through meditation. We gain it by our thoughts, by meditating on created things, by the labor of our minds. In short, it is
the result of our endeavors, and so makes the commotion I spoke
of earlier, while profiting the soul.

The other fountain, like divine consolations, receives the water
from the source itself (which signifies God). As usual when supernatural favors are bestowed on us, we experience the greatest
peace, calm, sweetness, in the inmost depths of our being. I know
neither where nor how.

This joy is not, like ordinary happiness, at once felt by the heart.
After gradually filling it to the brim, delight overflows throughout
all the mansions and faculties of the soul, until at last it reaches

the body. Therefore I say it arises from God and ends in ourselves, for whoever experiences it will find that the whole physical part of our nature shares in this delight and sweetness.

While writing this, I have been thinking that the verse *"Dilatasti cor meum"*—"You have opened my heart"—declares that the heart has been opened. This joy does not appear to me to originate in the heart, but in some more inner part; as it were, in the depths of our being. I think this must be the center of the soul, as I have heard and will explain later on. I discover secrets within us which often fill me with astonishment: How many more must there be that are unknown to me! O my Lord and my God! How stupendous is your grandeur!... How great are your mysteries!...

ROSE OF LIMA
PERU, 1586–1617

Isabel Flores, who was nicknamed Rosa by her nurse, is considered the founder of social work in Peru. Born to a Puerto Rican father and a mother part Spanish and part Incan, she came to understand the resentment of the Indians toward the Spaniards, led by Francisco Pizarro, who killed their people, crushed their culture, and mined their vast reserves of gold. In adolescence she dedicated herself to the spiritual life and helping the poor and ill. Like Clare of Assisi and Catherine of Siena, she cut off her long hair to avoid suitors and persuade her parents that she would not marry. Rose built herself a hermitage on the family grounds, establishing an infirmary in her parents' home to care for ill elderly people and poor children. As her fame grew, she did not escape the grave danger of scrutiny by the Inquisition, but being judged acceptable, she remained unharmed. She died at the age of thirty-one, most likely of "holy anorexia" (anorexia used in the service of Divine Love), like Catherine of Siena (see p. 84) and Simone Weil (see p. 187), having told her family on the day of her death: "I go to a great banquet tonight."

Rose wrote her enchanting mosquito tale toward the end of her brief years.

~ɔ

MOSQUITOES IN PRAISE

One summer, a [member of Lima's nobility] came to the garden
behind the home of Rosa's parents, to see her in her hermitage. He
sat by the door in the shade of young trees, and he and Rosa talked.
There were many mosquitoes bothering him, but not one touched
Rosa. Her face and hands, too, were free of welts. He inquired:
"My Mother, how is it that these mosquitoes bite guests but not my
Mother?" Rosa replied, "My Father, I have made friends with the
mosquitoes ever since I began coming to this cell. So, not only do
they not bite, they are in addition a motive for me to praise God.
For by night, they gather here inside the cell, and great swarms cling
to the walls. And when, in the morning I come and open the door,
they all rise, and I tell them it is time for us to praise God. And
really, . . . it seems that they do just that, raising their voices in concert, humming their praise."

ADAPTED FROM *THE ROSE AND THE LILY*
BY FRANCES PARKINSON KEYES

ANONYMOUS PAWNEE CHANT

NATIVE AMERICA, ORAL TRADITION

*A Pawnee household was composed of some thirty to fifty people living in
an earth lodge, a dome-shaped dwelling with a roof made of earth. Women
were separated into three sections of the structure, one for mature women
who performed most of the work; another for young women learning their
future tasks; and another for old women who cared for infants. The Pawnee
people numbered about twelve thousand and were established primarily in
present-day Nebraska. Women sang this chant at a blessing ceremony for a
child.*

~⁀

ANOINTING WITH SACRED OINTMENT

Look, my child! Lift your eyes,
Look at the one who is standing here,
Look, my child! At the one who is waiting
To set you here apart.
Awaken, my child, awaken!
Sacred ointment comes to you,
To set you apart.

ANNE BRADSTREET
ENGLAND, 1612–1672

Anne Bradstreet enjoyed the double fulfillment of a woman as devoted to her husband and eight children as to her work. She is the author of the first known book of poetry to be written in colonial America. In 1956, the American poet John Berryman honored her in a poem fifty-seven stanzas long: "Homage to Mistress Bradstreet."

Born in England to devout Puritans, Anne married Simon Bradstreet at the age of sixteen, and two years later they and her parents set sail on the Arabella *for the Massachusetts Bay colony. Anne's father became the second governor of Massachusetts, and her husband succeeded him seven years after Anne died. Like Dhuodana in the ninth century (see p. 46), who wrote a touching manual of good behavior for her son William, Anne Bradstreet left a book of moral guidance for her son Simon. Her dedication in the book reads in part: "You once desired me to leave something for you in writing that you might look upon when you should see me no more. I could think of nothing more fit for you nor of more ease to myself than these short meditations."*

In her poetry and all her work, Anne used her Puritan faith to see meaning and purpose in every event, joyful or sorrowful. In this poem, written when her family home in North Andover burned down with all her belongings, her immediate surrender recalls the Buddhist couplet:

Now that my house has been burned to the ground
I have an unobstructed view of the rising moon.

~)

ON THE BURNING OF OUR HOUSE,
JULY 10, 1666

In silent night when rest I took
For sorrow near I did not look
I wakened was with thunderous noise
And piteous shrieks of dreadful voice.
That fearful sound of "Fire!" and "Fire!"
Let no man know is my desire.
I, starting up, the light did spy,
And to my God my heart did cry
To strengthen me in my distress
And not to leave me succorless.
Then, coming out, beheld a space
The flame consume my dwelling place.
And when I could no longer look.
I blest the name that gave and took.
That laid my goods now in the dust.
Yea, so it was, and so 'twas just.
It was his own, it was not mine,
Far be it that I should repine;
He might of all justly bereft
But yet sufficient of us left.
When by the ruins oft I passed
My sorrowing eyes aside did cast,
And here and there the spaces spy
Where oft I sat and long did lie.
Here stood that trunk, and there that chest,
There lay that store I counted best.
My pleasant things in ashes lie.
And them behold no more shall I.
Under thy roof no guest shall sit,
Nor at the table eat a bit.

No pleasant tale shall e'er be told,
Nor thing recounted done of old.
No candle e'er shall shine in thee,
No bridegroom's voice e'er heard shall be.
In silence ever shall thou lie.
Adieu, adieu, all's vanity.
Then straight I 'gin my heart to chide,
And did thy wealth on earth abide?
Didst fix thy hope on mold'ring dust?
The arm of flesh didst make thy trust?
Raise up thy thoughts above the sky
That dunghill mists away may fly.
Thou hast an house on high erect,
Framed by that mighty architect,
With glory richly furnished,
Stand permanent though this be fled.
It's purchased and paid for too
By Him who hath enough to do.
A price so vast as is unknown
Yet by His gift is made thy own;
There's wealth enough, I need no more....

MARGARET MARY ALACOQUE
FRANCE, 1647–1690

The West's most sublime writer on the mystery of the heart of God, Margaret Mary Alacoque is scarcely known, and few of her writings have been translated, yet her mystical devotion to the sacred heart has swept across the world and today marks one of the most important feast days in the Catholic Church.

A child mystic acutely sensitive to the workings of the Spirit, Margaret Mary was born to a woman apparently incapable of nurturing and was sent at the age of four to her godmother, who lived alone in a large house staffed by servants. Margaret Mary found joy and refuge in her godmother's chapel, where her gift for prayer and mystical spirituality blossomed. Astonished servants observed her kneeling in the chapel in silence and solitude, almost immobile, for hours at a time.

In young adulthood, she entered the Visitation convent of Paray-le-Monial where, at twenty-two, she wrote of her decision to become a nun: "I felt like a slave freed from prison and chains entering the house of her Beloved to be joyful and absolutely free in his presence, his riches, his love." A vision urged her to follow the path of St. John the Evangelist by teaching her devotion to others. But no one, neither the nuns nor the doubtful theologians appointed to examine her, took her seriously, and Margaret Mary fell ill and took to her bed (a not-infrequent last resort of nuns when institutional structures block self-expression: Hildegard, for example, did the same). Finally a Jesuit, Claude de la Colombiere, recognized her mystical genius and through his own writing about her teachings took the first step in spreading her message around the world.

Margaret Mary's last words were "I need nothing but to lose myself in the heart of God."

~∂

FROM A VISION OF THE DIVINE HEART

Christ asked me for my heart which I implored him to take, which he did, placing it within his own sacred heart and showing it to me as a tiny speck consumed in a burning furnace. Then, taking it out as a burning flame shaped like a heart, He returned it to the place from which he had taken it.... And he said:

> Look at this heart which has so loved men and women that it has spared nothing, even to the point of suffering and dying to make this love known. Yet nothing is given back: instead of gratitude I receive ingratitude, irreverence and sacrilege. I am shown coldness and contempt in the very sacrament of love.

PRAYER TO THE SACRED HEART

I offer, dedicate, and consecrate wholly and purely to the Sacred heart . . . all the merit to be acquired or given me during my life and after death, that the intentions of the sacred heart may be fulfilled.

SOR JUANA INÉS DE LA CRUZ

MEXICO, C. 1648–1695

A multifaceted genius—scientist, mystic, writer, and poet—the earliest great woman we know of from Mexico, Juana Rabirez de Asbaje y Santillana was the subject of a 1997 film, Sor Juana. Born to a Spanish family living in Mexico 135 years after Cortes's brutal conquest of the Indians, when the dominant culture was Spanish and poor Indians performed most household work, Juana grew up free of the duties imposed on most Mexican girls. Ferociously intelligent, she spent much of her childhood reading books in the extensive library of her grandparents, who raised her in the small town of Panoáyan, southeast of Mexico City.

At thirteen, she was invited to the residence of the Spanish viceroy and vicerine, where a selection of especially gifted boys and girls were educated. Juana revealed so much talent and her performance so surpassed her peers' performance in all areas that the forty "most learned men" of the time were gathered to test her in an all-day oral exam. She dazzled the men, and the viceroy described the exam as "a great galleon under attack by a few small canoes."

Because further education and all professional paths were closed to women, and she did not want to marry, she considered dressing in men's clothes in order to study at the University of Mexico, but settled on entering the convent of San Jeronimo, where lax rules and comfortable surroundings allowed her to have an attractive suite of rooms, servants to care for her needs, and, eventually, a spectacular library of over four thousand books—reputedly the largest library in seventeenth-century Mexico. Here, for twenty relatively contented years, she studied, wrote prose and poetry, and performed "scientific" experiments; for example, to study transformation from semiliquid to semisolid states, she studied eggs frying in a pan. Ultimately she became suspect in church circles for her free-thinking individualism. Her spiritual director complained of her "secularism," and she let him go, stating that she needed only the guidance of the Spirit. When the Bishop of Puebla (using the pseudonym Sor Filotea) publicly counseled her to write on topics more appropriate for a woman and for her calling, Sor Juana wrote a defiant argument for women's intellectual freedom, Respuesta a Sor Filotea. In the end, church officials forced her to renounce her intellectual life, surrender her entire library, and succumb to a life of

silence and harsh physical penance. Not surprisingly, she died only a few
years later during an epidemic of probable plague.

~⁹

SELECTIONS

Seraphim, come,
come here and ponder
a Rose that, when cut,
lives all the longer.

Break the crystalline seal
On the clear, cold glass of this fountain
And allow my love to enter.
See how my golden curls
Are overspread with hoar-frost,
Are wet with dewy pearls.
Come, my Spouse, to your Love,
Rend that clear curtain,
Make your countenance seen,
let me hear your voice in my ear!

TRANSLATOR UNKNOWN

Oh, all the consideration,
the tenderness I have seen:
when love is placed in God,
nothing else can intervene.
From what is legitimate
it cannot deviate;
no risk of being forgotten
need it ever contemplate.
I recall—were it not so—
a time when the love I knew
went far beyond madness even,
reached excesses known to few,

but being a bastard love,
built on warring tensions,
it simply fell apart
from its own dissensions. . . .

TRANSLATED BY
ALAN S. TRUEBLOOD

RWALA BEDOUIN WOMEN

ARABIAN PENINSULA, ORAL TRADITION

This prayer from the Rwala Bedouin people belongs to a richly complex ritual performed by the women when drought threatens. Terrified and trusting, the women create a "Rain Mother" from a stick and women's clothing, and then girls, led by the woman selected to carry Rain Mother, process from tent to tent chanting a song such as the one that appears below. At each tent they collect a little food to offer to the god who is refusing them rain, hopefully appeasing its apparent anger at them. The bearer of the simulacrum begins the chant, alternating verses with the girls in traditional call-and-response fashion. In the third verse, the leader is weeping because she sees a beloved camel weakening from thirst, perhaps dying, which hints at the catastrophic loss of animals, crops, and human life that may lie just ahead.

∽♪

O MOTHER OF RAIN,
RAIN UPON US!

O Mother of Rain, rain upon us!
Moisten the cloak of our shepherd.
O Mother of Rain, rain upon us!
Quench our thirst with torrential rains.
O Mother of Rain, rain upon us!
Give us our portion from Allah's stores.
O Mother of Rain, rain upon us!
Cause torrents of water to fall over us.

O Mother of rain, rain upon us!
We are tormented by this thirst.
O Mother of Rain, have mercy on us,
Dust clouds are making us blind.
O Mother of Rain, come to our aid,
The specter of death speeds toward us.
O Mother of Rain, O famished one,
The great cold is destroying us.

Place me upon my camel.
Hold back whoever would restrain me.
The tears of my eyes are used up,
Spent for those who have already gone.

ANN LEE
ENGLAND, 1736–1784

Ann Lee founded the Shakers, or "shaking Quakers," who sang, chanted, shouted, laughed, and gyrated in lively dances as part of their daily worship ritual. In marked contrast to the dour Puritans, who banned "sinful" singing, dancing, and even card playing, Ann Lee's movement sprang from authentically mystical joy.

While imprisoned in England for supposedly "profaning the Sabbath," she had two forceful dreams, one of which revealed to her the Feminine Divine, which she identified with sophia, *holy wisdom. The other dream convinced her that the road to the fullest knowledge of the Divine demanded celibacy. A charismatic public speaker, she drew a number of disciples who migrated with her to the United States in the hope of conducting their ecstatic religious services without persecution. However, she was imprisoned in America as well, this time for refusing to take a loyalty oath during the American Revolution. Charged with possible witchcraft and spying for the enemy, she was suspect probably because of her unconventional spiritual leadership, wild rituals, and huge success. She continued to gain more and more converts, both men and women. Ann Lee is receiving renewed attention today from scholars interested in her theology and spirituality, especially her emphasis on simplicity—in dress, home furnishings, meals, and general lifestyle. Shaker songs are again popular—the one below was performed on the hit television show ER—and the distinctive style of furniture the Shakers developed can be seen today at the Shaker Museum in New Hampshire, among other places.*

~૭

'TIS THE GIFT TO BE SIMPLE

'Tis the gift to be simple,
'Tis the gift to be free,
'Tis the gift to come down to where we ought to be,
And when we find ourselves in the place that's right,
'Twill be in the valley of love and delight.

THE LORD OF THE DANCE

I dance in the morning when the world was begun,
And I dance in the moon and the stars and the sun,
And I came down from heaven and I dance on the earth.
At Bethlehem I had my birth.

I danced for the scribe and the Pharisee,
But they would not dance and they wouldn't follow me,
I danced for the fishermen, for James and John,
They came with me and the Dance went on.

I danced on the Sabbath and I cured the lame,
The holy people said it was a shame
They whipped and they stripped and they hung me high
And they left me on a Cross to die.

I danced on a Friday when the sky turned black.
It's hard to dance with the devil on your back.
They buried my body and they thought I'd gone
But I am the dance and I still go on.

SOJOURNER TRUTH
NEW YORK, C. 1799–1883

One of the most influential black leaders in women's fight for emancipation, Sojourner Truth was a forceful orator and dynamic leader whose life-long inspiration came from her mother's insistence that "there is a God who sees and hears you." She was born into slavery on a Dutch estate in the Hudson Valley of New York. Raised in deplorable conditions, crowded into a basement space with other slave families, undernourished, overworked, and forced to endure extreme suffering, she reinforced her faith and courage by taking refuge once a day near a hidden stream where the roar of a waterfall comforted her and she could pray. The more intimate she became with her God, the more rich her mystical experience and the bolder her spirit. Some years later, when women were gathering to hear black ministers preach on women's rights, with no woman daring to speak, Sojourner Truth would storm the podium and galvanize the audience with her frank eloquence.

On one occasion, she was the only black person attending a revival meeting in Northhampton, Massachusetts, when a local gang armed with clubs began harassing the crowd and threatening to burn down their tents. With panic spreading rapidly, Sojourner Truth determined to pacify the mob. Stepping up on a rise of earth, she threw out her strong arms and in her great powerful voice began to sing a gospel song. The gang leaders rushed to encircle her, so she climbed up on a wagon and shouted them down with her typical wisdom and wit:

> Well, there are two congregations on these grounds! It is written that there shall be a separation, that the sheep shall be separated from the goats. Seems the other preachers got the sheep, and I got the goats.

There was a burst of laughter, and peace was quickly restored. She preached for an hour, sang another hymn, and the mob quietly dispersed. The former slave, who was named Isabella at her birth and renamed herself Sojourner Truth, died at eighty-four in her own home in Battle Creek, Michigan, a free woman in every sense of the word.

~♪

AR'N'T I A WOMAN?

That man over there says that women need to be helped into carriages, and lifted over ditches, and to have the best place everywhere. Nobody ever helped me into carriages, or over mud puddles, or gave me any best place—and ar'n't I a woman?

Look at me! Look at my arm! I have plowed and planted and gathered into barns, and no man could head me—and ar'n't I a woman?

I could work as much and eat as much as a man—when I could get it—and bear the lash as well—and ar'n't I a woman?

I have born thirteen children and seen most of them sold into slavery, and when I cried out a mother's grief, no one but Jesus heard me—and ar'n't I a woman?...

That little man in black there [a minister] says woman can't have as many rights as man, 'cause Christ wasn't a woman. Where did your Christ come from? *Where did your Christ come from!* From God and a woman! Man had nothing to do with him.

IN DEFENSE OF EVE

If the first woman God ever made was strong enough to turn the world upside down all alone, these together [the women assembled in the audience] ought to be able to turn it back and get it right side up again. And now that they are asking to do it, the men better let them.

I AM GOING TO STAY RIGHT HERE AND STAND THE FIRE!

Here you are talking about being changed in the twinkling of an eye. If the Lord should come, He'd change you to nothing, for there is nothing in you. You seem to be expecting to go to some parlor away up somewhere, and when the wicked have been burnt, you are coming back to walk in triumph over their ashes—this is to be your New Jerusalem! Now I can't see anything so nice in that, coming back to such a mess as that, a world covered with the ashes of the wicked! Besides, if the Lord comes and burns—as you say He will—I am not going away. I am going to stay right here and *stand the fire,* like Shadrach, Meshach, and Abednego! And Jesus will walk me through the fire, and keep me from harm. No, I shall remain! Do you tell me that God's children *can't stand fire?* It is absurd to think so!

PYGMY WOMEN
ZAIRE (TODAY'S DEMOCRATIC REPUBLIC OF THE CONGO),
ORAL TRADITION

Certain groups of Pygmy women in Zaire chant this prayer in the morning as they walk to their work. The Pygmy people live mostly in equatorial rain forests in Africa, in small semi-nomadic bands and are hunter-gatherers. They number about 150,000 to 300,000. They have no chiefs or political structure, and respected male elders make decisions.

~♪

WOMEN'S MORNING SONG

Morning has risen;
O, Asobe, take away from our path
Every hurt
Every pain,
Every sickness,
All our cares.
O, Asobe, bring us home safely tonight.

CHANT FOR A SICK CHILD

[Here the mother recites her part of the prayer, holding her sick child. The other women respond like a chorus, chanting.]

Mother: O spirits of our ancestors, this little one I hold is my child. She is your child also. Be good to her.

Women: She has entered a world of trouble. There is sickness. There is cold and pain. The pain that you knew when you were here, the sickness with which you are familiar.

Mother: Let her sleep in peace. For there is healing in sleep. Let her be healed. Let no one have anger toward us.

Women: O spirits of the past, let her grow. Let her be strong. Let her become a woman. Then she will offer a sacrifice to you that will fill your hearts with delight.

ASHANTI WOMEN
GHANA, ORAL TRADITION

In this girl's rite of initiation into womanhood, a joyful spirit of celebration turns to concern that the girl might die before reaching adulthood. The women, who belong to the Ashanti people of Ghana, pray to the Divine Mother for length of life. The Ashanti are matrilineal, identity and inheritance passing through the mother rather than the father, and are ruled by a male king. Noted for the splendid quality of their gold work and the colorful kente *cloth that women weave, they are famed for their gold-encrusted stool that symbolizes kingship.*

~⁀

FROM THE MENSTRUAL
RITE OF PASSAGE

O divine Mother, we lean on you and do not fall.
We offer you wine.
Receive our wine, and drink.

O Earth Goddess, we worship you every Thursday.
We offer you wine.
Receive our wine, and drink.

O Spirits of our ancestors, you too,
Receive this wine, and drink.

This girl child, given to me from God

Today the *Bara* has come to her.

O Mother Who Lives in the Spirit Land,
Do not come to take her away from me,
Do not allow her to menstruate only to die.

LET ONE REMAIN

[This prayer comes from a sacred ritual that is performed by the women when a baby who is less than a week old dies. The infant's mother and her own mother bring eggs and mashed bananas or yams to a crossroads, where the prayer is offered.]

O Mother Who Lives in the Spirit Land, we offer you these bananas and eggs. Receive them and eat. We thank you very much that you allowed this child to come to us, and we beg you to send another.

And you, infant who has left, receive these eggs. They are yours. Now give back to your mother, saying: "Let one come to her again, but this time permit it to remain."

IN DESPERATION OF GRIEF

[This is a "wailing prayer," which a widow and other relatives recite soon after the death of the husband.]

My husband, you have abandoned me.
My husband is gone, and will never return.
I am lost. Where will I go?
You used to fetch water for me. You collected the firewood.
You clothed me and fed me with good things.
Why have you left me? Why have you done this to me?
Where will I go?

COVER ME WITH THE NIGHT

[This is a Christian prayer from Ghana.]

Come Lord,
and cover me with the night.
Spread your grace over us
as you assured us you would.
Your promises are more than
all the stars in the sky;
your mercy is deeper than the night.
Lord, it will be cold.
The night comes with its breath of death.
Night comes; the end comes; you come.
Lord, we will wait for you
day and night.

BIBI HAYATI
PERSIA (IRAQ), ?–1853

The daughter of a Muslim family with a long history of Sufi practice, Bibi Hayati began her spiritual training with her brother, who was a Sufi sheikh, a spiritual guide. She studied with other teachers and eventually with a leader of the Nimatullahi order named Nur Ali Shah, whom she married. She received initiation as a Sufi and wrote love poetry while devoting much of her time to cooking for the community and caring for people in need.

Her poems are a magnificent blend of deep, timeless insights and feelings that arise in Buddhism as much as Islam or Christianity. As poet Jane Hirshfield writes, the poems of Bibi Hayati "offer us the Sufi realization that the radiance of the Beloved shines in and through all the many things of the world, making temple and alley equal when seen in their original Face."

∼꙳

IS THIS DARKNESS
THE NIGHT OF POWER?

Is this darkness the night of Power, or the black falling of your
     hair?
Is the rising light daybreak, or the reflection of your face?

In the book of Beauty, is this a first line?
Or merely a fragment I scribble, tracing your eyebrows?

Is this boxwood gathered in the orchard, or the rose garden's
     cypress?
The Tree of Paradise, heavy with dates, or the shape of your
     standing?

Is this scent from a Chinese deer, or the fragrance of infused
     water?
Is it the breathing of roses carried on wind, or your perfume?

Is this scorching a lightning bolt's remnants, or the burning
     mountain?
The heat of my sighs, or your inner body?

Is this Mongolian musk, or the purest of ambergris?
Is it the hyacinth unfolding, or your plaited curls?

Is this magic, or a chalice of red wine at dawn?
Your narcissus eye drunk with the way, or a sorcerer's work?

Is it the garden of Eden, or some earthly paradise?
The temple of those who have mastered the heart, or an alley?

Others all turn to adobe and mud when they pray to the Sacred—
The temple of Hayati's soul turns toward the sun of your Face.

TRANSLATED BY JANE HIRSHFIELD

ESKIMO PRAYER

WEST GREENLAND, ORAL TRADITION

The Eskimo people of West Greenland used to chant this prayer-song in praise of the Creator for a safe delivery of a baby, either a boy or a girl.

~♪

THANKS FOR THE BIRTH
OF A BABY GIRL

That she was taken out of her mother,
Thanks be for that!
That she, the little one,
Was taken out of her, we say,
Thanks be for that!

A HOPI CREATION STORY

NATIVE AMERICA, ORAL TRADITION

It is impossible to estimate the age of this Hopi creation story, which undoubtedly was transmitted orally for hundreds of years before scholars recorded it in the nineteenth century. Like most aboriginal myths, it gives woman as well as man a role in creation and celebrates the sacredness of all life on earth in the here and now as well as in eternity.

~♪

IN THE WOMB OF EARTH-MOTHER

Spider Woman took earth of four colors, yellow, red, white, and black, and moistened it with liquid in her mouth. She then shaped a form and covered it with the white cloak of creative wisdom. Over the form she sang a creation song, and then uncovered what she had made. There were human beings made in the likeness of her father, Sotuknang. The first four beings that she made were male and so she created four female partners for them.

It was at the time of the purple light that the forms came to life, at the first dawn of creation when the mystery of human creation begins to glow.

Soon the humans awakened and began to stir. Their foreheads were still moist and there was a soft spot on their heads. This took place at the second phase of the dawn of creation, at the time of the yellow light, when breath entered the human form.

After a while, the sun rose at the horizon, drying the moisture from their foreheads, making the soft spot on their heads firm. This took place at the third phase of the dawn of creation, at the time of the red light, when man and woman were fully formed.

Spider Woman introduced man and woman to their father, the sun. "Remember always," she said to them, "the three phases of your creation. The time of the purple light, which reveals mystery; the time of the yellow light, the breath of life; and the red light, the warmth of love."

HARRIET A. JACOBS
NORTH CAROLINA, 1813–1897

In 1861, a recently freed slave named Harriet A. Jacobs made her way to the North and published what has been called a "revolutionary" account of her life as a woman, a mother, and a heroine. This extraordinary narrative exposes not only the well-known atrocities of slavery—from humiliation and degradation to torture and death—but also reveals the ugly story of sexual oppression of slave women by their masters. In many poignant passages, Jacobs describes her brave attempts to save her white-fathered children from slavery and to keep them connected to a supportive community consisting of her grandmother and a few free blacks in North Carolina. Harriet's book, Incidents in the Life of a Slave Girl, *which was copied by her daughter and published with the help of an abolitionist editor, Lydia Maria Child, can be read in its entirety in Jean Fagin Yellin's edition published by Harvard University Press in 2000.*

~♪

FROM INCIDENTS IN THE LIFE OF A SLAVE GIRL

Everywhere the years bring to all enough of sin and sorrow; but in slavery the very dawn of life is darkened by these shadows. Even the little child, who is accustomed to wait on her mistress and her children, will learn, before she is twelve years old, why it is that her mistress hates such and such a one among the slaves. Perhaps the child's own mother is among those hated ones. She listens to violent outbreaks of jealous passion, and cannot help understanding what is the cause. She will become prematurely knowing in evil things. Soon she will learn to tremble when she hears her master's footfall. She will be compelled to realize that she is no longer a child. If God has bestowed beauty upon her, it will prove her greatest curse. That which commands admiration in the white woman only hastens the degradation of the female slave. I know that some are too much brutalized by slavery to feel the humiliation of their position; but many slaves feel it most acutely, and shrink from the memory of it. I cannot tell how much I suffered in the presence of these wrongs, nor how I am still pained by the retrospect. My master met me at every turn, reminding me that I belonged to him, and swearing by heaven and earth that he would compel me to submit to him. If I went out for a breath of fresh air, after a day of unwearied toil, his footsteps dogged me. If I knelt by my mother's grave, his dark shadow fell on me even there. . . .

The secrets of slavery are concealed like those of the Inquisition. My master was, to my knowledge, the father of eleven slaves. But did the mothers dare to tell who was the father of their children? Did the other slaves dare to allude to it, except in whispers among themselves? No, indeed! They knew too well the terrible consequences.

FLORENCE NIGHTINGALE
ENGLAND, 1820–1910

Florence Nightingale's fame as the founder of modern nursing is legendary. Rejecting the posh lifestyle of her parents, she broke with the family's values and devoted her entire life to caring for the sick and for the injured on the front lines of battle, ignoring dangers to her own life and health. For all her fame, few people know that her motivation and energy sprang from a deep inner well of faith and a strong belief that she was "called" to her work. Today a movement in England's Anglican Church seeks to canonize Florence Nightingale, and books on her life and work are beginning to appear.

The following excerpt from her vast correspondence gives a glimpse of one of her favorite themes: the sad waste of priceless talent and energy when society blocks women's development and the responsibility of women to lead themselves out of stagnancy into full use of their gifts along lines of excellence.

~♪

FROM A LETTER ON WOMEN'S STAGNATION
IN THE NINETEENTH CENTURY

Jesus raised women above the condition of mere slaves... raised them by his sympathy, to be ministers of God. He gave them moral activity. But the age, the world, humanity, must give them the means to exercise this moral activity, must give them intellectual cultivation, spheres of action.

There is perhaps no century in which woman shows so meanly as in this [the nineteenth century]. Because her education seems entirely to have parted company with her vocation; there is no longer unity between a woman as inwardly developed and as outwardly manifested.

In the last century it was not so. In the succeeding one let us hope it will not be so. But now she is like the archangel Michael as he stands upon Saint Angelo in Rome. She has an immense provision of wings, which seem as if they would bear her over the earth and heaven; but when she tries to use them, she is petrified to stone, her feet are grown into the earth, chained to the bronze pedestal.

Nothing can well be imagined more painful than the present position of woman, unless, on the one hand, she renounces all outward activity and keeps herself within the magic sphere, the bubble of her dreams; or, on the other, surrendering all aspiration, she gives herself to her real life, soul and body. For those to whom it is possible, the latter is best; for out of our activity may come thought, out of mere aspiration can come nothing.

EMILY DICKINSON
MASSACHUSETTS, 1830–1886

The mystical genius of Emily Dickinson remains unrecognized, despite the innumerable studies of her poetry and life that have appeared in the past hundred years. While each decade brings new insights into her spiritual passion and force, the profundity of her psychological insight, the stunning originality of her style and poetic diction, and her unconventional freedom and perplexing solitude, few literary critics understand her illumination or the mystical grasp of "Immortality" that she poured into her brilliant quatrains.

Driven to the Divine by intense suffering, perhaps agoraphobia, Emily Dickinson used her holy neurosis to explore rooms of the soul that few people would choose to enter but that open onto the light of the Divine. Like her fellow mystic, Walt Whitman, she found a new language to express for future centuries what mystics of all centuries are always striving to teach us.

One of three children born to a long line of prominent Puritans, she grew up during the "Great Awakening" of evangelical religious fervor in the United States when there was immense pressure to "convert" to Christianity. Yet, when the headmaster of Amherst Academy asked "all students who want to be Christian" to rise, she was the only student who remained in her seat. She later remarked that she didn't like the Bible very much, because "it isn't very merry." (She loved the book of Revelations, but "her bible" was Shakespeare.) At the age of thirty Emily made a permanent decision to remain an unmarried recluse in the family home, which she did until her death at the age of fifty-six, obliged to leave on only two occasions, once to visit a doctor. Like Teresa of Avila, whose momentous decision to stop socializing in the convent parlor and devote herself totally to prayer released vast resources of creativity, so Emily Dickinson's choice to be alone set fire to the inner spark, fueling enormous productivity and love. At her death, her sister Lavinia found 1,776 poems sewn into small booklets tied with ribbons.

In the later decades of her life, she wore only white, a fitting symbol of the purest and highest possible degree of spiritual realization.

The first poem reprinted here prefigures the life-altering experience of Simone Weil (see p. 187), when she was reading George Herbert's poem "Love," and "Christ came down and took" her.

(see p. 187)

~

I HAD BEEN HUNGRY ALL THE YEARS

I had been hungry, all the Years—
My Noon had Come—to dine—
I trembling drew the Table near—
And touched the Curious Wine—

'Twas this on Tables I had seen—
When turning, hungry, Home
I looked in Windows, for the Wealth
I could not hope—for Mine—

I did not know the ample Bread—
'Twas so unlike the Crumb
The Birds and I had often shared
In Nature's—Dining Room—

The Plenty hurt me—'twas so new—
Myself felt ill—and odd—
As Berry—of a Mountain Bush—
Transplanted—to the Road—

Nor was I hungry—so I found
That Hunger—was a way
Of Persons outside Windows—
The Entering—takes away—

WILD NIGHTS—WILD NIGHTS!

Wild nights—Wild nights!
Were I with Thee
Wild Nights should be
Our luxury!

Futile—the Winds—
To a Heart in port—
Done with the Compass—
Done with the Chart!

Rowing in Eden—
Ah, the Sea!
Might I but moor—Tonight—
In Thee!

I SAW NO WAY

I saw no Way—the heavens were stitched—
I felt the Columns close—
The Earth reversed her hemispheres—
I touched the Universe—

And back it slid—and I alone—
A Speck upon a Ball—
Went out upon Circumference—
Beyond the Dip of Bell—

AFTER GREAT PAIN

After great pain, a formal feeling comes—
The Nerves sit ceremonious, like Tombs—
The stiff heart questions was it He, that bore,
And Yesterday, or Centuries Before?

The Feet, mechanical, go round—
Of Ground, or Air, or Ought—
A Wooden way
Regardless grown,
A Quartz contentment, like a stone—

This is the Hour of Lead—
Remembered, if outlived,
As Freezing persons, recollect the Snow—
First—Chill—then
Stupor—then the letting go—

THOUGHTS

I find ecstasy in living—the mere sense of living is joy enough.

The mind is so near itself—it cannot see, distinctly—

There's a noiseless noise in the Orchard—that I let persons hear—

When much in the woods as a little girl, I was told that the Snake would bite me, that I might pick a poisonous flower, or Goblins kidnap me, but I went along and met no one but Angels . . . .

The only News I know is Bulletins all day from Immortality.

I live in the Sea always and know the Road.

Time is a test of trouble but not a remedy—if such it prove, it prove too there was no malady.

I sing—as the Boy does by the burying Ground—because I am afraid—

Is it oblivion or absorption when things pass from our minds?

Perhaps you smile at me. I could not stop for that—My Business is Circumference.

If I read a book and it makes my whole body so cold no fire can ever warm me I know that is poetry. If I feel physically as if the top of my head were taken off, I know that is poetry...

The Landscape of the Spirit requires a lung, but no Tongue.

I found a bird this morning, down—down—on a little bush at the foot of the garden, and wherefore sing, I said, since nobody hears? One sob in the throat, one flutter of bosom—"My business is to sing"—and away she rose!

The withdrawal of the Fuel of the Rapture does not withdraw the Rapture itself.

A LETTER TO MRS. J. G. HOLLAND

early summer 1873

... Enclosed please find my gratitude.
    You remember the imperceptible has no external Face.
    Vinnie says you are most illustrious and dwell in Paradise. I have never believed the latter to be a superhuman site.
    Eden, always eligible, is peculiarly so this noon. It would please you to see how intimate the Meadows are with the Sun. Besides—

> The most triumphant bird I ever knew or met
> Embarked upon a twig today
> And till Dominion set
> I famish to behold so eminent a sight
> And sang for nothing scrutable

But intimate Delight.
Retired, and resumed his transitive Estate—
To what delicious Accident
Does finest Glory fit!

While the Clergyman tells Father and Vinnie that "the Corruptible shall put on Incorruption"—it has already done so and they go defrauded.

A LETTER TO SUSAN DICKINSON GILBERT

[Written after the death of Susan's eight-year-old son, Gilbert, Emily's nephew]

early October 1883

Dear Sue—
The Vision of Immortal Life has been fulfilled—
How simply at the last the Fathom comes! The Passenger and not the Sea, we find surprises us—
Gilbert rejoiced in Secrets—
His Life was panting with them—With what menace of Light he cried, "Don't tell, Aunt Emily"! Now my ascended Playmate must instruct *me*. Show us, prattling Preceptor, but the way to thee!
He knew no niggard moment—His life was full of Boon—The Playthings of the Dervish were not so wild as his—
No crescent was this Creature—He traveled from the Full—
Such soar, but never set—
I see him in the Star, and meet his sweet velocity in everything that flies—His life was like the Bugle, which winds itself away, his Elegy an echo—his Requiem ecstasy—
Dawn and Meridian in one.
Wherefore would he wait, wronged only of Night, which he left for us—

Without a speculation, our little Ajax spans the whole—

Pass to thy Rendezvous of Light
Pangless except for us—
Who slowly ford the Mystery
Which thou hast leaped across!

                                                        Emily

MYRTLE FILLMORE
OHIO, 1845–1931

The cofounder of Unity, an important nineteenth-century American religious movement, Myrtle Fillmore (with her husband, Charles) was seeking Christianity's essential oneness in its dozens of often conflicting denominations. The vision they shaped together of that oneness led to the Unity School of Christianity, which, a hundred years later, operates a vast global outreach. Headquartered near Kansas City, Unity sponsors a twenty-four-hour telephone prayer ministry responding to some two million annual requests for prayer. The Unity School enrolls fifteen hundred students each year and has a ministerial training program. The publishing company produces, among many other publications, the Daily Word, *which has a circulation of 1.2 million in 153 countries.*

Myrtle "caught her vision," as she put it, gradually realizing, like Job in the Old Testament, that suffering is not punishment for sin. She discovered in meditation that examining only her sins and flaws darkened her attitude toward life and made her feel ill, and in a life-altering spiritual experience she heard the words "You have looked among your faults; now look among your virtues." She began to redeem the negative mind states by deciding to "handle" whatever entered her experience before "swallowing" it. "I gained real poise," she wrote, "and the ability to keep my thoughts and feelings truly free." In order to sustain the new attitude, she used prayer and meditation for the rest of her life, especially "affirmations," a style of positive and hopeful prayer that is based in belief in the goodness and power of God in all creation and is widely practiced today both within and outside Unity. Her writings include the book How to Let God Help You, *pamphlets, and a large correspondence (published in part in* Healing Letters). *Her biography is called* Torch-Bearer to Light the Way.

~୨

GOD DOES NOT PUNISH

I found my dear ones did not have an understanding of God, who ruled in their lives, which satisfied me.... My mother was a very spiritual woman. She always kept the principles of right and wrong before us by her own example. But she...had such a devotional spirit that she felt that if her God saw fit to punish, or do any of the many things that were attributed to God, he must have a reason for it and it was all right. I marveled that my wonderful mother, who loved so devotedly, could have a God who might punish, or take the lives of his children.

OTHER TEACHINGS

I do not believe in want. I believe in Abundance.
I do not believe in death. I believe in Life.
I do not believe in ignorance. I believe in Intelligence.
There are no discords in my being. Being is peace.
My faith, understanding, and love are becoming one.
"What therefore God hath joined together, let not man put asunder."

1897

All of us sooner or later come to the place in our development where we are no longer satisfied to go on living the old life, without the knowledge of our oneness with God, the source of our being. Sometimes, when we reach this point in our soul's progress, we do not at first know what is taking place. We may become restless and dissatisfied. We may go through experiences that we do not understand. We may even be tempted to think that our good has gone from us. But just as surely as there is God the one Presence and one Power, we shall find that...we are going from one room, as it were, into another, larger and lighter room.

We need more often to think of our body as being the temple of divine love, the very substance of health and harmony in order that this truth may be implanted in the subconscious mind, which controls the body functioning.

It is my great joy to perceive somewhat of the mother side of God—the Divine love that never fails and that is equal to the drawing of souls to itself. It is my prayer to be able to radiate the qualities of this divine love to all. You too are the mother of Unity, because in your heart you have the same ideals, and the same great generous spirit, and the endless and tireless service, and the love that never fails! The mother of Unity is the universal mother. How happy we are to represent this Mother!

When men understand women and adore the divine qualities in them they will be endowed with power from on high to live so that perfect harmony results.

FRONTIER WOMEN ON THE OVERLAND TRAIL
UNITED STATES, 1840–1870

The recent publication of pioneer women's journals has revealed for the first time in 150 years something of women's experience on the Overland Trail. The trail was a grueling, 2,400-mile-long, dangerous, muddy path leading from the East Coast to Oregon and California that people crossed in fragile covered wagons to claim free land and hopefully "strike it rich." Until now attention was paid only to men's perspectives, and it was assumed the women shared their excitement at the adventure. In fact, women often held strong reservations about emigrating or opposed it altogether, setting out only because they were subject to the decisions of their husbands (the head of the family), having no freedom themselves to influence the course of events. They found the Overland Trail marked from beginning to end by graves of loved ones lost to cholera outbreaks, childhood illnesses, sunburn, skirmishes with Indians, childbirth, accidents, and inadequate food or medicine. Harsh rains often poured through the wagon's cotton cover, soaking bedding and ruining provisions. One woman noted that, even then, the Missouri River was "hard to ford, destitute of fish, too dirty to bathe in, and too thick to drink."

On the trail, pioneer women mustered formidable courage, physical stamina, and ingenuity to make their families as comfortable as possible and the trip as enjoyable as possible, even rolling out dough on the wagon seat to bake a pie on the campfire at night. (A popular travel book advised packing 20 pounds of sugar, 10 of salt, 10 of coffee, 150 pounds of bacon, and 200 pounds of flour; dried beans, fruit, and beef; rice, baking powder, and tea.) Women often befriended Indians, trading clothing for fish and berries, bread in return for canoe rides across flooded rivers. Many read the Bible for comfort and attended Sabbath services when ministers were present.

Many women never reached the West Coast; others arrived strengthened by hardship, with their own voices, independence, and spirituality fully released. The story is wonderfully told by Lillian Schlissel in Women's Diaries of the Westward Journey, *where the journal excerpted here appears.*

~❨

A PAGE FROM THE DIARY OF CATHERINE HAUN

[In contrast to poor emigrants, the young, middle-class bride Catherine Haun and her attorney husband made a fairly easy Overland Crossing in a "spacious, well-provisioned, and experienced" Wagon Train. Nevertheless they too met death along the way, and the usually lighthearted Catherine responded with inner reserves of mature religious faith.]

Across this drear [sic] country [a long stretch of suffocating dusty desert], I used to ride horseback several hours of the day which was a great relief from the continual jolting of even our spring wagon. I also walked a great deal and this lightened the wagon. One day I walked fourteen miles and was not very fatigued. . . .

Our only death on the journey occurred in this desert. The Canadian woman, Mrs. Lamore, suddenly sickened and died, leaving her two little girls and grief stricken husband. We halted a day to bury her and the infant that had lived but an hour, in this weird, lonely spot on God's footstool away apparently from everywhere and everybody.

The bodies were wrapped together in a bedcomforter and wound, quite mummyfied [sic] with a few yards of string that we made by tying together torn strips of a cotton dress skirt. A passage of the Bible (my own) was read; a prayer offered and "Nearer, My God to Thee" sung. Owing to the unusual surroundings the ceremony was very impressive. Every heart was touched and eyes full of tears as we lowered the body, coffinless, into the grave. There was no tombstone—why should there be—the poor husband and orphans could never hope to visit the grave and to the world it was just one of the many hundreds that marked the trail of the argonaut.

SARADA DEVI
INDIA, 1853–1920

Sri Sarada Devi was married at the age of five to one of the most realized mystics of the nineteenth century, the Indian saint and sage Ramakrishna, who was twenty-three at the time. When she turned eighteen, she moved to his temple compound, living in a tiny room some eight square feet in size until she was thirty-two, when Ramakrishna passed away. Her years with her husband were a time of demanding training in spiritual life and in the Vedantic philosophy of religion. Emerging as his foremost student, Sarada Devi was believed by everyone who knew her to incarnate the Divine Mother and came to be called "Holy Mother." At Ramakrishna's death, his students maintained that he had left Holy Mother in the world to reveal the Motherhood of God.

She spent the rest of her life in spiritual teaching and ministry, renowned for her love and the purity of her soul. The essence of her message, a key to understanding her love, is revealed in extensive teachings, which were written down by one of her students. Only five days before she died, she offered guidance to a young disciple: "If you want peace, do not see the faults of others. Rather, see your own faults. Learn to make the whole world your own. No one is a stranger.... This whole world is your own."

Saint Catherine of Genoa gave similar advice to her Western followers with her often-quoted words: "Fight yourself, and you need have no other foe."

~

TEACHINGS ON DAILY SPIRITUAL LIFE

One who makes a habit of prayer will overcome all difficulties and remain calm and undisturbed in the midst of life's trials.

One should be like the dabchicks floating on the water, swimming and diving without a drop of water sticking to them. Live in the midst of a materialistic world, but shake off all clinging to things.

It is the nature of water to run downwards, but the sun's rays lift it up toward the skies. Similarly, it is the very nature of the mind to go to lower things, but the grace of God can lift the mind toward higher things.

How can one's mind be healthy if one doesn't work? No one can spend all twenty-four hours in thought and meditation. To keep the mind cheerful, one must engage the mind in work.

The mind stays well in work, but worship, prayer, and meditation are also necessary. Sit at least once in the morning and in the evening. That acts like a rudder for a boat. When one sits in meditation in the evening, one gets a chance to think over what one has done during the day and to compare one's mind of the preceding day to the present day's.

One must practice meditation at regular times each day. While living at Dakshineswar I used to get up at 3:00 in the morning to meditate and worship. One day I felt a little indisposed and left the bed rather late. The next day I woke up late through laziness. Gradually I found that I did not feel inclined to get up early at all. Then I said to myself: "Ah, I have fallen a victim to idleness." So I had to force myself to get up early. Gradually I got back my former habit. You see how one must keep practicing with unyielding resolution.

Whether you jump into water or are pushed into it, your clothing will be equally drenched. So too, either regular meditation or constant meditation will make the mind one-pointed. Discriminate always between the real and the unreal. Whenever you find your mind clinging to one object, try to draw the mind back to the thought of God. The mind of a spiritual aspirant should remain fixed. . . . One gets everything when the mind becomes steady.

How does one receive the vision of God? It is through Divine grace. But one must practice meditation, worship, spiritual disciplines. Just as one receives the fragrance of a flower by handling it, or the smell of sandalwood by rubbing it against a stone, so in a similar way, one receives spiritual awakening by thinking of God.

People suffer endless miseries because of their egotism. But at last they say,

> Not I,
> not I;
> it is You;
> O God, it is You.

What is the purpose of your life? To realize God.

If one is without kindness, how can one be called a human being?

Work to remove the sufferings of the world.

CONCEPCIÓN CABRERA DE ARMIDA (CONCHITA)
MEXICO, 1862–1937

Born Concepción Cabrera de Armida, Conchita grew up in San Luis Potosí, a vivacious, pretty, popular girl who received a number of marriage proposals. She enjoyed a happy marriage for eight years until her husband died, leaving her at the age of thirty with eight children. Throughout her life Conchita retained an unusual balance between spirituality and daily life in the world. Obviously called to the full mystical journey and the heights and depths of mystical love, she remained grounded and extremely active in family, social, and communal life, founding two religious orders. For forty years she kept a diary, which amounted to sixty-six volumes and from which the present selections are extracted.

~*9*

FROM HER DIARY

March 26, 1897
I would like to stop writing, forget everything, turn the page, change my life! Such is the state of my spirit! Drowning in distractions, temptations to do other things, and pain. I have no control over myself and feel pitiless toward myself. I may die in this struggle, but I will keep my commitment.

March 21, 1901
There unrolled before me spiritual panoramas which left me mute in admiration. Suddenly I found myself involved in the most profound secrets of the spiritual life. I contemplated ravishing beauties, formidable abysses, delights and dangers. I do not know why or how I was taken into these so unknown spaces. . . . Why do these flashes of exquisite light explode in me at any moment at all? Why does the Divine present itself to me and appear in my consciousness so clearly? At times I think that all this is perfectly natural, appropriate for someone with intelligence like mine, and at other times I think that my spirit is too limited to receive such extraordinary illuminations. Perhaps I am receiving a special grace, even though I do not know what the purpose is.

February 19, 1911
I have heard of a hidden treasure, the greatest treasure that has ever existed in heaven or on earth. Because it remains unexplored, no one has any idea of its worth; no one can know its value. Not even the whole world of souls all together knows what it holds.

It is a Light that wants to shine in our intellects and a Fire that wants to blaze in our hearts; its work is Life, and its being is Love. This hidden treasure is the Spirit, and its purpose is to lead us into the heart of Love.

If we are sad, it is because we have not looked for the joy and comfort that the Spirit brings. If we are weak, it is because we have not found the energy that the Spirit offers us. If we are failing, it is because we are not living in that Light. If trust has been lost, this too is because of the absence of the Spirit.

We invite the Spirit into our lives through love. Not by loving lukewarmly, but with passionate love.

January 26, 1915
Some people think that the Spirit is very far away; way, way, way up above. Actually, it is closely present to every one of us, to every creature. We are accompanied everywhere. We are penetrated with Holiness. We are called. We are protected. We are helped. We are guarded from enemies and dangers. The Spirit is at work in all of that, intimately and directly. The Spirit is closer than our own souls, constantly giving us inspirations, illuminations and moments of grace. It is the Spirit, too, that moves us to say "thank you," to love fiercely, to know God, to want to give to others.

OSAGE CHANT
NATIVE AMERICA, ORAL TRADITION

This chant was handed down orally from Osage mothers to their daughters for many centuries before being recorded at the beginning of the twentieth century. It concluded a girl's initiation ritual into womanhood, and it alludes to her future life growing corn. The Osage people, who call themselves Wazhazhe, live in Oklahoma and number about eighteen thousand. Discovery of oil and gas on their land in the twentieth century brought them prosperity. They have a highly developed priesthood and cosmology.

PLANTING CHANT

I made a footprint: it is sacred.
I made a footprint: small green specks push through it.
I made a footprint: new green blades push upward.
I made a footprint: above it, blades wave in the breeze.
I made a footprint: over it grow new stalks.
I made a footprint: over it I bend to pick the ears.
I made a footprint: above it the blossoms lie gray.
I made a footprint: smoke rises from my house.
I made a footprint: there is laughter in my house.
I made a footprint: my family lives in good health.

GEMMA GALGANI
ITALY, 1878–1903

Gemma Galgani underwent more mystical phenomena than any other mystic we know of in the West. Beginning when she was five and lasting until her untimely death at the age of twenty-five, the events included visions, locutions, ecstasies, angelic visitations, demonic attacks, unusual bleeding, and the stigmata, wounds resembling those Jesus received in the crucifixion—all of which she regarded as accidental by-products of intense mystical prayer. Despite these disturbances, and with enormous effort, she focused her intentions on being and birthing love.

Like another nineteenth-century French mystic, Thérèse of Lisieux, who also experienced enormous suffering and died in her early twenties, Gemma exemplifies a rare stream of mysticism that people today tend to suspect of pathology: victim-soul mysticism. In Christianity, this type of calling relates to the mystic's prolonged contemplation of the mystery of the Crucified God and subsequent desire to suffer with or for the innocent Christ, as though sharing in his suffering could somehow remove or alleviate his pain. Such extreme compassion is seen in our own time in those German people who, having contemplated the Holocaust and the vast mystery of evil surrounding it, undertake a painful pilgrimage on their knees to Auschwitz or another concentration camp as though to atone for the suffering of the Jewish people in Third Reich Germany. A true mystic of this type *differs from the masochistic personality in the way they live their lives: the mystic's experience always issues in love, in compassionate caring and justice work, creation of hospitals, orphanages, monasteries or schools, or in simple service to others within their communities. Pathology without spirituality cuts off such a capacity to love.*

Gemma did not leave any books, but fortunately her spiritual director preserved her correspondence, which mirrors her development in Divine love. In the following passages from her letters, she tells her director about her expanding experience of the Spirit's inner fire.

~)

MYSTICAL BURNING

If I could only hear from you, Father Germano.... I feel like I am dying of Love! And I want to be consumed in it! I want my heart to turn into ashes!...

For the last eight days I have felt something mysterious in the region of my heart that I cannot understand. The first days I disregarded it, because it gave me little or no trouble. But today is the third day that this fire has increased. So much as to be almost unbearable. I should need ice to put it out, and it hinders my sleeping and eating. It is a mysterious fire that comes from within to the outside. It does not torment me, though; rather it delights me! But it exhausts me, consumes my energy.

In order to form an idea of it, imagine that into the very center of your heart a red-hot iron, kept continually heated in a furnace, has been introduced: That is how I feel.... [I find myself praying]: "You are a fire, Lord, and I am burning with your love—an infinitely happy Love! A sweet fire! Sweet flames! If my heart is meant to burn...then let it be.... I will open my heart to You. I will let Divine Fire in. My heart shall become a flame."

HOW I SEE OUR SOULS IN GOD

Imagine that you see a light of immense splendor that penetrates everything, and at the same time gives life and animation to all, so that whatever exists has its being from this light and lives in it. That is how I see God, and all creation in God.

Now imagine a fiery furnace, vast as the universe—no, infinitely greater than the universe—that burns everything without consuming anything, and burning, illuminates and strengthens. Those who are most penetrated by its flames are happiest and desire more ardently to be consumed. That is how I see our souls in God.

ELIZABETH OF THE TRINITY
FRANCE, 1880–1906

More and more influential today, especially with people seeking contemplative silence, Elizabeth Catez grew up in Dijon, a child whose family taught her to channel her soaring energies into music and spirituality. By adolescence she was a fine pianist whose vivacious charm was attracting suitors, and her mother began pressuring her to marry. But Elizabeth was following the footsteps of Teresa of Avila and Thérèse of Lisieux to the Carmelite order, which had a convent next door to her home, and at eighteen, unaware that she had only six more years to live, she entered the Carmel of Dijon, receiving the name Elizabeth of the Trinity. Quoting from Ephesians 1.11–12, she called herself a "praise of glory." When she learned that she was dying, she said she "would rush like a little rocket into the heart of God." And when asked if she, like Thérèse of Lisieux, would "spend her eternity doing good on earth," she replied that she would spend her eternity "drawing souls to interior recollection." Which is precisely what her memory is accomplishing today as people all over the world begin to embrace her spirituality of listening.

O MY BELOVED STAR

O my God, Trinity whom I adore, help me to forget myself entirely, that I may be established in you, still and peaceful, as though I were already in eternity. May nothing trouble my peace, or lead me away from You.

O Unchanging One, may each minute draw me further into the depth of Your mystery. Give peace to my soul. Make it your heaven, a home for your love, a place of rest. May I never leave you there alone; may I be there totally, awakened totally, trusting, adoring, opened totally to Your creative work.

O my Beloved, I would like to be a bride of your heart, I would like to honor you, I would like to love you until I die. But I am aware of my weakness. I ask you to clothe me with yourself, to make my soul a mirror of your soul, to let me sink in your being, be filled by you, so that my life will become but a radiance of your radiance. Come into me as Adorer, Restorer, the One Who Makes Whole.

O Eternal Verb, Word of my God, I want to spend my life listening to you, I want to be totally teachable, to learn everything from you. Through all the nights, all the emptiness, all the powerlessness, I want to place my attention on you, and live in your great light.

> O my beloved star,
> So fascinate me
> That I will not withdraw
> From your radiance.
> O consuming fire,
> Spirit of love
> Come upon me
> And re-create my soul
> Like an incarnation of the Word
> That I may be another being
> In whom the great mystery is born.

ELIZA CALVERT HALL
KENTUCKY, NINETEENTH CENTURY

Eliza Calvert Hall, whose real name was Eliza Calvert Obenchain, wrote a wonderful series of short quilting stories, which were compiled in 1907 in Aunt Jane of Kentucky, *from which the selection here is excerpted. She was the president of the Kentucky Equal Rights Association, a suffragette movement, and fought in particular for a woman's right to make her own will.*

PIECIN' A QUILT'S LIKE LIVIN' A LIFE

Did you ever think, child, ... how much piecin' a quilt's like livin' a life? And as for sermons, why they ain't no better sermon to me than a patchwork quilt, and the doctrines is right there a heap plainer'n they are in the catechism. Many a time I've set and listened to Parson Page preachin' about predestination and free will, and I've said to myself, 'Well, I ain't never been through Centre College up at Danville, but if I could jest get up in the pulpit with one of my quilts, I could make it a heap plainer to folks than Parson's making it with all his big words.' You see, you start out with jest so much caliker; you don't go to the store and pick it out and buy it, but the neighbors will give you a piece here and a piece there, and you'll have a piece left every time you cut out a dress, and you take jest what happens to come. And that's like predestination. But when it comes to the cuttin' out, why, you're free to choose your own pattern. You can give the same kind o' pieces to two persons, and one'll make a 'nine-patch,' and one'll make a 'wild-goose-chase,' and there'll be two quilts made out o' the same kind o' pieces, and jest as different as they can be. And that is jest the way with livin'. The Lord sends us the pieces, but we can cut 'em out and put 'em together pretty much to suit ourselves, and there's a heap more in the cuttin' out and the sewin' than there is in the caliker.

PART 2

VOICES OF
OUR TIMES

IRINA RATUSHINSKAIA

RUSSIA, TWENTIETH CENTURY

The poet Irina Ratushinskaia was detained for over five years in a Russian work camp. During her incarceration she came to know some of the most creatively courageous women we know of in all history: the Babushki (from the Russian word babushka, *meaning grandmother). Conscientious objectors, like Agape, Chione, and their friends in the fourth century (see p. 30), these heroic Roman Catholic women preferred imprisonment to renouncing their faith in the crucified Christ. Some of them were detained for twenty to thirty years. The Babushki refused any behavior that implied allegiance to the atheistic Soviet regime or to the state-supported Orthodox Church, which they perceived as a puppet of the government. They refused to carry Russian passports, and they would not use Russian money or work for Soviet institutions. Even when punished with hunger, inadequate clothing in the bitter Russian winter, or solitary confinement, they clung to their faith, forgiving and praying for the guards who tormented them. Irina Ratushinskaia's meditation below describes how the resourceful Babushki risked their lives to clothe women freezing in punishment cells.*

~)

THE BABUSHKI'S TROUSSEAU

In punishment cells you are stripped of your underwear and given a special smock: its low neckline rivals the most daring ballgown, and it has very wide, three quarter length sleeves to ensure that the wearer will freeze. That's what these cells are for: . . . [punishment and isolation]. Extreme cold is regarded as a necessary feature of the corrective process, but it never yielded the required results with the women in our Zone. The *babushki*—experienced [seamstresses] one and all—did everything possible to beat the cold. They sewed underwear out of flannel footcloths (long strips to be wound around one's feet) which were issued them in winter, and whenever possible quilted them on the inside with cotton wool. [For brassieres] they made something akin to shortened vests. Everything was multilayered for maximum warmth. All these garments were made out of a multitude of scraps of cloth, for large pieces of material were not obtainable in the camp.

So we inherited a box full of what we called the *"babushki's trousseau."* Looking at the shirts they had made, I found them to be a veritable patchwork of all shades and textures: here a scrap of cotton, here something knitted, here a small woolen insert—all painstakingly gathered and cobbled into a garment. The underwear they produced would hardly have merited that name elsewhere— at first glance, one was hard put to determine which part of the body it was supposed to cover. Everything was much worn, much washed, carefully darned again and again. In some cases, there were patches on patches, darns on darns. And all done with such care, such love for one's neighbor, as if for oneself! Not only were the *babushki* willing to sacrifice the shirts off their backs for others, they tried to prolong the life of every bit of clothing ad infinitum.

MARY MERCEDES LANE
CALIFORNIA, 1871–1965

In the early 1900s, high school girls enrolling in a small Catholic school north of San Francisco were assigned a legendary book on the art of "courtesy" written by an equally legendary nun, Sister Mary Mercedes Lane. Upperclasswomen assured newcomers that only the Bible held greater importance than A Book of Courtesy: The Art of Living with Yourself and Others.

The author came from the powerful tradition of Dominicans founded in France in 1207, and the code of conduct she taught revolved around the timeless spiritual principle and skill of putting oneself in the place of the other to know "what is needed in any situation." A revision of A Book of Courtesy *published in 2001—and updated with attention to such matters as electronic communications—introduces Sister Mary this way:*

Some people are born knowing how to live, knowing from the start what it takes to become a worthy human being. It is as if they have it

*stamped somewhere on their DNA: "Love your neighbor as yourself.
Do unto others as you would have them do unto you."*
    Sister Mary Mercedes Lane was one of those people.

The Golden Rule had come to primitive California in the heart of the
first Dominican woman to reach the United States, Sister Mary Goemaere,
who intrepidly crossed the ocean from France in 1849—at the height of the
Gold Rush—and arrived on the back of a mule. She founded what is today
California's oldest independent school, the San Dominico School in San
Anselmo, where some half a century later Sister Mercedes would begin
imbuing generations of teenaged girls with the keys to real happiness. Today,
Sister Mercedes' book of right living—like Dhuodana's in the ninth century
(see p. 46) and Sharon Lebell's in our own time (see p. 300)—poses an elo-
quent challenge to a world much in need of it.

~✑

ELECTRONIC COMMUNICATIONS

The Telephone
However useful it is, the telephone can be an intrusion that calls
for consideration and judgment. Be considerate about the time of
your call and its length. Ask yourself, "Does this person need to
hear this? Right now? Is the telephone the best way to communicate my message?" Ask the answering party, "Is this a good time to
call?" and do not go on for too long. . . .

Call Waiting
Know what you want to say before calling and do not interrupt the
call for other things. Call waiting, for example, can be an annoying
interruption. You can alleviate that either by having a message center that records your calls when you are on the line or by asking the
first caller to hold for a moment, then picking up the second call
and asking for a number where you can call right back. If the second call is more urgent than the first, ask the caller to hold; return to
the first caller and explain that you need to take the second call but
will call back as soon as you are done. The key is to show consideration to each caller and to return calls as soon as you can. . . .

The Cellular Phone

It is extremely rude and inconsiderate to take private or business calls at social meetings or any place where the sounds may be disruptive. For example, you can use a cell phone in a drugstore while waiting for a prescription to be filled, as long as you keep your voice low. Do not use it in a restaurant where you are sitting with a friend. To avoid being a nuisance to others, turn off your cell phone or set its ring very low before entering a church, a theater, or a restaurant. At the very least, excuse yourself and take a call in the restroom, the lobby, or near a public phone. The same rules apply to the use of beepers.

The Answering Machine

The answering machine is a way to communicate without inconveniencing the other person.... The outgoing machine message should be short and clear. Subjecting callers to a five-minute program of "witticisms" or children's babble may not be as amusing to others as it is to you, particularly if the call is long-distance or related to business. The person receiving the message should answer as soon as possible, within twenty-four hours.

FROM *A BOOK OF COURTESY*

SIDONIE-GABRIELLE COLETTE
FRANCE, 1873–1954

At the age of twenty, Colette Landoy married a prominent literary critic in Paris, Henri Gauthier-Villars, who persuaded her to write novels and then signed them with his own name. Parisians loved the "Claudine" series, as the books came to be known, but Colette suffered immensely in the marriage and eventually left Gauthier-Villars to begin writing under her own name. For almost fifty years she published one novel after another as well as essays and literary criticism. By the end of her life she was revered as "The Great Lady" of French literature. A few readers have begun to notice her spirituality, especially in relation to the beauty of nature, as in this remark-

able letter written the year before she died, which honors a plant's blossoming as a divine epiphany.

~❧

LETTER CONCERNING HER PINK CACTUS

Monsieur,

You invited me to visit you for a week, which means that I would be near my daughter, whom I adore. You who live with her know how rarely I see her, how much her presence delights me, and I am touched that you should ask me to come to see her. All the same, I am not going to accept your kind invitation, for the time being at any rate. The reason is that my pink cactus is probably going to flower. It is a very rare plant that was given to me and I am told that in our climate it blossoms only once every four years. Now I am already a very old woman, and if I went away when my pink cactus is about to flower, I am certain that I shouldn't ever see it flower.

So I beg you, Sir, to accept my sincere thanks and my regrets, together with my kind regards.

Sidonie Colette, née Landoy

EVELYN UNDERHILL
ENGLAND, 1875–1941

Evelyn Underhill is the author of one of the great classics of spiritual literature of all time, the dense and lyrical compendium of mystical knowledge, Mysticism, *which has been widely read for close to a hundred years. Published in 1911, it was rejected by the academic establishment for a long time. By the 1930s, however, Evelyn had become the first woman in twentieth-century England to be taken seriously as a theologian, a stunning feat in an era when women were forbidden to even teach theology. An only child whose upper-class parents often left her at home while they went yachting, she took to Plotinus at an early age, perhaps finding in his idea of "the flight of the alone to the Alone" a solution to her own loneliness and an impetus to study the mystics—Christian, Sufi, and Hindu.*

Not until many years after her death did people realize that Evelyn Underhill herself was a mystic of the most intense and intellectual kind. Not the negative imprint of the Neoplatonists or her otherworldly spiritual director, Baron Von Hugel, and not even a personal tendency toward sternness prevented her from experiencing personally the states of joy and rapture, and the dark nights she loved to read and write about. Among her other books are The Mystic Way *(1913),* Practical Mysticism *(1915), and* Concerning the Inner Life *(1926). The passage here comes from* Mysticism.

~ 9

THE GOAL OF THE MYSTICAL JOURNEY

The mystic . . . would say that his long-sought correspondence with Transcendental Reality, his union with God, has now been fully established: that his self, though intact, is wholly penetrated—as a sponge by the sea—by the Ocean of Life and Love to which he has attained. "I live, yet not I but God in me." He is conscious that he is now at length cleansed of the last strains of separation, and has become, in a mysterious manner, "that which he beholds."

In the words of the Sufi poet, the mystic's journey is now prosecuted not only *to* God but *in* God. He has entered the Eternal Order; attained here and now the state to which the Magnet of the Universe draws every living thing. Moving through periods of alternate joy and anguish, as his spiritual self woke, stretched, and was tested in the complementary fires of love and pain, he was inwardly conscious that he moved towards a definite objective. In so far as he was a great mystic he was also conscious that this objective was no mere act of knowing, however intense, exultant, or sublime; but a condition of being, fulfillment of that love which impelled him, steadily and inexorably, to his own place. In the image of the alchemists, the Fire of Love has done its work: the mystic Mercury of the Wise—that little hidden treasure, that scrap of Reality within him—has utterly transmuted the salt and sulphur of his mind and his sense. Even the white stone of illumination, once so clearly cherished, he has resigned to the crucible. Now, the great work is accomplished, the last imperfection is gone, and he finds within himself the "Noble Tincture"—the gold of spiritual humanity.

THE MOTHER
FRANCE, 1878–1973

*F*ew people know the real name of the radiant woman at Sri Aurobindo's ashram in Pondicherry, India, who was referred to as "The Mother" and seen as an incarnation of the Divine Mother. She was born in Paris to a wealthy family with materialistic values and received an excellent education, especially in art and higher mathematics, studying painting with the French artist Gustave Moreau and associating with the innovative French Impressionists of her era. She became friendly with Max Theon, who introduced her to occultism at his estate in Algeria. In 1914 she traveled to the French colonial city of Pondicherry, where she met the sage Aurobindo for the first time and forged a strong connection with him. In 1920 she returned there permanently, reading and studying as well as organizing and developing the ashram, while Aurobindo researched and wrote on complex evolutionary issues.

After Aurobindo's death in 1958 until her own death fifteen years later, she withdrew from ashram activities to grapple intellectually with the issue that had fascinated her for many years: body consciousness—more specifically, cellular consciousness, or the cellular mind—and the transformation of that consciousness in the body's cells in the direction of a new species. She wanted to find the precise doorway through which humankind would grow to the next stage in evolution, or the next "species." She narrated her thought to an author at the ashram named Satprem, who had put himself at the service of the Mother and Aurobindo, and the resulting work, a masterful accomplishment that unfolded over the years, comprised six thousand pages published in thirteen volumes under the title Mother's Agenda.

Satprem had been arrested by the Gestapo at the age of twenty and imprisoned in German concentration camps until the war ended. By the time he was released, he was shattered, physically, mentally, and spiritually. Healing began when he met the Mother and Aurobindo. In 1953 he became a Sannyasin, or renunciant.

When the Mother passed away, Satprem set himself to furthering her work.

∽૭

A DREAM

There should be somewhere on earth a place that no nation could claim as its own, a place where every human being of good will, sincere in his aspiration, could live freely as a citizen of the world, obeying one single authority, that of the Supreme Truth. A place of peace, concord, harmony, where all the fighting instincts of man would be used exclusively to conquer the causes of his sufferings and miseries. To surmount his weakness and ignorance; to triumph over his limitations and incapacities; a place where the needs of the spirit and the concern for progress would take precedence over the satisfaction of desires and passions, the search for pleasures and material enjoyment. In this place, children would be able to grow and develop integrally without losing contact with their souls; education would not be given with a view to passing examinations or obtaining certificates or posts, but to enrich one's existing faculties, and bring forth new ones. In this place, titles and positions would be replaced by opportunities to serve and organize; everyone's bodily needs would be provided for equally, and in the general organization, intellectual, moral, and spiritual superiority would be expressed not by increased pleasures and powers in life, but by greater duties and responsibilities. Beauty, in all its art forms— painting, sculpture, music, literature—would be accessible to all equally, the ability to share in the joys it brings being limited solely by one's capacities and not by social or financial position. For in this ideal place, money would no longer be the sovereign lord; individual worth would have a far greater importance than material wealth and social position. There, work would not be for earning one's living, but the means to express oneself and develop one's capacities and possibilities. While at the same time being of service to the group as a whole, which would in turn provide for everyone's subsistence and field of action. In short, it would be a place where human relationships of collaboration and real brotherhood could be formed.

The earth is not ready to realize such an ideal, for humanity does not yet possess either the knowledge necessary to understand

and adopt it or the conscious force indispensable for its execution. This is why I call it a dream.

Yet this dream is on the way to becoming a reality, and it is what we are endeavoring to do at the Sri Aurobindo Ashram, on a very small scale and in proportion to our limited means. The achievement is indeed far from being perfect but it is progressive; little by little we are moving toward our goal, which, we hope we shall one day be able to show to the world as a practical and effective means of emerging from the present chaos to be born to a new life, more harmonious and truer.

ISADORA DUNCAN
CALIFORNIA, 1878–1927

The founder of modern dance, Isadora Duncan saw all dance as a sacred art. She formed her spirituality of art growing up in San Francisco in a family where imagination was encouraged and art was honored. After moving to Europe with her mother and siblings, she began to dance at private gatherings, and as her popularity grew, she performed on major stages throughout the continent. Her dances were created from free and natural movements inspired by Greek arts, folk dances, and her spirituality of nature, as well as the athleticism of skipping, running, jumping, leaping, and tossing. With her innovative and controversial style, her free-flowing costumes, bare feet, and loose hair, and her focus on the solar plexus and torso as the source of dance movement, she came to be credited with inventing modern dance but has barely begun to be recognized for her spirituality of dance. Isadora's entire life was an adventure, a challenge of the status quo, and a radical revisioning of what it means to be a woman and an artist. Her celebrated love life caused her both pain and ecstasy, and both of her children and their governess were tragically killed in a drowning accident. Her own life ended at fifty-nine in a car accident along the Riviera. The material below comes from her autobiography, My Life, *published by Horace Liveright in 1927.*

～♫

I LIVE IN MY BODY

How mysterious it is to feel the life of the body, all through this weird journey on earth. First the timid, shrinking slight body of the young girl that I was and the change to the hardy Amazon. Then the vine-wreathed Bacchante drenched with wine, falling soft and restless under the leap of the Satyr, and growing, expanding; the swelling and increase of soft, voluptuous flesh, the breasts grown so sensitive to the slightest love emotion as to communicate a rush of pleasure through the whole nervous system; love now grown to a full blown rose whose fleshly petals close with violence on their prey. I live in my body like a spirit in a cloud—a cloud of rose fire and voluptuous response.

In the first performance of "Tannhauser," my transparent tunic, showing every part of my dancing body, had created some stir amidst the pink-covered legs of the Ballet and at the last moment even poor Frau Cosima lost her courage. She sent one of her daughters to my loge, with a long white chemise, which she begged me to wear under the filmy scarf which served me for a costume. But I was adamant. I would dress and dance exactly my way, or not at all.

...at that time, there was much contention and hot discussion about my beautiful legs, whether my own satiny skin was quite moral or whether it should be covered with horrid salmon-coloured silk tights. Many times I declaimed myself hoarse on the subject of just how vulgar and indecent these salmon-coloured tights were and how beautiful and innocent the naked human body was when inspired by beautiful thoughts.

I believe that in each life there is a spiritual line, an upward curve, and all that adheres to and strengthens this line is our real life— the rest is but chaff falling from us as our souls progress. Such a spiritual line is my Art. My life has known but two motives— Love and Art—and often Love destroyed Art, and often the imperious call of Art put a tragic end to Love. For these two have no accord, but only constant battle.

Fine art comes from the Human Spirit and needs no externals. In our School we have no costumes, no ornaments—just the beauty that flows from the inspired human soul, and the body that is its symbol.... Beauty is to be looked for and found in children; in the light of their eyes and in the beauty of their little hands outstretched in their lovely movements.... These are my pearls and my diamonds; I want no others. Give beauty and freedom and strength to the children. Give art to the people who need it. Great music should no longer be kept for the delight of a few cultured people, it should be given free: ... it is as necessary as air and bread, for it is the Spiritual Wine of Humanity.

What nonsense to sing always of Love and Spring alone. The colours of autumn are more glorious, more varied and the joys of autumn are a thousandfold more powerful, terrible, beautiful. How I pity those poor women whose pallid, narrow creed precludes them from the magnificent and generous gift of the Autumn of Love. I was once the timid prey, then the aggressive Bacchante, but now I close over my lover as the sea over a bold swimmer, enclosing, swirling, encircling him in waves of cloud and fire.

VIRGINIA WOOLF
ENGLAND, 1882–1941

Virginia Woolf was born in London into a privileged, but not happy, literary and intellectual family. She was sexually abused by her half-brother, emotionally scarred by her father, and wounded by the neglect of her mother. Tormented by illnesses that are now seen as symptoms of a bipolar disorder (manic depression), which writers frequently suffer, she finally took her own life at fifty-nine. In her active writing years, she is credited with helping reinvent the modern novel by her use of stream of consciousness techniques, which allow the reader access into the characters' inner lives. Woolf, who was happily married to Leonard Woolf (also a writer and publisher), formed intense emotional attachments to several women and an erotic relationship with Vita Sackville-West. She spoke with a feminist voice in the male-dominated literary world of her time, where, as one critic

put it, she "presumes to enter, as few women have done, the sphere of criti-
cism, argument and theory." Her essay, A Room of One's Own, *which*
defines the importance of women's independence, economically and psycho-
logically, has become a classic of feminist thought. However, it is the beauty
and power of her novels that enlighten and entrance most readers.

~ 9

FROM MRS. DALLOWAY

In people's eyes, in the swing, tramp, and trudge; in the bellow and
uproar; the carriages, motor cars, omnibuses, vans, sandwich men
shuffling and swinging; brass bands; barrel organs; in the triumph
and the jingle and the strange high singing of some aeroplane overhead was what she loved; life; this moment in June.

FROM A ROOM OF ONE'S OWN

The beauty of the world has two edges, one of laughter, one of
anguish, cutting the heart asunder.

When . . . one reads of a witch being ducked, of a woman possessed
by devils, of a wise woman selling herbs, or even a very remarkable
man who had a mother, then I think we are on the track of a lost
novelist, a suppressed poet. . . . Indeed, I would venture to guess
that Anon, who wrote so many poems without signing them, was
often a woman.

FROM TO THE LIGHTHOUSE

Then indeed peace had come. Messages of peace breathed from the
sea to the shore. . . . Through the open window the voice of the
beauty of the world came murmuring, too softly to hear exactly what
it said—but what mattered if the meaning were plain? entreating the
sleepers . . . if they would not actually come down to the beach itself
at least to lift the blind and look out. They would see then night

flowing down in purple; his head crowned; his sceptre jeweled; and how in his eyes a child might look. And if they still faltered... if they still said no, that it was vapour, this splendour of his, and the dew had more power than he, and they preferred sleeping; gently then without complain, or argument, the voice would sing its song. Gently the waves would break (Lily heard them in her sleep); tenderly the night fell (it seemed to come through her eyelids). . . .

Indeed the voice might resume, as the curtains of dark wrapped themselves over the house. . . . [W]hy not accept this, be content with this, acquiesce and resign? The sigh of all the seas breaking in measure round the isles soothed them; the night wrapped them; nothing broke their sleep, until, the birds beginning and the dawn weaving their thin voices in to its whiteness, a cart grinding, a dog somewhere barking, the sun lifted the curtains, broke the veil on their eyes, and Lily Briscoe stirring in her sleep. She clutched at her blankets as a faller clutches at the turf on the edge of a cliff. Her eyes opened wide. Here she was again, she thought, sitting bolt upright in bed. Awake.

I have done with phrases. How much better is silence; the coffee-cup, the table. How much better to sit by myself like the solitary sea-bird that opens its wings on the stake. Let me sit here for ever with bare things, this coffee-cup, this knife, this fork, things in themselves, myself being myself. . . .

GEORGIA O'KEEFFE
WISCONSIN, 1887–1986

I'm going to be an artist!" was Georgia O'Keeffe's answer at age thirteen when asked what she was going to be when she grew up. By the time she was twenty-nine, O'Keeffe (as she was always known in the art world) had her first exhibit in New York, arranged without her knowledge by the artist and gallery owner Alfred Stieglitz, whom she later married. Though she found inspiration in the cityscapes of New York City, she longed for wide open spaces and found them first in northern Texas and later in New Mexico, where she lived and painted for many years.

O'Keeffe is known for her large flower paintings (which quickly became commercially successful) and for her paintings of bones, trees, and sky and the landscape near the towns of Taos and Abiquiu, where she lived alone in an adobe house, unconcerned with critical success and fame. To the end, she followed her heart in matters of love and her own instincts in matters of art, looking through her own eyes, painting the reality she knew. As Stieglitz said, her work "could only have come from a woman and from America." In her struggle to balance love and work, and in her profound vision of the "wideness and wonder of the world," she continues to inspire generations of artists.

A wonderful book about O'Keeffe is Anita Pollitzer's A Woman on Paper: Georgia O'Keeffe, published by Touchstone in 1988. The author gives O'Keeffe's answer to the constantly asked question, "Why did she paint the flowers so big?"

> *I painted the flower big to give the feeling I had in me when I looked at it. At the time it seemed to me as though the flower I was painting was the only thing in the world.... When the bloom came out, I felt as though a skyscraper had gone up overnight.*

Catalogs often quote another remark she made about her flowers: "I have painted it big enough so that others would see what I see."

Georgia O'Keeffe's spirituality was a pure creation-centered spirituality.

~ච

ABOUT PAINTING DESERT BONES

I have wanted to paint the desert and I haven't known how. I always think that I can not stay with it long enough. So I brought home the bleached bones as my symbol of the desert. To me they are as beautiful as anything I know. To me they are strangely more living than the animals walking around—hair, eyes and all their tails switching. The bones seem to cut sharply to the center of something that is keenly alive on the desert even tho' it is vast and empty and untouchable—and knows no kindness with all its beauty.

FROM AN EXHIBITION CATALOG, 1944

ON THE WIDENESS AND WONDER
OF THE WORLD

I have picked flowers where I found them—Have picked up sea shells and rocks and pieces of wood where there were sea shells and rocks and pieces of wood that I like.

When I found the beautiful white bones in the desert I picked them up and took them home too.

I have used these things to say what is to me the wideness and wonder of the world as I live in it.

FROM AN EXHIBITION CATALOG, 1939

ON SAYING WHAT SHE WANTED TO

I grew up pretty much as everybody grows up and one day seven years ago found myself saying to myself—I can't live where I want to—I can't even say what I want to—Schools and things that painters have taught me even keep me from painting as I want to. I decided I was a very stupid fool not to at least paint as I wanted to and say what I wanted to when I painted, as that seemed to be the only thing I could do that didn't concern anybody but myself—that was nobody's business but my own.... I found I could say things with color and shapes that I couldn't say in any other way—things that I had no words for.

FROM AN EXHIBITION CATALOG, 1923

FROM A LETTER TO ANITA POLLITZER,
JANUARY 1916

I half way have a new job out in Texas—hope I get it—I'll have a cat and a dog and a horse to ride if I want it—and the wind blows like mad—and there is nothing after the last house of town as far as you can see—there is something wonderful about the bigness and the loneliness and the windyness of it all—mirages people it with all sorts of things at times—sometimes I've seen the most wonderful sunsets over what seemed to be the ocean....

I'm disgusted with dreams now. I want real things, live people to take hold of—to see—and to talk to. Music that makes holes in the sky.

FROM A LETTER TO ANITA, SEPTEMBER 1916

Tonight I walked into the sunset—to mail some letters. The whole sky—and there is so much of it out here—was just blazing—and grey-blue clouds were rioting all through the hotness of it—and the ugly little buildings and windmills looked great against it.

...The Eastern sky was all grey-blue—bunches of clouds...and the whole thing lit up, first in one place, then in another with flashes of lightning—sometimes just sheet lightning—and sometimes sheet lightning with a sharp bright zigzag flashing across it.

I walked out past the last house—past the last locust tree—and sat on the fence for a long time—looking—just looking at the lightning. You see there was nothing but sky and flat prairie land, land that seems more like the ocean than anything else I know. There was a wonderful moon.

FROM A LETTER TO ANITA, OCTOBER 1916

...I discovered that by running against the wind with a bunch of pine branches in your hand you could have the pine trees singing right in your ears....

FROM A LETTER TO ANITA, 1929

In the evening I go up in the desert where you can see the world all around—far away. The hours I spend each evening watching the sun go down—and just enjoying it—and every day I go out and watch it again. I draw some and there is a little painting and so the days go by.

ANNA AKHMATOVA

RUSSIA, 1889–1966

Anna Akhmatova is revered as one of Russia's three greatest twentieth-century writers, and, like the others, Boris Pasternak and Marina Tsvetaeva, she suffered bitterly from the country's century-long political tumult. Expelled from the Writer's Union, persecuted and imprisoned for her political stands, her friends executed, her son imprisoned, she held relentlessly to her convictions and stood for human rights throughout her life. The Russian people celebrate her courageous spirituality and integrity as well as her literary genius.

Anna Akhmatova grew up in Tsarkoye Selo, the imperial summer residence near St. Petersburg, and planned a career in law, although the circumstances of her life led to her earning a living primarily as a translator. Graduating from law school in Kiev, she married the literary critic Nikolei Gumilev, but the unhappy marriage ended in divorce after eight years, not long before Gumilev was executed. A volume of poetry published when she was twenty-five, Rosary, *brought her fame, but the publication of* Anno Domini *led to her being silenced for eighteen years. In 1946, because of her activism, her son was arrested and imprisoned until the death of Stalin, when she herself was "rehabilitated" and readmitted to the Writer's Union. Oxford University conferred an honorary degree on her the year before she died.*

"What could be worse than this century?" she asked in a poem. "Bewildered with sorrow and anguish, it touches a sore so deep it cannot heal."

~ɔ

SELECTIONS

During the terrible years of Yezhovshchina [the chief of Stalin's secret police], I spent seventeen months in the prison lines in Leningrad.

One day someone recognized me. Then a woman with lips blue with cold, who was in line behind me, and had never heard my name, came out of the numbness which affected us all and whispered in my ear—we all spoke in whispers there:

"Can you describe this?"

I said, "I can!"
Then something like a smile slipped over what had once been
her face.

TRANSLATED BY RICHARD MCKANE

Sunset in the ethereal waves:
I cannot tell if the day
Is ending, or the world, or if
The secret of secrets is inside me again.

TRANSLATED BY JANE KENYON

And the miraculous comes so close
To the ruined, dirty houses—
Something not known to anyone at all,
But wild in our breast for centuries.

TRANSLATED BY STANLEY KUNITZ
WITH MAX HAYWARD

Until I collapse by the fence
And the wind deals me the final blow,
The dream of salvation close at hand
Will burn me like an oath.

TRANSLATED BY ALIKI BARNSTONE

There my white nights
Whisper of someone's discreet exalted
Love.
And everything is mother-
Of-pearl and jasper,
But the light's source is a secret.

TRANSLATED BY D. M. THOMAS

GABRIELA MISTRAL

CHILE, 1889–1957

In 1945, Gabriela Mistral became the first Latin American to win a Nobel Prize in literature. Hailed for her poetry all over the world, she was also a social and political activist with strong convictions who held a number of diplomatic posts for some twenty years, in Italy, Brazil, the United States, and other countries. Throughout her poetry, correspondence, interviews, articles, and speeches, written and extemporaneous, she expounds a powerful doctrine of human rights that greatly expands our understanding of the range of her creative genius. A committed Christian, she identified herself with the poorest of the poor, speaking out with a forceful voice against the exploitative, often bloody, interventions of rich nations in poor countries. She firmly believed that justice and beauty would one day be established on earth.

Gabriela Mistral was born in a small town in Chile and denied an education on the grounds that she lacked intellectual gifts. Self-educated, she became a teacher and at the age of twenty-one fell in love with a young man who took his own life (a tragedy repeated some years later when her adopted son committed suicide at the age of seventeen). She began writing poems as an outlet for her grief and almost immediately won her first prizes. The books that established her literary standing are Desolación *(1923), about a spiritual crisis, and* Tala *(1946). She spent the last four years of her life in the United States.*

~⁀

FROM "PRAYER"

Like those jars that women put out to catch the dew of night,
I place my breasts before God. I give Him a new name, I call
Him the Filler, and I beg of Him the abundant liquid of life.
Thirstily looking for it, will come my son.

TRANSLATED BY LANGSTON HUGHES

THE POWERFUL AGAINST THE POOR, 1928

You ask me what I think about General Sandino's resistance against North American forces.... I am becoming convinced that the time is fast approaching when I must say that not only women but even children will have to speak out about politics, because only politics can bring about just distribution of the wealth of our nations; the destruction of the landed class which today prevents a dignified and equitable division of land; the death of the old educational system which does not teach skills to the poor child;... and the rejection of foreign interests.

[The U.S. president, Herbert Hoover] has declared Sandino an "outlaw," oblivious to what is called international law. The United States government speaks of Nicaraguan territory as if it were its own, since declaring someone an "outlaw" cannot be understood except as it applies to one of its own citizens.

Mr. Hoover's marines are going to hold in their hands a trophy in which nearly all of us from the South will see our own blood.... We are cursing them, quietly and loudly, in words we have never used before, despite Santo Domingo and Haiti.

When they execute Sandino, there will be a unity [that will renew our resolve to fight]. In Sandino, we see our Paez, our Morelos, our Carrera, our Artigas [revolutionary heroes in other Latin American countries]. The task is the same, as is the predicament.

Mr. Hoover will cause us to experience a feeling of continental unity never achieved before, not even in 1810.... Mr. Hoover is going to attain, without intending to do so, something which we ourselves have not been able to accomplish: to see ourselves, from first to last, from the beginning to the end, as one person in Augusto Sandino's death.

FROM "THOSE WHO DO NOT DANCE"

God asked from on high,
"How do I come down from this blueness?"
We told Him:
come dance with us in this light.

TRANSLATED BY MARIA GIACHETTI

ANITA SCOTT COLEMAN
NEW MEXICO, 1890–1960

This compelling story shines with the beauty of the spirit and the beauty of racial pride. Its author, Anita Coleman, was a poet, essayist, and short story writer of the Harlem Renaissance in the first half of the twentieth century. For over two decades she published in such journals as Opportunity, Crisis, *and* Half Century, *winning both second and third prizes one year in a contest sponsored by* Crisis. *In her unforgettable story "The Eternal Quest," from which the following excerpt is taken, a famous surgeon is making a scientific study of faith.*

~9

NO. 60 IN WARD 400

No. 60 in Ward 400 was one of the strangest cases ever admitted to the county hospital. His was [a] unique malady and of a far-reaching scope. Plainly it came within the category of the cases wherein the great Evan Given had labored so magnificently. It was known that the famous English surgeon was sojourning in the American city. If he could be prevailed upon to grant no more than an hour of his time, if for no more than a consultation, if only for an observation, anything he might choose to do would be a priceless gift to the medical profession.

At last when all arguments had failed, someone mentioned that—which seemed to him, the strangest phase of the case in question—that this great hulking giant of a fellow—No. 60 was well over forty—should lay day after day, calling for his mother.

"That," said Evan Given, instantly, "is faith. Wait. I will come."

The span of No. 60's shoulders came near to over-taxing the width of the white iron cot. His massive head pressed against the headpost. His feet protruded through the foot rails. He was easily six foot ten, and he was delirious when Evan Given saw him first. He was strapped, but yet the strong thongs were proving inadequate, the motions of the man lifted the cot until it tossed about like a frail craft on a windy sea. And always, he screeched the one word, "mom-mer."

"Too late...Nothing can be done!" proclaimed the great man. "At least, he can be made comfortable. Send for his mother!"

"There can be no visitors." Head Nurse of Ward 400 voiced a protest that was curbed at a glance of the surgeon.

No. 60's mother arrived when he was at his worst. It was the crucial hour. He was seeking with maniacal strength to break his bonds, and screaming fiendishly. The mother, after a brief period with the great London physician, hurried to her son's bedside.

She was a small woman, a tightly shrivelled hard little person, not unlike a black walnut.... her timidity fell from her, as she drew near the bed. She became no longer an uneasy visitor among countless strangers, but a mother with her only son, and it was he and she against the world.

The great Evan Given was a close observer of all that passed. This was a pregnant moment to him, in his study of faith.

The mother said quickly and a little shrilly, "Lie down 'dar." Then in firmer tones, and quieter, "Be still. Didn't ah tells you!"

Magically, the huge form upon the bed grew calm.

"What's you a-laying here fo', disturbin' these yere folks; ain't yo' Mammy done taught yo' better'n 'at..." Her voice was crooning. "Ain't yo' shame yo'self. Here's yo' Mammy done come this long ways to see yo', and yo' is lyin here yellin' like yo' is possessed."

"Mommer. . . ."

To the amazement of those watching, the man on the bed was muttering in his turn to the old woman. The mother down on her knees bent her head to hear. Quickly she stood erect, and called loudly.

"Nurse...Doctor...somebody come quick and take off dese bindings. My boy wants to die free...Come quick, somebody quick."

Evan Given came—interns and nurses together removed the straps. No. 60 heaved a great sigh of relief. His head jerked back convulsively, and his eyes rolled wildly toward his mother. "De Lord's done come," he intoned majestically, and fell into his final sleep, peacefully as a babe.

"Faith," jotted Given, mentally.

The old woman sat beside the cot with folded hands. Evan cleared his throat. Surely this was a strange manner in which to meet death, not a tear, in no wise did she betray regret.

"Why-er, why-er," began Evan.

"Blessed lamb...Sweet Jesus, done come and set my po' suf-f'ring boy free," chanted the old woman, almost gaily.

"Faith," tabulated Given in his scientific mind.

"What will you do?" he inquired curiously, and not unkindly.

"Do heah this man," exclaimed No. 60's mother, "I'se goin'er do my wo'k." As an afterthought, "I'se got'er wo'k for sho' now, 'cause dis boy a-lying heah is my sole suppo't. But de Lord will provide."

"Faith," said Evan Given audibly in the voice of a man who talks often to himself. "I must find it."

ANANDAMAYI MA
INDIA, 1896–1982

Anandamayi Ma was the spiritual mother of Indira Gandhi and hundreds of thousands of other people, although she refused to be promoted as a guru or religious authority. People saw her as an avatar, or incarnation of God: the Divine Mother in human form. Because she was illiterate, she signed her name with a dot, noting that "it contains all that is," which expresses her self-understanding as "a God-realized being."

Born to a poor Bengali family who named her Nirmala Sundari, she was married at the age of twelve to an equally poor boy whom she served for about a dozen years. Ecstatic gifts and a strong personality unfolded gradu-ally until by the end of her twenties she had initiated her husband, who now considered her his guru, and abandoned all household duties. She embraced the life of an itinerant monastic, wandering around India for ten years, attracting devotees and assisting people wherever she went.

A natural contemplative with an iron will, capable of the most advanced meditative practices even in youth, Nirmala took a three-year vow of silence while still in her twenties. Forced to break the silence on a few occasions, she would seat herself in a yoga position, draw an imaginary circle around herself, recite a mantra, then say what needed to be said. When finished, she would erase the circle in the same way and resume her silence. She healed sick people as many healers will, by taking on the illness herself— until her husband, fearing for her life, begged her to give up the practice. As the circle of devotees surrounding Nirmala enlarged, she changed her name to Anandamayi Ma, which means "Mother of Bliss." Today a non- profit foundation established in her name supports twenty-eight ashrams all over India, a hospital, medical dispensaries, and schools for the poor. Her burial site in Kankhal on the banks of the Ganges has become a center of pilgrimage and worship for growing numbers of disciples around the world. Her "sayings" are excerpted from Matri Vani *by Atmananda.*

~ᴐ

SAYINGS AND ADVICE

The universal remedy is contemplation of the One.

As the intention, so the reward.

Whatever happens is welcome.

With the name of the One on your lips, perform your work in the world.

See the people [prostrating like sticks at the feet of] Ma? They do that because they think that their souls are different from the one to whom they are paying homage. But in fact, both are one and the same.

What is the method for drawing closer to God? Recite the name for your beloved that you like best. That is all. You have to call your beloved. Do that in whatever way you want.

To concentrate on the One brings release from all anxiety.

It is incumbent on humankind to consider everything that happens to be for the best; "the best" denoting what is most helpful towards realization of the Divine.

In all forms, in all diversity and disparity is the One. The infinite variety of appearances and manifestations, of modes of becoming and states of being, of species and types, all the numberless distinctions as well as all identity are but the One. With whom then are you angry?

Remain calm and at peace under all circumstances.

Pray for the power of endurance.

Try your utmost to never succumb to anyone's influence.

In order to become firm, calm, deeply serious, full of courage, with one's personality fully intact, . . . one must be centered in the One.

Only actions that kindle your divine nature are worthy of the name of action; all the rest are non-actions—a waste of energy.

Stay quietly in one place and do your *sadhana* [spiritual practices], as a sincere and earnest aspirant, and first of all to fill your own emptiness. Then the treasure you have accumulated will of its own accord seek an outlet and communicate itself to others.

It is by seeking to know one's Self that the Great Mother of all may be found.

Memorize chants and verses in praise of God and repeat them while you move around. Never allow your mind to be idle.

SATOMI MYODO
JAPAN, 1896–1978

Satomi Myodo is an example of the modern Japanese woman who struggles to attain enlightenment through the ageless practices of Zen Buddhism. She began her mystical journey with pregnancy and a miserably unhappy marriage to a man who abandoned her, after which she lost her child. Unable to live up to the motto of the school she attended, "Good Wives and Wise Mothers," she suffered a breakdown, succumbing to madness, though not for long.

Healing came when she left behind the roles she could not fulfill and found the contemplative path that she was meant to follow. Her first teacher was a Shinto priest who trained her in shamanism, and she became an exorcist and oracle. By midlife, feeling a need to delve deeper, she embraced the teachings of Zen Buddhism, which she practiced ardently for the rest of her life.

When Satomi met her principle teacher, Zen master Yasutani Roshi, she attained an early state of enlightenment known as kensho, *with the dramatic, lasting result that she "felt as if a chronic disease of forty years had been cured in an instant."*

Continuing to practice diligently, she successfully solved the entire series of koans, the riddles pondered in meditation that intuition (but not reason) can penetrate. With this test passed, she had earned the right to become a Zen teacher though she chose not to. She remained in a relationship with Yasutani Roshe, continually deepening her meditation practice, until she was almost eighty, when she returned home to Hokkaido for the last two years of her life.

The selection reproduced here comes from her book, Passionate Journey: The Spiritual Autobiography of Satomi Myodo, *which was translated in 1987 by Sallie B. King.*

As this selection begins, Satomi learns she is pregnant and must end her education, since she is unmarried, and return home to work in the field with her parents. Believing she has destroyed her parents' high hopes for her, their only child, she no longer desires to live. Her pregnancy is obvious, but according to the mores of the time, not a word is spoken about it, which heightens her agony. Suddenly one day, her father breaks the silence with a wise, compassionate, and illumining intervention.

~᠑

A LIBERATING EXPERIENCE

One day I went as usual to the field, working and getting covered with dirt. From a distance, my father urgently called my name. I went to see what he wanted and found Father squatting at the edge of the field, gazing intently at something. A moment passed. I felt a little strange, squatting quietly by my father's side. Absently my eye caught his line of vision. There was nothing but a single weed growing there. Softly Father began to speak.

"I've been watching this for some time... it's quite interesting... Look! A winged ant is crawling up the weed. It climbs up, little by little... it seems to want to reach the top. Oh, it fell! There—it's climbing again! For some time now it's been doing this over and over again." Just as he said, a winged ant was climbing up the weed and falling; falling and climbing up again.

"Here! Climbing again! Look, it must be tired now. When it's tired, it stretches its legs and beats its little wings up and down like that. That's how it restores its energy. Then, when it's rested, it starts climbing again. . . ."

Suddenly it hit me—I understood what my father was getting at! It was unbearable! I quickly got up and left his side. I ran to the shady side of the field where no one could see me and fell down wailing. I cried and cried in anguish.

"Oh, Father, I understand; I really understand! Do you love me so much? I'm so unfilial! Do you still cherish such hope for me, when I am so disgusted with myself? How... grateful I am!" I determined to repay my father's love, no matter what. Just then, an iron shackle was broken and at once a broad expanse of light burst upon the world.

MARIA VALTORTA

ITALY, 1897–1961

Maria Valtorta, whose work is virtually unknown outside of Italy, left some fifteen thousand pages of writings about her visions of Mary the mother of Jesus. Her mystical life began at the age of four when, as she noted in her journals, "I met the face of God and God's love." The experience never left her. Paralyzed at the age of thirty-seven, she was confined to her home for the rest of her life, devoting herself to prayer and to elucidating her visions in writing, forging in the process an original Mariology that has been acclaimed as the finest work on Mary of the twentieth century.

Gabriel Roschini, one of the foremost Roman Catholic Mariologists, a professor at the Pontifical Lateran University in Rome, the author of over 125 books, wrote of Maria: "The Mariology found in all of Maria Valtorta's writings—both published and unpublished—has been a real discovery for me. No other Marian writings, not even the sum total of everything I have ever read and studied, were able to give me as clear, as vivid, as complete, as luminous, or as fascinating an image, both simple and sublime, of Mary."

~⁀

A VISION OF MARY

On October 24, [1947], I saw the symbol of what Mary is in God: an incandescent triangle—the Most Holy Trinity—in which was Mary. The voice of the Eternal Father said to me, "This is how Mary is in us. Let learned theologians understand what this vision means. Let them understand all that it contains about Mary's power and wisdom. To her, Love gave Himself completely, Wisdom revealed Itself completely, and Power deigned to bestow Itself completely."

GOD SPEAKS TO MARY DURING CREATION

I am looking at you and I give [the blue of Your eyes to the sea and the firmament], [the color of Your hair to the holy wheat], whiteness to the lily, and a rosy color to the rose, like Your silky skin. I copy the pearls from your minute teeth, I make the sweet strawberries [while looking at] Your mouth, and I give the nightingale Your notes, and the turtle-doves your weeping. And reading Your future thoughts, and listening to the throbs of Your heart, I have [My theme, My guide for creation]. Come and see sheep and lambs, eagles and doves being created. Stay beside me when I make the hollow of the seas and the grooves of the rivers, and as I raise the mountains and adorn them with snow and forests. Stay here while I sow [grain-bearing plants, trees and vines.]... Run, fly, rejoice, My Beauty. And may the universe which is created hour by hour learn from You to love Me, My Love. May it become more beautiful owing to Your smile, Mother of My Son, Queen of My paradise, Love of Your God.

DOROTHY DAY
NEW YORK, 1897–1980

Dorothy Day was a natural activist, not given to self-analysis, with no intention of becoming the legend she has become. A bright young woman appalled by the hunger and homelessness she saw all around her in New York—before, during, and after the Depression era of the 1930s—she converted to Catholicism, making a commitment to herself to somehow live out the New Testament message of feeding the hungry, clothing and sheltering those who have nothing, soothing the anguish and confusion of those who can find no work. Like the saints of Assisi, she literally followed Christ's injunction to "give away all that you have and come follow me." The proximity to us of her language, photographs, and justice work—the fact that her life could be filmed—makes the saints of all centuries seem closer to us in time and more real, Christ's message more immediate. Dorothy Day had no desire to be a monastic or take religious vows; she was a single mother who never married, but she made the extreme choice of "voluntary poverty" and spent her life without personal comfort or security to be a servant of the poor.

With her French intellectual friend, Peter Maurin, she founded the Catholic Worker Movement, publishing an eight-page monthly newspaper, The Catholic Worker, *founding "houses of hospitality" to shelter the homeless and agitating tirelessly for social justice. In the first volume of her autobiography,* The Long Loneliness—*a second volume,* Loaves and

Fishes, *came later—she relates how, in 1917, she and a group of women undertook a defiant hunger strike while imprisoned for picketing the White House. The women had been demanding certain rights for political prisoners, who at the time received brutal treatment no longer permitted in the United States.*

Dorothy Day died at the age of eighty-three. Thomas Merton, the Trappist monk who wrote The Seven Storey Mountain *and some sixty additional books, wrote that she was "a credit to American democracy and a credit to American Catholicism."*

She made an important distinction between poverty as a "social phenomenon" and poverty as a "personal matter," which is the subject of the first selection here.

~◌

VOLUNTARY POVERTY

We know the misery being poor can cause. St. Francis was "the little poor man" and no one was more joyful than he; yet Francis began with tears, in fear and trembling, hiding out in a cave from his irate father. He appropriated some of his father's [belongings] (which he considered his rightful inheritance) in order to repair a church and rectory where he meant to live. It was only later that he came to love "Lady Poverty." Perhaps kissing the leper was the giant step that freed him not only from fastidiousness and a fear of disease but from attachment to [material possessions] as well....

I have "kissed a leper"—consciously—but I cannot say I am much better for it.... A woman with cancer of the face was begging...and when I gave her money, passing on alms someone had given to me, she tried to kiss my hand. The only thing I could do was to kiss her dirty old face with the gaping hole in it where an eye and a nose had been. It sounds like a heroic deed, but it was not. We get used to ugliness so quickly. What we avert our eyes from today can be borne tomorrow when we have learned a little more about love. Nurses know this, and so do mothers....

FROM *LOAVES AND FISHES*

JAIL

Each cell was made for one prisoner.... [T]here were no meals to break the monotony, and if the women tried to cry out to one another, there were always guards on hand to silence them harshly. We had no idea how many were in the punishment block but estimated there could be no more than 12 since there were only so many single cells. The older women had been taken elsewhere. "Keep the strike," one of the girls called once. "Remember, if it's broken we go back to worms in the oatmeal and the workshop."

Personally I would have preferred the workshop and prison clothes to the hunger strike. Those first six days of inactivity were as six thousand years. To lie there through the long day, to feel the nausea and emptiness of hunger, the dazedness at the beginning and the feverish mental activity that came after. I lost all consciousness of any cause. I had no sense of being a radical, making protest against a government, carrying on a nonviolent revolution. I could only feel darkness and desolation all around me. The bar of gold which the sun left on the ceiling every morning for a short hour taunted me; and late in the afternoon when the cells were dim and the lights in the corridor were not yet lit, a heartbreaking conviction of ugliness, of the futility of life came over me so that I could not weep but only lie there in misery.

I lost all feeling of my own identity. I reflected on the desolation of poverty, of destitution, of sickness and sin. That I would be free after 30 days meant nothing to me. I would never be free again, never free when I knew that behind bars all over the world there were women and men, young girls and boys, suffering constraint, punishment, isolation, and hardship for crimes of which all of us were guilty. The mother who had murdered her child, the drug addict, who were the mad and who the sane? Why were prostitutes prosecuted in some cases, and in others respected and fawned on? People sold themselves for jobs, for the paycheck, and if they received a high enough price they were honored. If their cheating, their theft, their lie, were of colossal proportions, if it were successful, they met with praise, not blame. Why were some caught, not others? Why were some termed criminals and others good businessmen? What was right and wrong? What was good and evil? I lay there in utter confusion and misery.

I [have written] of my identification with those around me. I was that mother whose child had been raped and slain. I was the mother who had borne the monster who had done it. I was even that monster, feeling in my own breast every abomination. Is this exaggeration? There are not so many of us who have lain for six days and nights in darkness, cold and hunger, pondering in our heart the world and our part in it. If you live in great cities, if you are in constant contact with sin and suffering, if the daily papers print nothing but Greek tragedies, if you see on all sides people trying to find relief from the drab boredom of their job and family life in sex and alcohol, then you become inured to the evil of the day, and it is rarely that such a realization of the horror of hate can come to you. . . .

There were stories told of prisoners being left in these cells for six months. Six months! The 30 days stretched out before me interminably. I would be utterly crushed by misery before I was released. Never would I recover from this wound, this ugly knowledge I had gained of what men were capable of in their treatment of each other. It was one thing to be writing about these things, to have the theoretical knowledge of sweatshops and injustice and hunger, but it was quite another to experience it in one's own flesh. There were those stories too of a whipping post and of bloodhounds wandering through the grounds to terrorize the prisoners. These things had been sworn to by a former matron of the workhouse, and the superintendent did not deny them.

I had no sense as I lay there of the efficacy of what I was doing. . . .

The hunger strike lasted for 10 days. . . . On the 10th day the strike was broken by the announcement that all our demands would be granted.

FROM *THE LONG LONELINESS*

ELSA GIDLOW

ENGLAND, 1898–1986

Elsa Gidlow, a poet and journalist relatively unknown in the United States, was born in England, emigrated to Canada with her family as a child, and later settled in the United States. In the 1920s she built her *famous California home, Druid Heights, overlooking the Pacific Ocean amid majestic redwood trees on the top of Mount Tamalpais, a mountain just north of San Francisco that was once sacred to Native Americans. Among her books are her autobiography,* Elsa, I Come with My Songs; Sapphic Songs: The Love Poetry of Elsa Gidlow; *and* Shattering the Mirror.

~⌒⌒

FROM "CHAINS OF FIRE"

I know myself linked by chains of fire
To every woman who has kept a hearth. In the resinous smoke
I smell hut, castle, cave,
Mansion and hovel,
See in the shifting flame my mother
And grandmothers out over the world.

IRINA TWEEDIE

RUSSIA, 1907–1999

An ancient saying in the Golden Sufi tradition holds that there are only forty Sufis in the world at any one moment in time. Irina Tweedie, during the last four decades of her life from about the age of fifty-five to ninety-three, clearly belonged to this group of great souls. Today her first student, Llewellen Vaughan Lee, who teaches at the Golden Sufi Center in Inverness, California, merits the same distinction.

Irina Tweedie received a privileged education in Vienna and Paris and then left her native Russia permanently to marry a British naval officer and settle into an upper-class social life of parties and vacations. The death of her husband when she was forty-five led her on a spiritual quest that ended in India in 1961 when she became the student of a great Muslim teacher in the

Golden Sufi tradition, Bhai Sahib. She told him that she "wanted the Rootless Root, the Causeless Cause of the Upanishads," instead of the harsh and concrete images of God that she had imbibed since childhood. Bhai Sahib recognized in her a formidably strong ego and, paradoxically, the potential to "accomplish in one year what most people can in twenty years," and he inducted her into a supremely strenuous Sufi training. He ignored and insulted her; persuaded her to give away her money so she would experience hunger and India's stifling summer heat without relief; assigned her deliberately humiliating tasks; and convinced her to give up her lipstick so she would look "old and ugly," telling her all the while to "love whatever happens."

Bhai Sahib used the very strength of Irina Tweedie's ego to shatter it. And this strategy, which would drive away most of us, worked, for as she held her ground and refused the temptation to run away, her stubbornness melted into perseverance, her arrogance dissolved, and, by the time Bhai Sahib passed away, she was indeed a Golden Sufi, set free on the path of love.

Since she did not know Persian and could not study essential texts, Bhai Sahib instructed her to keep a detailed journal of her spiritual experiences, dreams, reflections, and his teachings. Her own experiences alone, he taught her, would bring her the knowledge she was seeking. The journal appeared in 1986 in a gripping nine-hundred-page book, Daughter of Fire: A Diary of a Spiritual Training with a Sufi Master (which was published at her students' center in Inverness).

The diary describes repeated bouts of extreme heart disturbance—wild fibrillation, pain, breathlessness, nausea, and dizziness—that she fearlessly endured without complaint and interpreted as mystical phenomena. Not surprisingly, London physicians diagnosed heart disease, yet she lived to be ninety-three, performing the best work of her life in her sixties, seventies, and eighties. In London during these decades, her reputation spread rapidly, attracting a wide circle of students and lecture invitations from all over England.

~)

CIRCULATION OF LIGHT IN THE BODY

16th February, 1962
I noticed something completely new.... At first I thought that my blood was getting luminous, and I saw its circulation throughout the body. But soon I became aware that it was not the blood; the

light, the bluish-white light, was running along another system which could not have been blood vessels. For I could see the blood vessels too; they were pulsating with every beat of the heart, doing their work of supplying blood to the tissues. But they were not the carriers of light. This strange unearthly light, clearly seen in a semi-transparent body, used other channels.... But of course! I suddenly understood; it was running along the nerves!

The whole nervous system was clearly visible, and the light was circulating in it just as the blood does in the blood vessels. Only, and here was the substantial difference, the circulation of the blood stops at the skin, but this light did not stop at the skin level; it penetrated through it, radiating out, not very far, say about nine inches (I couldn't be quite sure, for it kept fluctuating, increasing and diminishing with some kind of flares). As I say, it came out and re-entered the body again at another place. Observing closely I could see clearly that there were many points, as though agglomerations of light in various parts of the body, and light came out of one of them and re-entered through another one. As those points seemed to be countless, it looked like a luminous web encircling the body, inside and outside. It was very lovely. The Web of the Universe, I thought, and was fascinated by the unusual and the very beautiful sight.

Soon, however, I became aware of something rather alarming. Because I was so absorbed and enchanted, or perhaps the heat at the beginning was not great, I became increasingly aware that the body seemed to be on fire. This liquid light was cold, but in spite of it being cold by itself (and for some inexplicable reason I was sure that it was cold), it was burning me... as if currents of hot lava were flowing through every nerve, every fiber, hotter and hotter, more and more unbearable, more and more luminous, faster and faster,... shimmering. Increasing and decreasing. Fluctuating, expanding and contracting all at the same time. And I could do nothing but lie there. Watching helplessly, as the intense suffering increased with every second. "Burned alive," flashed through my mind. This must be the end. Surely this time I will die. Hot light circulating everywhere, leaving not one particle of my body alone.

Everywhere it went. And when I concentrated on some part of my body, I noticed that the light and the heat increased to an unbearable degree, concentrating where my thought was concentrating. How long this intense and at times unbearable suffering lasted, I don't know.... [I]t was all gone in the morning, leaving a great tiredness behind.

[At the peak of her training ordeal, at the point of surrendering, Irina Tweedie copied in her diary this beautiful poem.]

Like a tree struck by lightning, I crashed before Thee;
Like a star which falls from the sky, its light spent forever;
So I spent myself before Thee like this star....
As a stone thrown into the lake by the playful hand of a
    child
Goes down into the utmost depth, never to come up
    again—
So I went down before Thee once and for all....

THIS IS A PROMISE, AND I WILL KEEP IT

9th March, 1967
My infinite One, I am asking for help. I am going to a life dedicated to You. It is said that the river takes no rest, the wind knows no fatigue, and the sun can only shine and shine forever. [So] I will go on. I know that the states of Nearness will increase, will become more permanent, but also the state of separation will become more painful, more lonely, the nearer one comes to Reality. This cannot be avoided; it belongs to this school of training. But it does not matter anymore. The memory of nearness to [You] will remain and will give me strength to go on. I know I go back to a life of fire; for you, my dear [Teacher], before accepting me, you told me what to expect. And I said "yes" and sealed my destiny. I know health will fail me sometimes, I know I will be burned and it will not matter, for always, always, I will remember that I belong somewhere and that will give me strength to go on. I know one must not impose

one's own experiences on other people, for each of us is intensely individual, and experiences are unique for each of us. I remember that after your death, I felt like screaming at the thought of returning to the West. I could not reconcile the states of oneness and the world around me. Solitude was the only way out. To be able to find myself again; which was not a self at all. I know now that I can never be alone anymore, for you are with me always. I know now that God is silence and can be reached only in silence. I will try to help people to reach this state: This is a promise, and I will keep it.

SIMONE WEIL

FRANCE, 1909–1943

A passionate servant of the poor and the rarest kind of cerebral mystic, Simone Weil was the author of Waiting for God, *a twentieth-century classic of astonishing depth and sheer brilliance. She earned distinction for "genius in philosophy" at the Ecole Normale Superieure in Paris, competing for first place with the great French existentialist Simone de Beauvoir (author of* The Second Sex). *Raised in a family of well-to-do, secular Jews, she "felt like a Catholic" for most of life because she loved Jesus' teachings but refused entry into the church because of the accretion of dogmas around the historical Jesus and the church's abuse of power. Driven by passionate outrage over the unjust plight of the poor, she flirted with Marxism, becoming known at university as "the red virgin." She also made her physical appearance as unattractive as possible, insisting that "a beautiful woman, looking at her image in the mirror, may very well believe the image is herself. An ugly woman knows it is not."*

In her early twenties, when she began her career as a philosophy teacher and writer, Simone spent summers working as a farmhand in order to share the lot of the poor. At twenty-six, despite severe headaches and worsening health, she spent an entire year working on an assembly line in a Renault factory. Her descriptions of the staggering stress and mind-numbing boredom on the assembly line are a classical exposé of life without enough money, education, medical care, relief, or hope. A year later she went to war, direct to the front lines, where the French Republican Army, or "Reds," fought the "Francoites." When she returned, understanding "in the very depths

of my being" the full horror of war and its atrocities, she continued her fight
until her death for the rights of the poor.

During the early years of the Second World War, Simone's mystical nature
was steadily opening. She was studying Greek philosophy and Hinduism and
was mentored for two years by Father Perrin, a Dominican who asked her to
expound on her thoughts on Plato and the Pythagoreans in a circle of Catholic
intellectuals who met in the crypt of an old Dominican convent. In 1942, she
accepted an invitation to be a member of the French Provisional Government
in England, where her health continued to decline, and she fasted excessively
to be in solidarity with people who had only war rations or less.

Her last fast turned into self-starvation, and on August 29, 1943, at the
age of 33, she died of the same illness that also took the life of Catherine of
Siena at thirty-three: "holy anorexia," or anorexia made sacred by the mys-
tic's use of it for others.

~⁀Ͻ

FROM WAITING FOR GOD

At the end of my year in the factory, before returning to teaching, I
had been invited by my parents to Portugal and while there, I left
them to go to a small village alone. I was, as it were, in pieces: soul
and body. That year of daily contact with affliction had killed my
youth. Until then I had not had any experience of affliction, unless we
count my own, which, since it was my own, seemed to me of little
importance, and which moreover was only partial, being physical, but
not social. I certainly knew that there was a great deal of affliction in
the world, I was obsessed with the idea of affliction, but I had not yet
any prolonged or immediate experience of my own. While I worked in
the factory, indistinguishable from the anonymous mass, in the eyes
of everyone including my own, the affliction of others penetrated into
my flesh and my soul. There was no relief from it, since I had truly
forgotten my own past and could not look ahead to any future, finding
it too difficult to imagine the possibility that so much fatigue could be
survived. What I endured that year imprinted me so irrevocably that
still today when any human being, whoever it is, speaks to me without
brutality, I sense that there must be a mistake, and that, unfortu-
nately, the mistake will probably be discovered and disappear. In the

factory, I received forever the mark of a slave, like the branding by a red-hot iron that the Romans pressed onto the foreheads of their most despised slaves. Since then I have always considered myself a slave.

In this state of mind then—and in wretched physical condition—I arrived at the little Portuguese village which was very wretched also, even though it was the feast-day of its patron saint. I was all alone. It was evening and a full moon was shining over the sea. The wives of the fishermen were processing around the ships, holding candles and singing what must have been very ancient hymns of a heart-breaking sadness. No words can convey an idea of it. I have never heard anything so poignant except perhaps the song of the boatmen on the Volga. There the conviction suddenly came to me that Christianity is pre-eminently the religion of slaves, that a slave cannot be anything but Christian, I included.

DIVINE LOVE IN THE MIDST OF AFFLICTION

In 1938, I spent ten days at Solesmes, from Palm Sunday to Easter Tuesday, following all the liturgical services. I was suffering from splitting headaches. Every sound hurt me like a blow. By an extreme effort of concentration I was able to rise above this miserable flesh, to leave it to suffer by itself, heaped up in a corner, and to find a pure and perfect joy in the unimaginable beauty of the chanting and the words. By analogy, this experience enabled me to understand more deeply the possibility of loving with Divine love in the midst of affliction. It goes without saying that over the course of these liturgies, the thought of the passion of Christ entered into my being once and for all.

There was a young English Catholic there from whom I gained my first idea of the spiritual power of sacraments because of the truly angelic radiance with which he seemed to be clothed after going to communion.... [H]e told me of those English poets who are named metaphysical. Reading them later on I discovered [George Herbert's poem] "Love." I learned it by heart. Often when a violent headache reaches its peak, I force myself to say it over and over, focusing all my attention upon it and clinging with all my soul to the tenderness it enshrines. I used to think I was reciting it as a beautiful poem, but without my becoming aware of it, reciting it had the nature of a prayer. During one of these recitations, ...Christ himself came down and took possession of me....

In this sudden possession of me by Christ, neither my senses nor my imagination played any role; I only felt in the midst of my suffering the presence of a love—like that which one can read in the smile of a beloved face.

MAE V. COWDERY
PENNSYLVANIA, 1909–1953

An award-winning poet who published her first poetry at the age of seventeen, Mae Cowdery won a coveted place in the Philadelphia High School for academically gifted girls. She moved to New York in the 1920s to participate in the Harlem Renaissance with some of the most gifted artists of the era, publishing in such journals as Opportunity *and* Crisis. *A book of her poems,* We Lift Up Our Voices, *was published when she was twenty-five. Tragically, at forty-four, she took her own life.*

The selection below comes from a short story she published in 1928 in the first volume of Black Opals, *the journal of a distinguished black writers' group in Philadelphia. The story weaves a dream of sacred love that stands the test of time. A theme relevant to all peoples, it would hold special meaning to black people in the first half of the twentieth century, with memories of slavery all too close and painful, family structures shattered, segregation raging, most social assistance withheld, and limited opportunities for professional or artistic self-expression.*

~

A DREAM OF LOVE

Lai-li was dancing in the moonlight...Once more. Her brown body gleamed like gold in his path.

Fearfully he whispered her name.........Once more,

"Lai-li........Lai-li........"

She did not answer...Ah! There was no need.........she was

coming nearer, nearer. Slowly she danced. There was no sound save for the pounding of his heart and the magic melody of the waves rolling slowly to shore . . . . all was as on that night when first he saw her. Lai-li . . . . "Moon flower."

Many, many years had passed since then. Time had dealt gently with her. She was even more beautiful.

He could feel her breath on his cheek, fragrant as the perfume imprisoned in the crimson petals of the flowers she wore in the ebony coils of her hair. Close she came, her tiny feet making no sound as she beat her love song on the silver sands.

Would she know him? Would she forgive? . . . . Had her heart forgotten the wound he had dealt in the reckless days of his youth? . . . . He surely had suffered.

And again he whispered her name.

"Lai-li . . . . Lai-li . . . . "

Her golden arms were twining around his neck. Her body yielded, on that night—so long ago. Her lids drooped over eyes like midnight pools, hiding the fire within . . . . Her lips were cool, like dew, on his feverish ones . . . . As on that night . . . . so long ago.

Once more they would dance the strange jungle dance she had taught him . . . . once more they would dance . . . . she had forgiven.

God! He had forgotten he was no longer young. Time had dealt roughly with him. . . . It was his punishment. His limbs could no longer bend and whirl . . . . his arms could no longer hold close their precious burden, as he sought to lift her and dart to the shadows . . . . once more.

"Lai-li! Lai-li! Do not go! Stay! Stay! I am coming. I . . . . am . . . . coming."

The moon passed behind a cloud: the waves paused an instant on their homeward flight. Air hung silent.

Again two figures danced a jungle dance in the moonlight . . . . gold and ivory blending, caressed by the moon's silver breath . . . . Two figures slept once more in the embrace of the sand, watched over by the cool shadows . . . . Two loved once more . . . .

MOTHER TERESA
ALBANIA, 1910–1997

When the woman who would become Mother Teresa of Calcutta was a Catholic sister in her native Europe, she felt impelled to live a more Christ-like life. What she was seeking appeared in India when she spontaneously ministered to an old man who was dying of illness and starvation on a Calcutta street. Before long, she left her European order behind and moved permanently to Calcutta to serve destitute people dying on the streets. She opened a primitive shelter where people who had previously known only hunger and squalor could die with dignity. Women, and later men, came to assist her, and soon there was a hospital and the beginnings of a new religious order, the Society of the Missionaries of Charity, which now has over a hundred and twenty-five communities throughout the world, including the United States. The Sisters of Charity dress in simple white saris trimmed in blue and dedicate their lives to "holy poverty" while giving dignity, love, food, clothing, shelter, medical treatment, and other kinds of help to the dying and the poor. Many "dying" people are unexpectedly healed and enabled to leave the hospitals. Mother Teresa was awarded the Nobel Peace Prize, and as she walked to the podium to receive it, reporters noticed that her shabby sweater was held together with a safety pin.

~~)

BE A CANDLE

How wonderful it is to think that we have all been created for a purpose! We have not come into the world to be a number; we have been created for a purpose, for great things: To love and be loved.

In our congregation in India, we deal with thousands and thousands of people who die of hunger, of loneliness, of being unwanted, unloved. Once I picked a man up from the street, from an open drain, and I took him to our home. He did not complain, he said, "I have lived like an animal in the street, but I am going to die like an angel, loved and cared for." Two or three hours later, he did die— with a smile on his face.

Now about 70 young American sisters have joined us in India who are so dedicated, and through that dedication take care of lepers, the dying, the crippled, unwanted, shut-ins, the poorest of the poor. And there is so much joy! Because God wants us to be happy. "That my joy may be with you," the Scriptures say.

And when our sisters started a congregation in Yemen, a Muslim country, the governor wrote and said: "The presence of the sisters has lit a new light in the hearts of our people."

So my prayer for you is that you go out into the world today and love the people you meet. Let your presence light new light in the hearts of people.

FROM A GRADUATION ADDRESS AT THOMAS
AQUINAS COLLEGE, CALIFORNIA, 1984

WHO ARE THE POOR?

The poor are the materially and spiritually destitute
The poor are the hungry and the thirsty
The poor are those who need clothing
The poor are the homeless and the harbourless
The poor are the sick
The poor are the physically and mentally handicapped
The poor are the aged
The poor are those imprisoned
The poor are the lonely
The poor are the ignorant and the doubtful
The poor are the sorrowful
The poor are the comfortless
The poor are the persecuted
The poor are those who suffer injustice
The poor are the ill-mannered
The poor are the bad-tempered
The poor are the sinners and the scoffers
The poor are those who do us wrong
The poor are the unwanted, the outcasts of society
The poor are somehow or other—we ourselves.

FROM *LIFE IN THE SPIRIT,*
EDITED BY KATHRYN SPINK

SIVANANDA RADHA

GERMANY, 1911–1995

The woman who is known as Radha was born to a Jewish family in Berlin and became a solo concert dancer. Feeling the need of a deeper inner life, she traveled to India where she remained for many years, undergoing a demanding training with a Hindu spiritual teacher. A gifted pupil, she was eventually initiated as a swami in the Sarasvati order and sent to Canada to "update the teachings of western mind." In 1962 Swami Radha founded the Asodhara Ashram in British Columbia, dividing her time between teaching and writing such books as Hatha Yoga; The Hidden Language: Symbols, Secrets and Metaphors; *and* The Divine Light Invocation.

~_9_

WHY PRACTICE YOGA?

The meaning of *Yoga* is "union," the bringing together of the various polarities within, in order to reach a state of balance and transcend our limited vision. But Truth is approached by degrees. We have first to know the truth about ourselves. We have learned to cover up our many fears very well. In Hatha Yoga we confront our fears as well as our potentials by balancing attention between the body and the mind; for example, a person who has a neck and shoulders as unyielding as a piece of steel is probably unyielding in daily life. *Asanas* [yoga postures] might loosen up the neck and shoulders temporarily, but becoming aware of the psychological implications will help to make the change more permanent. By observing and dealing with the mental-emotional processes, awareness and understanding are increased. Reverence for one's body, as for all life, is an antidote to abuse and violence.

Through the practice of *asanas*, students will become aware of stress in the body and, by the use of their own minds, discover many of their problems. Changes can then be made in life by a conscious decision on the basis of will and self-analysis. The inability to cope with stress, and the sense of helplessness and hopelessness that many people experience, can be counteracted by recognizing the options and applying the power of choice.

MAHALIA JACKSON

LOUISIANA, 1911–1972

Mahalia Jackson brought gospel music to a large audience and has been described as one of the great voices of the twentieth century, as well as "the greatest gospel singer of all time." Born in New Orleans into a Baptist family (her father was a part-time preacher), she was influenced by blues music but never sang it. "The blues are fine for listening. But I never would sing them. I was saved." She refused to sing any but religious songs and would not perform in surroundings she considered inappropriate. She gained popularity and success with her powerful singing and soulful compositions, including her personal anthem, "I'm Going to Move on Up a Little Higher." Eight of her records sold more than a million copies each. She was a favorite of Dr. Martin Luther King Jr. and at his request sang to an audience of two hundred thousand people immediately before his "I Have a Dream" speech in August of 1963. She won a Lifetime Achievement Grammy, was inducted into the Rock and Roll Hall of Fame, and was honored with a stamp issued by the U.S. Postal Service in 1998.

The excerpt here comes from her 1966 book, Movin' On Up, *written with Evan McLeod Wylie.*

～

FROM MOVIN' ON UP

I say this out of my heart—a song must do something for me as well as for the people that hear it. I can't sing a song that doesn't have a message. If it doesn't have the strength it can't lift you. I just can't seem to get the sense of it....

I know now that a great influence in my life was the Sanctified or Holiness Churches we had in the South. I was always a Baptist, but there was a Sanctified Church right next door to our house in New Orleans.

Those people had no choir and no organ. They used the drum, the cymbal, the tambourine, and the steel triangle. Everybody in there sang and they clapped and stomped their feet and sang with their whole bodies. They had a beat, a powerful beat, a rhythm we held on to from slavery days, and their music was so strong and expressive it used to bring the tears to my eyes.

I believe the blues and jazz and even the rock and roll stuff got their beat from the Sanctified Church. We Baptists sang sweet, and we had the long and short meter on beautiful songs like "Amazing Grace, How Sweet It Sounds," but when those Holiness people tore into "I'm So Glad Jesus Lifted Me Up!" they came out with real jubilation....

Once at church one of the preachers got up in the pulpit and spoke out against me. I got right up, too. I told him I was born to sing gospel music. Nobody had to teach me. I was serving God. I told him that I had been reading the Bible every day most of my life and there was a Psalm that said: "Oh, clap your hands, all ye people! Shout unto the Lord with the voice of a trumpet!" If it was undignified, it was what the Bible told me to do.

CLARE BUCKLAND, 1914–
AND
DIANA DOUGLAS, 1960–
CANADA

Diana Douglas and Clare Buckland met for the first time in 1986 when Clare, a Jungian analyst, then seventy-four, asked Diana, a writer and editor, to edit Clare's autobiography. When they completed the book, Always Becoming: An Autobiography, *they decided to work together on a book that would describe Clare's experience of dying consciously. Diana would act as witness, recording notes of weekly meetings, asking questions, pointing out repeated patterns, and listening to Clare's struggles and breakthroughs. The result was* Always Becoming—Forever: A Journal of Conscious Dying/Conscious Living, *published in 1999 in the form of a dialogue between the two women. A highlight of the book lies in Clare's decision not to die alone but to share the sacred process with her family and closest friends.*

CONSCIOUS DYING

[Clare has completed the preparations for the time after her physical death—will, memorial service, giving away possessions—and is reflecting on the actual experience of dying.]

Clare: Wednesday, July 29, 1998
I've begun to . . . think about my physical death in a way that will be most meaningful for everyone. As a result, I am becoming more aware of my part in the process. At dinner on Monday with friends I spoke of my reluctance to have family and friends involved in the physical ministrations to the body after death. Immediately, Sylvia said, "That can be an act of love." I didn't allow that thought to enter, but said again, "I don't feel good about it, I feel too private."

But later, especially the next morning, the awareness came: "That is the ego's concern." I've always wanted to be immaculate— clean, attractive, fresh. I never minded cleaning up my babies, but I've never cared for or nursed an adult who is bed-ridden and incontinent. If this is an ego concern, I need to, and *want* to, let go of it.

Diana: Thursday, July 30
Today we talked about the process of the physical body dying and how Clare would like that to happen. Her son's earlier remark, "I'd like to be there when you die," has stayed with her. She wants her dying to be meaningful for everyone. We talked about what those who are with her might do to support her in the process. I said that I would like to have a focus for my thoughts. Clare suggested that each person could read something precious to them.

Clare: Thursday, July 30
The visit with Diana this morning and our discussion of the final death-of-the-body process moved me deeper into the "open heart" dimension. I know that I have left behind the ego concerns about physical care—and that I begin to sense how rich those last days could be for me and all those close to me. I have "let them in" to the most intimate part of my life—and it feels so much better than

the head-level talk about dying in the spring of last year. I feel very sad about those clumsy first attempts to talk about my dying to my family and friends. Now, I look forward to talking with my children about how *they* would like those last days to be. And I will prepare a list of readings and music that could be meditative and inspiring to anyone with me. I am thinking about prayers I would like them to say as my consciousness moves out of my body.

Clare: Sunday, August 2
Yesterday at a memorial gathering for a friend, a young man asked me what is involved in "conscious dying," and I stumbled around about "spiritual preparation." I felt awkward.

Now, as I sit listening to music this is what arises. The questions that led to my search were: What is my true nature? Who am I? Where did I come from? Where am I going when I die? Where do I fit into the Universe? What is it that continues after death?

Clare: Tuesday, August 4
The biggest question of all, of course, has been: What is conscious dying? Diana reminded me of this fact this morning. My understanding has certainly changed over the months.

Diana: Thursday, August 6
I reported to Clare my conversations with the medical officer of health and a coroner as to whether there are any legal restrictions to dying at home and allowing the body to remain untouched for three days. They both said that they couldn't see any impediment to that. The only time a coroner is called is when death is sudden and unexpected. Clare's would be expected. They suggested finding a doctor who would sign the death certificate and support the process.

Clare: Tuesday, August 11
Last evening I began to talk with my family about the actual dying process, and we plunged directly into the topic, comfortably. I shared with them how I had been shifting from wanting to die alone to including them and my closest friends in this final intimate experience. What emerged was a consensus that felt "right"

for all of us: not to attempt a three-day vigil, as in Buddhist practice, but a ritual of a maximum of twenty-four hours, depending on the circumstances. We *all* want an experience of privacy and intimacy with not too many people present at any one time. My children will try to orchestrate the comings and goings so that each person can be alone with me for whatever time they need.

I had been very ambivalent about the three-day type of vigil: it felt alien to me, and to go that route would be to follow a practice not my own. When I came home, I meditated and experienced briefly my own dying, a very beautiful foreshadowing. I imagined family and friends being around, people reading to me. It felt wonderful. I have never been comfortable being guided in this process by someone else. This happened naturally within my own meditation, and felt authentic and meaningful.

Diana: Winter 2000
Clare and I still meet weekly. Clare's physical energies are greatly diminished as she adapts to being blind. She now uses her time to focus on her inner world. Her core practice of letting go of old patterns and attachments as her way of living and dying consciously continues. She is at peace with not knowing what may happen as she is dying, trusting that all of us close to her will be in tune with what is needed in the moment.

MARY CAROLINE RICHARDS
OREGON, 1916–1999

A poet, potter, teacher, and mystical philosopher who said that all of her art was "a celebration of the numinous," M. C. Richards often remarked, "We live in the universe, not just on Maple Avenue." Supremely self-confident, renowned for her warrior personality, she attributed much of her lifelong fearlessness to her mother's wisdom. When she was an impressionable eight-year-old, for example, a distraught neighbor came running to M. C.'s mother to tell her that M. C. had climbed up on the roof and was perched precariously at the edge. Her mother went out and called up to her daughter, "Oh, M. C., you look so beautiful up there all silhouetted against the sky."

She received a doctorate in English from the University of California at Berkeley in the 1940s, when few women received more than a high school education, and later taught at the innovative Black Mountain College and other universities. She left two marriages and a number of unsatisfactory love relationships and started a new career at the age of seventy by joining the faculty of Matthew Fox's Institute for Culture and Creation Spirituality. As a seventieth birthday gift to herself, she had her ears pierced. Among her books are Imagine Inventing Yellow *and* Centering in Pottery, Poetry, and the Person.

~*ɔ*

SEEING WITH THE INNER EYE

Picture in your inner eye, your inner sight, four avocado seeds on the window sill. Three are suspended in a glass of water and have sprouted. One is still dry and papery and brown. Each of the sprouting seeds has its own character. One has two long roots, like two rubbery legs folding around each other in the bottom of the glass. Out of the top rises a cluster of tiny seedling leaves, and surprisingly, on this one, these leaves are white—little tight white albino avocado seedling leaves, coming out of that big hard seed knob. Another has one short straight root and one straight shoot bearing green leaves at the top. The third has neither root nor shoot, but the whole seed has been split open by a thrust from inside, and the two halves shoved apart by the geminating seed force—that little bunch of stuff, big as the end of your pinkie, shoving those big doors aside like a tiny Samson. It is a wonderful sight. And now let us look at the fourth seed, dry and papery and brown, nothing showing on the outside. But within are a life force and a living plantness which we cannot see with our ordinary eyes. If we are to behold the wrinkled old seed in truth, we have to behold it with imagination, with our inner eye. Only with the inner eye of imagination can we see inner forms of Being and Becoming. In this lifeless-looking seed there is a germinating center, totally alive and totally invisible.

FROM *THE CROSSING POINT:*
SELECTED TALKS AND WRITINGS

HOW CAN WE TEACH LOVE?

Once I had a dream, a short one. I like it because it isn't often that we get a really good look at ourselves in a way that makes us smile, however ruefully. In this dream I am sitting literally on the edge of a chair, talking urgently with someone. I am bending forward, my hands are active. "But we don't know anything about love," I am saying; "if we did, we could teach it."

Well, perhaps we do not know much about love. And surely we cannot as yet put it on the curriculum, Freshman Love, Sophomore Compassion, Junior Moral Imagination, Senior Enlightenment, with Freedom as an elective. With required courses in Second Sight and Speaking with Tongues. And a graduate program leading to a master's degree in Union with the Cosmos!

What is this love? I think it is a spiritual being acting within the person, and through the person. What we call mutual love is the experience of contact between persons when the spirit of love, dwelling in each, moves through the walls of resistance and separation into contact. Like great golden springs which gush into us from some single central source, and which in certain moments spill through us in transformed streams to meet again in a golden circuit.

For part of the mystery is the recognition we feel. It bespeaks an occult saying, that friends and lovers have been companions in ancient corridors of time: we come upon each other suddenly and lo! The unheard-of becomes potential. Possibility becomes power.... It is the enchantment of paradise. Rather than the witchcraft of hell. Or the dull suspensions of belief in the in between.

At the center, Christ, *Atman,* I and It.

FROM *CENTERING IN POTTERY,*
POETRY, AND THE PERSON

TWYLAH NITSCH
NEW YORK, 1920–

A Seneca elder now in her eighties, a member of the Wolf Clan, Twylah Nitsch did not begin sharing the sacred teachings and traditions of her people until she was in her seventies. Today she lectures widely, using her Seneca name, Yehwehnode, "she whose voice rides the wind." She is often told by her audience how perfectly she exemplifies the sacred wisdom that develops in elderhood for those who seek it. Inner guidance comes to her through a precise experience in the solar plexus, an actual sense of movement occurring there. The following excerpt is from The Feminine Face of God, *by Sherry Ruth Anderson and Patricia Hopkins.*

~⁀

DIGGING A HOLE BIG ENOUGH TO SIT IN

I must have been under five when I spent one whole summer digging a hole with a large spoon in the side of a bank near our house. I had to dig and dig because the ground was so full of roots and my goal was to make a hole big enough to sit in—like a cave. And that took a lot of hard work. Digging through all those roots was tough.

What I remember most about the experience is something my grandmother said. "When you take the dirt out, make sure you have a place for it," she cautioned me, "because the dirt is used to being in that particular place, and it is at home there. Don't take anything that is part of something and just scatter it around. Remember you are disturbing the home of the worms and the insects. You are moving them out of the place where they have been living, and you need to make sure that they are happy about where you are taking them." So I would scoop the dirt into a little basket I had and take it around to various spots. "Is this where you would like to be?" I'd ask. And if the answer was yes, I would leave it. Otherwise, I'd pick up my basket, go to another spot, and ask again.

When I had finally made the hole deep enough to sit in, I would crawl in there and listen. I could hear the earth talking.

AYYA KHEMA

GERMANY, 1923–

Born to Jewish parents living in Berlin, Ayya Khema at the age of fourteen escaped Hitler's Germany with a group of children sent to Glasgow, Scotland. For the next two years she was separated from her parents, who fled to China. By her midthirties, feeling the need for a spiritual path that would meet both her emotional and intellectual needs, she traveled to Aurobindo's ashram in India. There she learned meditation from the Mother (see p. 157) and for the next ten years continued to meditate while living a traditional lifestyle as a homemaker raising a son and daughter. Backpacking in Burma, Thailand, and Sri Lanka introduced her to Theravada Buddhism and the Buddhist nun's lifestyle. In 1979, in Sri Lanka, she was ordained a nun and took the name of Ayya (Sister) Khema, which means "safety," a poignant name for a woman who had escaped Nazi death camps.

Theravadan monks have fiercely resisted Ayya Khema's ordination. She counters their oppression by ignoring insults and working determinedly for Buddhist women's rights. She founded and became abbess of Parappuduwa Nuns' Island, an island off the coast of Sri Lanka, given to her by the Sri Lankan government, the first monastery for women and men from both the East and the West to be run by women. (Laypeople make three-month-long retreats at Nuns' Island.) She also organized the first international conference of Buddhist nuns. In 1986, Nuns' Island published her book, Be an Island.

∼⁊

FROM BE AN ISLAND

Sometimes one doesn't feel well physically. That's no reason for discontent. "I am of the nature to become diseased." We chant it every night. It doesn't say we have to become unhappy and discontented about it. It's the nature of the body. So the body doesn't feel good—that's all. The body has some problems. The body always has problems. Other times there may be ideas of wanting in the mind. Let the mind have ideas of wanting. It doesn't mean that one has to get involved in the wanting. If one starts believing the *dukkha* (suffering) which mind and body generate, there will never be any contentment. Where can one find it? It's not to be found within buildings, nature, or other people. Contentment has only one resting place and that is within one's own heart. And it has nothing at its base except the understanding that giving love and approval creates a field of harmony around oneself and gives a feeling of contentment. That is skillful living.

Skillful living is something one trains oneself in. It can only be done when we confront ourselves in others. If we have no mirror, how will we know what we look like? We need the mirror of confrontation, of the reflection of our own being in others in order to see ourselves. When there is disharmony with another person, it is a reflection of our own mirror image. There can be no disharmony with others if one feels harmonious in oneself. It's not possible. Our own mirror image does not lie.

We would never have a religion unless its founder were a mystic and knew a consciousness which is boundless.

[I]n order to realize the teachings of the founders of great religions one does need to have that contemplative meditative interiority which brings one to a different level of consciousness.

After having read Meister Eckhart and Teresa of Avila, I realized that they in their Christian approach have realized the same truth in their mystical experiences that I have come to know as meditative realities.

[The mystic's life] includes transcending the world—not by leaving it, but by seeing it as it really is.

Drop whatever you're hanging on to.

On the meditation pillow, there has to be an understanding that the impossible is possible.

[Joy is] like the yeast in bread: Without it, full expansion is impossible.

Impurity must be removed. What do I mean by "impurity"? Clinging and craving.

We must be contemplative and political; Buddha and Jesus Christ
were both.

CARMEN BERNOS DE GASZTOLD

FRANCE, C. 1925–?

*Long before Carmen de Gasztold had settled into a life of prayer and work
at the beautiful Benedictine Abby of Limon-par-Igny not far from Paris, she
began composing an enchanting series of animal poems,* Prayers in the
Arc. *Her country was occupied by enemy forces and scarcity forced her to
earn a harsh living in a silk factory. Carmen wrote primarily to distract herself, never dreaming of the critical acclaim her prayers would someday
receive or the joy she would give to the world.*

~~~

PRAYER OF THE CAT

Lord,
I am the cat.
And I don't really want to ask anything of you.
No,
I never was one to ask for anything.
However —
If you should by any chance have,
In one of heaven's barns,
A small bowl of milk,
Or a little white mouse,
I know someone who would delight in them.
And —
By the way,
Couldn't you one of these days
Place a curse on the whole class of dogs?

To that, I would gladly say:
Amen.

FROM *PRAYERS IN THE ARC*

PRAYER OF THE BEE

Lord,
I'm not one of those
ungrateful for your gifts,
I want to praise you
For the sweetness in my zeal;
Please
let my little parcel of fervent life
dissolve in the great
communal activity.
Please raise up to your glory
this temple of sweetness,
this citadel of incense,
this candle of tiny glowing cells,
forged only by your graces
And my hidden work!
  Amen

FROM *PRAYERS IN THE ARC*

PRAYER OF THE BUTTERFLY

Lord,
I lost my train of thought.
O, yes.
This flower, this sunlight,
O, thank you. Your world is so beautiful.
The scent of this rose.
Where was I?
A sparkling drop of dew
is sliding down
to twinkle in a lily's heart.
I must go now.

O, where do I have to go?
The wind has painted fantasies
On my wings.
Fantasies.
O, yes!
I had something to say to you, Lord:
    Amen

FROM *PRAYERS IN THE ARC*

LEILA HADLEY

NEW YORK, 1925–

An explorer of both the inner world and the outer world, Leila Hadley has ventured into remote areas of India, North and South Africa, the Far and Middle East, Central America, and Southeast Asia in search of learning, fullness, and mystical life. She is also a journalist, editor, author of several travel books, and an expert on traveling with children. In her sumptuous book, A Journey with Elsa Cloud, *she undertakes a triple exploration: of India's ravishing beauty; of her relationship with her twenty-five-year-old daughter, Veronica, who is living in India and studying Buddhism; and of the mystical intimations in her own soul. While Veronica searches for emptiness and greater distance from her mother through Buddhism, Leila seeks greater closeness to her daughter. Both quests seem to be honored in moments of endearing tenderness that bridge the intergenerational communication gap, as when the two women are examining a statue of the goddess Kali in her destructive aspect:*

"Buddhism, the kind practiced by Tibetans, has a particular love and reverence for the mother's love," Veronica says soothingly. "Tibetans feel that a mother's love for her children has no rewards or ulterior motive, and so no gain can be gotten. Love just flows out from the mother and that in itself brings the mother happiness."

"Oh," I say, warming to Tibetan Buddhism.

Veronica's nickname, Elsa Cloud, originated in her remark at the age of eight that she wanted to be "the sea, the jungle, or else a cloud." Leila

Hadley is the mother of three other children and lives in New York with her husband.

~⁀⁊

FROM A JOURNEY WITH ELSA CLOUD

Veronica wants me to buy a roll of the hand-woven, grosgrain rib-bonlike material Tibetan women cut and sew together to make their striped ornamental aprons, called *pangdens.* . . .

The *pangden's* durable colors—"the rainbow threads," Veronica calls them—and its varied combinations of woven stripes sing out to me, the fabric has what garment manufacturers call a good "hand," a good feel. Hand: the word conflates the feel of the product and hand on the shuttle of the loom. Great Mother, Maya, Weaver of the World. I remember lines from William Blake's *The Keys of the Gates (of Paradise)*:

> Thou'rt my mother, from the womb:
> Wife, sister, daughter, to the tomb;
> Weaving to dreams the sexual strife,
> And weeping over the web of life.

Veronica says that threads woven and spun are Tantric in their significance, that Tantrism—from the Sanskrit word *tantra,* which means the warp of threads on which the weft is woven—is a "teaching that stresses the interwovenness of things and actions." Tantrism teaches that everything in the world is inter-related, inter-connected, spun, woven, threaded together like tapestries, like the fabrics and rugs the Tibetans are "so talented" at weaving.

I think of the symbolism of weaving in other cultures, how the woman is associated with the loom and sometimes even insepa-rable from it, like the Mayan women of Guatemala with their looms attached to themselves and to trees, so that woman, tree, and loom are one. I think of how the long twisted threads of desoxyribonucleic acid, that master chemical of heredity, require both women and men to pleach their lives together to weave new worlds.

In *All's Well That Ends Well,* Shakespeare says that "The web of life is a mingled yarn, good and ill together." As a schoolgirl, I asked a schoolteacher how bad things like war could happen if God was Love. "It is as though you were sitting under a tapestry and seeing the tangled threads on the wrong side," she said. "Only God can see the real picture."

Is that what Buddhism is all about, seeing things as they are?

When I first came to India, the same age as Veronica is now, all the monumental genitalia sensuously carved in sandstone and granite in delicate shades of honey, pink, and cocoa brown; all those melon-and-mango shaped breasts, all those permutations of sexual activity, all those arching backs and dazzling erections made me flush, blush, laugh with surprise. It all seemed like one vast sculptural blue movie, until Mulk explained that the sculpture's symbolism was really more cosmic than sexual. "Sculpture of explicit sensuality derives from the female principle of Shakti," he said "and wound its way into the traditions of Tantric Buddhist art." I whisk out this fig-leaf phrase now as I do whenever anyone takes a close look at the gilded iconographical statue of Hevajira I have in my New York apartment. Hevajira . . . is embracing his Dakini in divine and mystical love, and stepping on four copulating forms of Mara, Tantric Buddhist demons who try to make men prefer earthly life with all its attachments rather than the path to enlightenment.

JOSÉ HOBDAY
TEXAS, 1928–

Sister José Hobday is a Seneca elder, a prominent Roman Catholic leader, and a Franciscan sister who adheres fully to St. Francis's radical ideal of holy poverty. She is a consummate artist in the arts of teaching, writing, and storytelling; she is also a mystic and contemplative; she is an earth warrior and elder guide on the wisdom path; and above all, she is an impassioned servant of the poor, especially poor Native Americans.

Sister José lives in the maximum simplicity of voluntary poverty in a tiny house in Gallup, New Mexico, surrounded on all sides by Indian reservations and pueblos. As people once flocked to Julian of Norwich's cell or to Dorothy Day's Hospitality House, so people today come to Sister José's warm hearth for spiritual guidance and material help, and no one leaves without assistance. Now in her seventies, her warrior power still intact despite less-than-ideal health, she travels a broad lecture circuit many months each year, earning substantial money to give to the poor. Two years ago, when she suddenly found herself hungering for a vacation without any funds to spend on herself, she managed a brief vacation by driving her jeep and sleeping either in the jeep or on couches in church-related places along the way.

Sister José—who often signs letters "Your Sis, José"—for many years has written wonderful books, among them Stories of Awe and Abundance. *The selection here comes from that book and originally from* Praying *magazine, for which she was a weekly columnist for ten years.*

~◯

A "BEGGAR'S" GIFT: A LOW-BUDGET AFFAIR

One morning [on a low-budget trip to the Holy Land with nine other sisters], a very, very old man approached me. He looked more like a shriveled up dwarf than a man. His back had a hump; his head and feet were bare. He wore only a dirty white rag wrapped around his body. When he smiled, I saw he had two teeth. He held out a bowl. At first, I thought he wanted money. Then I realized he was offering food. I looked in the bowl and saw an awful looking mixture of chicken bones, an animal skin, grain, and a milky-looking liquid. Smiling, he pulled a dirty little spoon from the bowl, and, with anticipation, invited me to help myself.

I didn't know what to do. The stuff in the bowl looked awful. It didn't smell any better. Finally, I tried the spoon but got very little of the mixture out of the bowl with it. I experienced a momentary sense of relief. But I could see the man still looking at me. His sense of anticipation showed no signs of diminishing. Slowly, I put the bowl to my mouth and half drank and half ate—and half gagged. When I finished, I smiled, and he smiled, and then—and I'll never forget this—he offered it to me again. I forced myself to take another helping. We smiled and nodded in a kind of semi-bow—and he walked on, thank goodness. . . .

Almost immediately three guards descended on me. I thought they had come to nab me for violating a code of some kind. But they commended me for taking the beggar's food. The man frequently came to the square to offer people food, they said, but no one ever accepted it until I did. As we talked, the guards, who seemed touched by what I had done, asked if they could do anything for me. I said I wanted to get into the mosque, then closed to visitors. No, no, they said, only dignitaries could get in and they had to have a pass from the security chief. Would they take me to see him? Reluctantly, they did. Reluctantly, too, he gave me a pass.

Inside, I saw a thing of beauty—lovely tiles and windows, the words of the Koran gracefully carved into the walls. Worshippers said morning prayer. As I watched, I had a profound sense of the holy. I would call it a religious experience. Afterward, I insisted on going back and thanking the chief. He expressed surprise, saying no one had returned before to thank him for a pass.

Over the years, in reliving this experience, I have had these reflections:

1. following in the footsteps of Jesus will lead us to the poor;
2. the poor will lead us to God, as my acceptance of this poor man led me to a religious experience in the mosque;
3. even the lowliest among us have gifts to share and, I suspect, their gifts often become the ones we really need, even though we almost automatically discount them;
4. nothing surpasses sharing food, in church or out, for experiencing our oneness with each other and with God. . . .

DOROTHY WALTERS
OKLAHOMA, 1928–

In the year 2000, at the age of seventy-two, long into retirement from an academic career, Dorothy Walters surprised the world by publishing a beautiful book of mystical poetry, Marrow of Flame. *Until then only a few friends had recognized that her quiet bearing concealed a daughter of Rumi, a soul profoundly illumined and drenched in love. One of those* friends was Andrew Harvey, who wrote in the introduction to her book that Dorothy is his most dearly beloved spiritual mother and muse, one of the few people he has ever met in his life with the humility and the capacity for ordeal demanded on a genuine mystical path: "Part of her, I felt, was always kneeling in silence before the vastness of the mystery that had clearly claimed her for its own."

   Among her books are Flannery O'Conner, a study of the Catholic short story writer, and Unmasking the Rose, an account of her Kundalini awakening and the ensuing twenty years (to be published by Hampton Roads in 2002).

~○

WHY

Something inside me
constantly bleeds toward god.

That's why I keep writing,
Slipping messages under the door.

THE RUNAWAY

The place you are right now
God circled on a map for you.
                              — HAFIZ

The poet tells you
god has put a circle around you on a map
to locate you in sacred space.
Then why do you keep tunneling
underground,
carving labyrinths for your escape?

WAITING

The jeweled cloud sways overhead,
Waiting.
Meanwhile, our cells are turning to air,
finer and finer arrangements of light.

A KUNDALINI AWAKENING

In 1981 I experienced an inner emotional crisis which culminated in an abrupt, profound, and totally transfiguring Kundalini awakening. One Sunday morning, in late May, I was reading in my living room in the mid-western city where I taught; the sun was streaming in through my high clerestory windows; the elm-lined street was quiet. I was now 53 years old, and facing the imminent breakup of a long-term relationship. Once more I was undergoing a kind of spiritual death. . . .

The book I was reading that day mentioned Kundalini but did not describe it in great detail. It spoke of the ancient yogis who could raise the "serpent power" from the base of the spine to the head. On impulse, I decided to see if I could lift my own energies this way. I meditated on an image of the god and goddess in union (from an illustration in the text) and focused on my breathing. Almost instantaneously I felt a great surge of ecstatic energy in the lower chakras and then, within seconds, this intense force rushed upward and into my head. My very crown seemed to open in rapture, and, for many minutes, I felt the energies of the unseen immensity flow in, as if petal after radiant petal were unfolding in my crown. . . .

Everything was now lit by an inner beauty surpassing everything I had experienced before. Every face was my own, every leaf or bloom an aspect of my being. I felt that I had, at last, fused at all levels; I knew, finally, and incontrovertibly, that spirit and flesh are one.

FROM *UNMASKING THE ROSE:*
AN ACCOUNT OF A KUNDALINI INITIATION

MARION WOODMAN

CANADA, 1928–

Marion Woodman graduated from the C. G. Jung Institute in Zurich in 1979 and since then has gained international prominence as a writer, lecturer, and workshop leader on such topics as conscious femininity, addiction and spirituality, and healing through metaphor. Among her many books are Addiction to Perfection, Leaving My Father's House, *and* Dancing in the Flames *(with fellow Jungian analyst Elinor Dickson).*

~_ɔ_

DANCERS: YOU ARE
PRIESTS AND PRIESTESSES

The dancer develops the body with infinite patience and hard physical discipline, in order to create a container that is strong enough and flexible enough to receive the penetration of the divine energy from the unconscious. Archetypally, feminine matter opens itself to masculine spirit. However well disciplined the muscles are, however perfect the technique, without the spontaneous opening to transcendent power, the dance lacks life. The form is not filled with spirit.

My own memories of Margot Fonteyn illustrate this point. In 1952, I saw her in what was to have been her final performance. Her movement was exquisite, her technique flawless. But she was not in the movement, not in a deep soul connection that would allow her body to transmit archetypal light. She was a magnificent diamond, brilliant but cold.

In 1961 the young Tatar, [Rudolf] Nureyev, arrived and a new Fonteyn was born. He constellated her innermost soul connection and the woman and the dancer became one, not only with herself, but with him and the audience. I was in Covent Garden the first night they danced *Marguerite and Armand,* the ballet created by Fredrick Ashton for Nureyev. Both of them were totally concentrated. Then a hush fell over the audience. The two bodies danced as one body. Some presence came through them that filled the audience with what I can only describe as a mystical experience of

God. When it was over, there was a long silence. They were as still as we. Then the audience burst into tears, into applause, into the aisles, into the foyer to gather daffodils from the jardinieres to throw onto the stage. For twenty minutes, Covent Garden was a yellow waterfall, with daffodils splashing from the box seats and the galleries. Fonteyn was a luminous pearl and Nureyev every inch a man, part animal, part divine.

THE CRONE

[The Crone can be thought of as the third stage in a woman's life, after maiden and mother. She is detached, wise, spontaneous, surrendered, and often outrageous.]

While age does not necessarily create a crone, the "slings and arrows of outrageous misfortune" do have something to do with her maturing. She evolves out of the conscious Mother and the conscious Virgin. As we, men and women, respond to what life brings, the Crone very gradually presents herself. She can shock us when we hear what comes out of her mouth. She speaks her blunt truth and lets the chips fall where they may. Not that she is without feeling, certainly not without sensitivity. But she has seen enough to be able to separate the irrelevant from the essence. And she has neither the time nor energy to waste on superficialities.

Having passed through her crossroads, the divine intersecting the human, the Crone will have learned to accept the surrender of her ego desires and, having accepted her own destiny, she is free and fearless. She no longer has to justify her existence, nor fear the judgment of others. The deep acceptance of herself unites her with the Virgin—the Virgin forever transforming into the maturity of the Crone. The new sense of freedom brings with it a childlike energy— spontaneity, play, creative ideas. With her well-developed masculinity, she may put her ideas into action in the world, ideas that confront causality with what Jung called synchronicity.

In a well-honed crone, we may feel the transparency of her body that is open to another reality. Being with her, we feel the presence of a timeless, spaceless world. We begin to see everything from two sides—the side that is totally in life and the side that is already dwelling in disembodied soul....

Because she has learned to love without any personal agenda, she makes an excellent guide. She knows how tough and how gentle we have to be to enter into this life and to leave it.

JOANNA MACY
CALIFORNIA, 1929–

Joanna Macy is a prophet and a mystic, a renowned and beloved Buddhist teacher with the heart of a bodhisattva, an earth warrior who fights for ecological healing and justice at every level of life, a superb scholar, a staunch advocate for the Tibetan people driven out of their homeland by Chinese expansionists, and the recipient of countless, well-deserved awards and honors for the breadth and depth of her work.

Born to a Protestant family in Los Angeles, she grew up in New York and majored in biblical history at Wellesley College. She received a Fulbright grant to study nationalism in the so-called Third World and earned her doctorate in religion with a concentration in Buddhism. In India in the 1960s, where Joanna's involvement with the Tibetan community in exile began, she decided to undertake a meditation practice in the Buddhist Vipassana tradition, never suspecting the fame, challenges, or calling to international leadership that would follow that decision.

Joanna received a Ford Foundation grant to study the Sarvodaya Buddhist movement in Sri Lanka for a year, which resulted in her first book, Dharma and Development. *Among her other books is the best-selling classic* World as Lover, World as Self, *and her autobiography,* Widening Circles: A Memoir. *The great Buddhist monk, Thich Nhat Hahn, wrote of her: "Let us join the buddhas and bodhisattvas in congratulating Joanna Macy by enjoying [her writing] and by practicing the fruit of her insights."*

~∂

FROM WORLD AS LOVER, WORLD AS SELF

Just as lovers seek for union, we are apt, when we fall in love with our world, to fall into oneness with it as well. Hunger for this union springs from a deep knowing, to which mystics of all traditions give voice. Breaking open a seed to reveal its life-giving kernel, the sage in the *Upanishads* tells his student: "*Tat tvam asi*—That art thou." The tree that will grow from the seed, that art thou; the running water, that art thou, and the sun in the sky, that art thou, and all that is, that art thou.

"There is a Secret One inside us," says Kabir, "the planets in all the galaxies pass through his hands like beads." Mystics of the Western traditions have tended to speak of merging self with God rather than with the world, but the import is often the same. When Hildegard of Bingen experienced unity with the divine, she gave it these words: "I am the breeze that nurtures all things green...I am the rain coming from the dew that causes the grasses to laugh with the joy of life."

In times like our own recent centuries, when the manifest world is considered less real and alive than ideas inside our heads, the mystic impulse reaches beyond it and seeks union with a transcendent deity. But once the bonds of limited ego snap, that blazing unity knows no limits. It embraces the most ordinary and physical of phenomena. The individual heart becomes one with its world, and expresses it in imageries of circle and net. The fifteenth-century cardinal, Nicholas of Cusa, defined God as an infinite circle whose periphery is nowhere and whose center is everywhere. That center, that one self, is in you and me and the tree outside the door. Similarly, the Jeweled Net of Indra, the vision of reality that arose with *Hua Yen* Buddhism, revealed a world where each being, each gem at each node of the net, is illumined by all the others and reflected in them. As part of this world, you contain the whole of it.

URSULA K. LEGUIN
CALIFORNIA, 1929–

*U*rsula K. LeGuin's writings encompass several genres: novels, short stories, science fiction, children's fiction, poetry, essays, and criticism. The phrase "science fiction" does not do justice to her achievement in such works as the novel Always Coming Home, where she creates a new world,

*complete with geography, language, music, myths, social structures, and
memorable characters. The depth and beauty of this work earn it a better
descriptive phrase: "guiding visions for the future" or "the anthropology yet
to come." Both her parents were professional anthropologists, and Ursula
grew up with a reverence for the truths to be found in cultures other than
our own. She also leads us deeper into the truths of the natural world, especially the animal world, where she animates coyotes, cats, ants, beetles, spar-
rows, and gulls and finds messages in the foam left on the shore by the waves
of the ocean. The lovely selection here appeared in* Always Coming Home.

~⁹

OWL, COYOTE, SOUL

Owl was flying in darkness. Its wings made no sound. There was
no sound. Owl said itself to itself: "hu, hu, hu, hu." Owl hears
itself; that makes sound be; sound comes into time then, four
times.

Sound circles out on the waters of darkness, the airs of darkness, gyring outward from the open mouth of the owl. Like scrum
and broken twigs and wings of insects on pond water, things come
to be, pushed by the circles moving outward. Near the owl's mouth
the sound is strong and things move quickly and firm and are distinct and strong. Moving outward the circles grow large and weak,
and things out there are slow and mixed and broken. But the owl
flew on and went flying on, listening, hunting. One is not all, nor
once always. Owl is not all, but only owl.

Coyote was going along in the darkness very sad, lonesome.
There was nothing to eat in the darkness, nothing to see, no way.
Coyote sat down in the darkness and howled: "yau, yau, yau, yau,
yau." Coyote hears herself; that makes death be; death comes into
time then, five times.

Death shines. Death makes shining. Death makes brightness in
water, brightness in air, brightness in being. Near Coyote's heart
the shining is strong and things grow strong and warm and take
fire. Farther outward things are burnt, weak, dim, and cold. Coyote
went on and goes along, hunting live things, eating dead things.
Coyote is not life or death, but only coyote.

Soul singing and shining goes outwards towards the cold and dark. Soul silent and cold comes inward to the shining, to the singing at the fire. Owl flies without sound; coyote goes in darkness; soul listens and holds still.

They say in the Grass singing: The universe is, and all there is is inside that house of houses.

THEA O'BRIEN

CANADA, 1930–

Thea O'Brien is a seventy-year-old woman who took up yoga in her fifties and continues to practice it every day. She was introduced to yoga by her mother, who took up the practice in her late sixties. Both mother and daughter became avid practitioners, and Thea believes that yoga has made her healthier than she was at fifty. She is a good example of the growing number of elders today who keep themselves strong through spiritual practices. Her remarks are adapted from a report in Health Wisdom for Women, *the newsletter published by Dr. Christiane Northrup (see p. 260).*

~♪

THE DELIGHT OF OLD AGE

It was in a small town outside of Ottawa that I first went to a yoga class, and I experienced *shavasana* for the very first time. It felt so relaxing and so peaceful and so liberating that I continued to go to class. One reason it felt so good, I think, was because I had always been active, but I was too intense when I did things. I have to continually work on relaxing myself.

[Also], before practicing Hatha Yoga, I had no help at all with my unruly mind. But a release in the body slowly transfers to the mind. The two are connected. When there is something wrong in my body, my mind doesn't function properly. So it is important that I keep my body functioning well.

For me, Hatha is not a discipline, it's a joy. . . . [I]t keeps me going. I feel I have very little control over [people or the town or things around me], but if I do Hatha every day I have control over my body. If there is an *asana* [posture] that I can't do, and I am persistent and faithful, eventually I am able to do it. This gives me a feeling of security. It gives me self-confidence.

I am much more flexible now at 70 than I was at 50....

I feel that as long as I do the *asanas,* I will not feel old.

ANNE BARING
ENGLAND, 1931–

Raised in love of the arts and the intellectual life and educated at Oxford as an academic, Anne Baring traveled to the East in her twenties in search of the Sacred Feminine and an enduring faith. Disillusioned with the bleak Christianity that she knew in her youth, she found in her travels to India, Cambodia, Indonesia, Japan, and China magnificent temples, massive stone statues of the Buddha, and enthralling frescoes of gods and goddesses that awakened her to the abundance of Divinity in all life. She returned home mystically transformed, her heart imprinted permanently with the ancient mystery of humankind's most sacred accomplishments, in the West as well as the East.

For twelve years following a Jungian analysis, Anne Baring designed dresses modeled on India's dazzling colors and fabrics, which she sold in her own shop in London called Troubadour. She later became a Jungian analyst, writer, and mystic of the most profound kind. In 1991, she coauthored (with Jules Cashford) an eight-hundred-page masterpiece, The Myth of the Goddess: Evolution of an Image, *which shows how the feminine principle of feeling, spontaneity, intuition, and instinct continues to exist "in disguise" even during the most oppressive historical eras. For example, when God is stripped of all goddess traits in the figure of Yahweh, she reappears as Yahweh's wisdom, Sophia. Similarly in Christianity, she reemerges beside the all-male trinity in Mary, the mother of Jesus.*

~𝒪

THE BLACK MADONNA

The symbolism of the black virgin returns us . . . to the Song of Songs, to the bride who is "black but beautiful." ["I am black but beautiful, O you daughters of Jerusalem," Song of Songs 1:50]. It returns us to Cybele, whose symbol was a blackstone, a meteorite, and the black images of Demeter, Artemis and Isis, and the black-robed, exiled Shekhinah [Yahweh's feminine presence], the "Precious Stone." It evokes the blackness of the night sky in which the moon and the evening star are the brightest luminaries, and the mystery of space as a mother who gives birth each night to the moon and stars and each morning to the sun. Above all, the black virgin holding her son, Christ, on her lap, gives us the image of the light shining in darkness, and the esoteric, hidden teaching of Gnosticism and Alchemy. . . .

Black is the color that is associated with Wisdom, as the dark phase of the lunar cycle, where light gestates in the womb, is transformed and brought forth anew—an association that is as old as the Black Stone of the Ka'aba, which was once the epiphany of the Great Goddess, and as the robe or veil of Isis. The image of the Black Virgin embodies the ageless Wisdom of life, the ageless Wisdom of an invisible dimension hidden within the outward form of nature, which brings it into being, informs and guides it, or contains it, as a mother her child. The child she holds is life itself to which eternally she gives birth; she is *zoe* holding *bios*. At the same time the Black Virgin symbolizes the fathomless mystery of the soul, which must follow the star that guided the wise men if it is to understand these mysteries and itself give birth to the divine child.

FROM *THE MYTH OF THE GODDESS*

TRAVELS THAT KINDLE SPIRIT

I discover that places move me to write and writing helps me to see. The meaning is clear years later but I follow the thread of love. I long to travel so that I may love what I discover. It is a way out of the labyrinth.

While I am at Oxford, acquiring more knowledge, preparing for yet another exam, answering always questions like—"With what success did the English in the 16th century attempt to reach the East by a northern passage?"—Instead of the inner ones, there are journeys south to the light.

There the fire of the mind dies for awhile and the fire of the heart can burn. There I meet St. Francis in the paintings of his contemporaries, and the great red Angel who hovers in the Umbrian skies. In Siena and all the towns of Tuscany and Umbria I see the work of [people] to whom the air itself is revelation and to whom rock and earth and sky and [humankind] and angel are one. I feel that painting as a praising, a loving, a longing, is communication with and a method of discovering God.

FROM *THE DREAM OF THE WATER*

WHERE SHOULD I TURN FOR GUIDANCE?

Where should I turn for guidance?

I appeal to those who have gone before, who have shown the Way. At first I love them for the beauty of their work alone and for a depth in it that draws me to them magnetically. I do not understand but I love. Then as I gather the fragments of many pasts and piece them together and try to ponder the meaning of the events of my own life, I begin to understand that there is something to be understood that will help me; and then what that "something" is.

They are isolated when I begin. In China there is Lao-Tze and Chuang-Tze. There are the painters of the Sung Dynasty and the fragments of T'ang. There are the paintings in the caves of Tun-Huang and the sculptures of Lung-Men. Instinctively I feel they express the destiny of man. In Persia there are the mystic poets, Rumi, Attar, and Hafiz. In India there are the temple sculptures and the *Upanishads* and the Bhagavad Gita. In Tibet, there is *The Book of the Dead*. In Egypt there are the gods and temples and in Greece the myths and the mysteries. In Europe there are fairy-tales and a tradition of heresies. There are the Alchemists and many saints and poets without number. There are the Legend of the Holy Grail and Gothic churches and there are Holy Mountains, as in the East.

I am drawn to each of them in turn with a thirst for truth. I love them because they help me to continue my search. But they need a key. I must find the key. I must learn how to understand them. Meanwhile I love and love and love them and fly to them from the dead philosophies of Europe and the churches of unwarmed stone.

FROM *THE DREAM OF THE WATER*

TONI MORRISON
OHIO, 1931–

In Toni Morrison's elegant, original, and deeply moral fiction, she struggles urgently to find value and meaning in a tragically flawed world from a black and female perspective. She has said, "I want to participate in developing a canon of black work...where blacks are talking to black people." And "I really think the range of emotions and perceptions I have had access to as a black person and a female person are greater than those of people who are neither.... My world did not shrink because I was a black female writer. It just got bigger." She was born in 1931 in Lorain, Ohio, attended Howard University and Cornell University, and has taught since 1989 at Princeton, earning many awards and prizes. Her talent and imagination were recognized internationally when she was awarded a Nobel Prize for Literature in 1993. Toni Morrison has written seven novels, a play, and a book of criticism over a period of more than thirty years. Her novel Beloved *was made into a powerful movie. She has two grown children.*

FROM BELOVED

[Baby Suggs preaches her weekly Saturday afternoon "sermon."]

[S]he shouted, "Let the children come!" and they ran from the trees toward her.

"Let your mothers hear you laugh," she told them, and the woods rang. The adults looked on and could not help smiling.

Then "Let the grown men come," she shouted. They stepped out one by one from among the ringing trees.

"Let your wives and your children see you dance," she told them, and groundlife shuddered under their feet.

Finally she called the women to her. "Cry," she told them. "For
the living and the dead. Just cry." And without covering their eyes
the women let loose.

...In the silence that followed, Baby Suggs, holy, offered up to
them her great big heart.

She did not tell them to clean up their lives or to go and sin no
more. She did not tell them they were the blessed of the earth, its
inheriting meek or its glorybound pure.

She told them that the only grace they could have was the grace
they could imagine. That if they could not see it, they would not
have it.

"Here," she said, "in this place, we flesh; flesh that weeps, laughs;
flesh that dances on bare feet in grass. Love it. Love it hard. Yonder
they do not love your flesh. They despise it. They don't love your
eyes; they'd just as soon pick em out. No more do they love the skin
on your back. Yonder they flay it. And O my people they do not love
your hands. Those they only use, tie, bind, chop off and leave empty.
Love your hands! Love them. Raise them up and kiss them. Touch
others with them, pat them together, stroke them on your face
'cause they don't love that either. You got to love it, you!"

A WEDDING SERMON OF THE
REVEREND SENIOR PULLIAM

"There is nothing in nature like [love]. Love is divine only and difficult always. If you think it is easy you are a fool. If you think it is
natural you are blind. It is a learned application without reason or
motive except that it is God.

"You do not deserve love regardless of the suffering you have
endured. You do not deserve love because somebody did you
wrong. You do not deserve love just because you want it. You can
only earn—by practice and careful contemplation—the right to
express it and you have to learn how to accept it. Which is to say
you have to earn God. You have to practice God.... Love is not a
gift. It is a diploma. A diploma conferring certain privileges: the
privilege of expressing love and the privilege of receiving it.

"How do you know you have graduated? You don't. What you do know is that you are human and therefore educable, and therefore capable of learning how to learn, and therefore interesting to God, who is interested only in Himself which is to say He is interested only in love. Do you understand me? God is not interested in you. He is interested in love and the bliss it brings to those who understand and share that interest.

"Couples that enter the sacrament of marriage and are not prepared to go the distance or are not willing to get right with the real love of God cannot thrive. They may cleave together like robins or gulls or anything else that mates for life. But if they eschew this mighty course, at the moment when all are judged for the disposition of their eternal lives, their cleaving won't mean a thing. God bless the pure and holy. Amen."

FROM *PARADISE*

FROM HER NOBEL LECTURE, DECEMBER 7, 1993

The systematic looting of language can be recognized by the tendency of its users to forgo its nuanced, complex, mid-wifery properties for menace and subjugation. Oppressive language does more than represent violence; it is violence; does more than represent the limits of knowledge; it limits knowledge. Whether it is obscuring state language or the faux-language of mindless media; whether it is the proud but calcified language of the academy or the commodity driven language of science; whether it is the malign language of law-without-ethics, or language designed for the estrangement of minorities, hiding its racist plunder in its literary cheek—it must be rejected, altered and exposed. It is the language that drinks blood, laps vulnerabilities, tucks its fascist boots under crinolines of respectability and patriotism as it moves relentlessly toward the bottom line and the bottomed-out mind. Sexist language, racist language, theistic language—all are typical of the policing languages of mastery, and cannot, do not permit new knowledge or encourage the mutual exchange of ideas. . . .

Word-work is sublime . . . because it is generative; it makes
meaning that secures our difference, our human difference—the way
in which we are like no other life.

We die. That may be the meaning of life. But we do language.
That may be the measure of our lives.

AUDRE LORDE

NEW YORK, 1934–1992

*A brilliant black lesbian writer who won an American Book Award in
1987, Audre Lorde is a major source of the twentieth-century spirituality of
eroticism. She sees the erotic as sacred because it connotes relating, connecting, community, and inter-dependence; circularity rather than linearity, attachment rather than detachment, intimacy instead of distance. Audre Lorde is
the author of many volumes of poetry, including* Coal *(1976),* The Black
Unicorn *(1987), a "biomythography," and* Zami: A New Spelling of My
Name *(1982). She titled her book of essays* Sister Outsider *(1984).*

~⁀

THE EROTIC AS SACRED

The erotic functions for me in several ways, and the first is in providing the power which comes from sharing deeply any pursuit
with another person. The sharing of joy, whether physical, emotional, psychic, or intellectual, forms a bridge between the sharers
which can be the basis for understanding much of what is not
shared between them, and lessens the threat of their difference. . . .

Another important way in which the erotic connection functions
[for me] is the open and fearless underlining of my capacity for joy.
In the way my body stretches to music and opens into response,
hearkening to its deepest rhythms, so every level on which I sense
also opens to the erotically satisfying experience, whether it is dancing, building a bookcase, writing a poem, examining an idea. . . .

During World War II, we bought sealed plastic packets of white,
uncolored margarine, with a tiny, intense pellet of yellow coloring

perched like a topaz just inside the clear skin of the bag. We would leave the margarine out for awhile to soften, and then we would pinch the little pellet to break it inside the bag, releasing the rich yellowness into the soft pale mass of margarine. Then taking it carefully between our fingers, we would knead it gently back and forth, over and over, until the color had spread throughout the whole pound bag of margarine, thoroughly coloring it.

I find the erotic such a kernel within myself. When released from its intense and constrained pellet, it flows through and colors my life with a kind of energy that heightens and sensitizes and strengthens all my experience.

JANE GOODALL
ENGLAND, 1934–

Jane Goodall is the world's foremost authority on chimpanzees, having closely observed their behavior for the past quarter century in the jungles of the Gombe Game Reserve in Tanzania, Africa, where she was able to gain the chimps' confidence and live in their forest environment.

Her dream of working in Africa appeared at the age of eleven when, as she often puts it, she "was passionately in love with Tarzan" and wanted to be with animals. Her family was too poor to support her dream financially, but her mother gave her lasting emotional support and encouragement. "If you really want something," she would say, "you will find the way. You have to work hard and take advantage of every opportunity that comes along."

The opportunity she was waiting for arrived in the form of a letter when she was in her early twenties. It was from a friend inviting Jane to visit her on a farm that her family had purchased in Kenya. Jane worked as a waitress to pay her way, spent a short visit with her friend, then earned a job at the Natural History Museum in Nairobi by impressing Louis Leakey, the famous paleontologist, with her extensive knowledge of African animals.

Her observations and discoveries regarding chimps and the evolution of human beings have gained international recognition for her as an innovative scientific thinker. Her 1986 book, The Chimpanzees of Gombe, *helped convince the scientific community that the behavior of animals is*

*not just programmed at birth; like humans, animals also learn. Jane
Goodall has also become an advocate for animal welfare in the wild, in
zoos, and in laboratories. In 1984 she received the J. Paul Getty Wildlife
Conservation Prize for "helping millions of people understand the importance of wildlife conservation on this planet." She founded the Jane
Goodall Institute, whose motto is "Every individual matters. Every individual has a role to play. Every individual makes a difference." The institute,
through Roots & Shoots, educates young people to take action to make the
world a better place for the environment, animals, and local communities.
Her latest book,* Reason for Hope, *reveals the depths, unknown until now,
of her Franciscan-like spirituality.*

~9

SELECTIONS ON WORKING
WITH CHIMPANZEES

The longer I spent on my own, the more I became one with the
magic forest world that was now my home. Inanimate objects
developed their own identities and, like my favorite saint, Francis
of Assisi, I named them and greeted them as friends. "Good morning, Peak," I would say as I arrived there each morning; "Hello,
Stream" when I collected my water; "Oh, Wind, for Heaven's sake,
calm down" as it howled overhead, ruining my chance of locating
the chimps. In particular I became intensely aware of the being-
ness of trees. The feel of rough sun-warmed bark of an ancient forest giant, or the cool, smooth skin of a young and eager sapling,
gave me a strange, intuitive sense of the sap as it was sucked up by
unseen roots and drawn up to the very tips of the branches, high
overhead. Why, I used to wonder, did our human ancestors not
take to the trees, like the other apes? Or, if we started as arboreal
primates, why did we ever come down?

FROM *REASON FOR HOPE*

[At first] the chimpanzees were terrified of me. They'd never seen a
white ape before. . . . [Then one day] David Greybeard—whom I
knew from the forest and could identify from his white frilly

beard—came to my camp.... He came the second day and the third. He was coming to eat the fruit of an oil-nut palm.... After that he would sometimes meet me in the forest and he would sit. Sometimes he'd even approach to see if I had a banana....

After about a year when I could actually follow him through the forest, I got myself...tangled in thorns and fronds, and thought I'd lost him. I spent a lot of time wiggling on my tummy, not to mention crawling, until there he was, almost as if he'd been waiting for me....

I saw a ripe red palm nut lying on the ground, and I held it out to him in the palm of my hand. He obviously didn't want it, but with one hand he took it, dropped it, and with the very same movement very gently held my hand with a gentle pressure.

This is how chimpanzees reassure each other. So it was as though he was saying, "I don't want the nut, but I understand your motive in giving it to me." That was an [ancient form of communication] that went right back to...our ape-like, human-like ancestors.

FROM AN INTERVIEW FOR *NEW DIMENSIONS*,

RADIO PROGRAM, 1999

One female chimpanzee, living in a large captive group in a zoo in Holland, became amazingly skillful at restoring peaceful relations. Whenever two of the adult males were sitting tense after a conflict, avoiding each other's gaze, there would be noticeable agitation running throughout the entire group. This old female would then initiate a grooming session with one of the rivals, during which she gradually moved a little closer to the second male—followed by her grooming partner.... Eventually the two males were so close that both could groom her at the same time. When she was thus the only thing separating them she quietly moved away, and, calmed by the grooming, and neither having to be the first to break the deadlock, they started to groom each other.

Surely, I thought, if chimpanzees can control their aggressive tendencies, and diffuse the situation when things get out of hand, so can we.

FROM *REASON FOR HOPE*

Chimpanzees now are being hunted commercially for food in Central Africa, which is their last stronghold. . . . The meat goes to the markets in towns, not to feed starving people—that's so important for people to understand—but to cater to this cultural preference for bush meat. You see chimpanzee sold next to a piece of goat. And people will pay more for this piece of bush meat.

FROM AN INTERVIEW FOR

NEW DIMENSIONS

MARY OLIVER
OHIO, 1935–

A Pulitzer Prize–winning poet, Mary Oliver has a radiant gift for joy that makes her poetry seem like praise for life's sacredness. Even when dealing with the most painful themes, such as the Holocaust, she retains the illumined quality of Spirit. She studied at Vassar College and has been a teacher or visiting professor at a number of colleges and universities. She received the prestigious Pulitzer in 1983 for her book American Primitive. *Among her other books are* No Voyage, The River Styx, *and* Dream Work, *where the following poem appeared.*

~つ

WILD GEESE

You do not have to be good.
You do not have to walk on your knees
for a hundred miles through the desert, repenting.
You only have to let the soft animal of your body
    love what it loves.
Tell me about despair, yours, and I will tell you mine.
Meanwhile the world goes on.
Meanwhile the sun and the clear pebbles of the rain
are moving across the landscapes,
over the prairies and the deep trees,
the mountains and the rivers.

Meanwhile the wild geese, high in the clean blue air,
are heading home again.
Whoever you are, no matter how lonely,
the world offers itself to your imagination,
calls to you like the wild geese, harsh and exciting—
over and over announcing your place
in the family of things.

LUCILLE CLIFTON
NEW YORK, 1936–

A distinguished and prolific writer, the recipient of many awards for poetry and children's fiction, Lucille Clifton was educated at the State University of New York and Howard University and has taught at several colleges and universities in the United States. Among the prizes she has received are an Emmy from the American Academy of Television Arts and Sciences, the Juniper Prize for poetry, and fellowships from the National Endowment for the Arts. Her first collection of poetry, Good Times, *was selected as one of the ten best books of 1969 by the* New York Times, *and in 1979 she was poet laureate of the state of Maryland. Her gift for using the black idiom to create dramatic immediacy and spiritual beauty is unparalleled, as in the exquisite biblical re-creation reprinted here.*

HOLY NIGHT

joseph, I afraid of stars,
their brilliant seeing.
so many eyes. such light.
joseph, i cannot still these limbs,
i hands keep moving toward i breasts,
so many stars. so bright.
joseph, is wind burning from east
joseph, I shine, oh Joseph, oh
illuminated night.

SYLVIA BOORSTEIN

NEW YORK, 1936–

A Buddhist teacher known for her down-to-earth methods of presenting and demystifying Buddhist subtleties, Sylvia Boorstein studied with Jack Kornfield, Joseph Goldstein, and Sharon Salzberg and is the author of best-selling books such as Don't Just Do Something, Sit There; That's Funny, You Don't Look Buddhist; *and* It's Easier Than You Think. *In the latter book she humorously and provocatively adds to Buddhism's Four Noble Truths a "Noble Truth # 3¹/₂, Suffering is manageable." (The Four Noble Truths state in essence that: (1) There is suffering; (2) Suffering comes from clinging; (3) Cessation of suffering is possible; and (4) Suffering can cease through practice of the eightfold path.) She enlarges Buddhist inclusivity and practicality by also revising the eightfold path into an "eightfold circle." Sylvia Boorstein currently teaches at Spirit Rock Meditation Center in Marin County, California, and lives nearby with her husband, Seymour, whom she refers to as her "lifelong best friend."*

~ 2

RIGHT EFFORT: "REMEMBER, BE HAPPY"

Once, many years ago, I drove to the Oakland airport in the middle of the night to meet my husband, who was arriving home on a late flight. The deserted freeway was monotonous. I began to feel drowsy, and then I felt alarmed that I would fall asleep at the wheel. Suddenly, in the passing flow of my thoughts, I remembered a problem I was having with a distant relative and felt annoyance over what that person presumably had said about me.

"Some nerve, she has," I thought, and in that moment I felt myself awake. A hit of righteous indignation had banished the drowsiness.

"Wow, this is great," I congratulated myself on my new discovery. "Mind states are interchangeable. I can replace one with another. I can wake myself by thinking angry thoughts."

And I did. All the way to the airport I thought angry thoughts and replayed different dialogues: what I said, what she said I said, what I could tell everyone about what she said I said. By the time I pulled into the airport parking lot, I was wide awake. I don't remember for certain, but my guess is I was probably a bit feisty and irritable as well—not the best mind states for a homecoming reunion.

Two days later, I recounted the whole driving episode to my teacher, assuming he would congratulate me on my new insight into the mind and body relationship. "Sure it's true about replacing mind states. However, " he added, "you could have woken yourself up with a sexy thought as well, and that would have been more fun. It probably would have put me in a better mood for a homecoming."

PEMA CHÖDRÖN
NEW MEXICO, 1936—

One day in 1967, when Pema Chödrön was a thirty-one-year-old flower child standing alone on top of a sunny hill in New Mexico, her long blond hair blowing freely in the breeze, she did not notice a young man standing below looking up at her. She was startled when he came up to her and told her, "I've just had a vision of you as a nun."

Pema took the vision seriously, recalling it vividly years later when she became the first American woman ordained a nun in the Vajrayana tradition of Tibetan Buddhism, her head shaved, her shining blond hair gone forever. So few women had ever been permitted to take vows in this tradition, even in the East, that the ordination rite had long been buried in history. Pema undertook painstaking research to discover the ancient formulas for the initiation ritual, and she was ordained in Hong Kong in 1981 after a long and grueling training. The ceremony concluded with her sitting in silent meditation while three pieces of incense burned on top of her shaved head. Today three permanent scars remind her of her proven capacity to endure pain and feel compassion for others' suffering.

Pema is a resident teacher at Gampo Abbey, on the wild Cape Breton coast of Nova Scotia. Her latest book is The Places that Scare You: A Guide to Fearlessness in Difficult Times. *Among her other books are* The Wisdom of No Escape, Start Where You Are, *and* When Things Fall Apart: Heart Advice for Difficult Times.

FROM START WHERE YOU ARE

We already have everything we need. There is no need for self-improvement. All these trips that we lay on ourselves—the heavy-duty fearing that we're bad and hoping that we're good, the identities we so dearly cling to, the rage, the jealousy and the addictions of all kinds—never touch our basic wealth. They are like clouds that temporarily block the sun.... This is who we really are. We are one blink of an eye away from being fully awake.

... From this perspective we don't need to change: You can feel as wretched as you like, and you're still a good candidate for enlightenment. You can feel like the world's most hopeless basket case, but that feeling is your wealth.... There's a richness to all of the smelly stuff that we so dislike and little desire. The delightful things—what we love so dearly about ourselves, the places in which we feel some sense of pride or inspiration—they are also our wealth.

As meditators we might as well stop struggling against our thoughts and realize that honesty and humor are far more inspiring and helpful than any kind of solemn religious striving for or against anything. In any case, the point is not to try to get rid of thoughts, but rather to see their true nature. Thoughts will run us around in circles if we buy into them, but really they are like dream images. They are like an illusion—not really all that solid. They are, as we say, just thinking.

When we look into our own hearts and begin to discover what is confused and what is brilliant, what is bitter and what is sweet, it isn't just ourselves that we're discovering. We're discovering the universe. When we discover the Buddha that we are, we realize that everything and everyone is Buddha.

FROM WHEN THINGS FALL APART

When the bottom falls out and we can't find anything to grasp, it hurts a lot. It's like the Naropa motto: "Love of the truth puts you on the spot." We might have some romantic view of what that means, but when we are nailed to the truth, we suffer. We look in the bathroom mirror, and there we are with our aging face, our aggression and timidity—all that stuff.

This is where tenderness comes in. When things are shaky, and nothing is working, we might realize that we are on the verge of something. We might realize that this is a very vulnerable and tender place, and that tenderness can go either way. We can shut down and feel resentful or we can touch on that throbbing quality. There is definitely something tender and throbbing about groundlessness.

It's a kind of testing, the kind of testing that spiritual warriors need in order to awaken their hearts. . . . I have a friend dying of AIDS [who said]: "I hated this, and I was terrified of this. But it turns out that this illness has been my greatest gift. . . . Now every moment is so precious to me. All the people in my life are so precious to me. My whole life means so much to me." Something had really changed and he felt ready for his death. Something that was horrifying and scary has turned into a gift.

Things falling apart is a kind of testing and also a kind of healing. We think that the point is to pass the test or to overcome the problem, but the truth is that things don't really get solved. They come together and they fall apart. Then they come together again and fall apart again. It's just like that. The healing comes from letting there be room for all of this to happen: room for grief, for relief, for misery, for joy.

CHAN KHONG

VIETNAM, 1938–

The foremost student and trusted adviser of the great Buddhist monk and peace activist, Thich Nhat Hanh, Chan Khong was born to well-to-do, highly respected landholders who taught her to care for the poor. She met Thich Nhat Hanh in 1959 when he was already a prominent monk and she, at twenty-one, was a deeply committed social activist, planning to eventually become a nun. He called her aside and asked her, "Don't you have a better dress?" Startled, she burst into tears, thinking that he of all people should understand that she wore an old gray dress several sizes too big for her in order to share the lot of the poor. He explained:

> *If you shaved your head, you would wear a beautiful nun's robe. But now your hair is long, and you should wear a simple beautiful dress like other young people your age. It will encourage those who might like to join you in your work. One's mind, actions, and dress should all communicate one's quality of being. This is the correct way for a Boddhisattva.*

Soon after this precious teaching, well-dressed, she had attracted seventy people to work with her in Saigon slums.

Chan Khong, whose name means "True Emptiness," has practiced nonviolent resistance all her life: against the corrupt Roman Catholic regime of President Diem, who tried to stifle all Buddhism; against the communists; and against the Vietnam War. When Buddhist monks and nuns were committing self-immolation to protest the war, she objected to their sacrifice but saw the numbers of peace activists swell after each such death. She decided to forgo marriage to care for children in the slums and remote areas and became a university professor. In 1966 she and five friends were ordained by Thich Nhat Hanh as the first members of his Order of Interbeing, in which men and women vow to practice mindfulness sixty days a year and to live according to fourteen precepts emphasizing compassion. She has spent the rest of her life working with him politically and spiritually, writing, counseling, coleading retreats, often singing haunting Buddhist chants in her high bell-like voice (today widely available on audiotape).

~♪

IN THE WAR ZONE

[Here Chan Khong, a university professor, describes one of her many acts of conscientious objection in the face of the Tet Offensive by North Vietnamese communists.]

During the days of the Tet Offensive, when fighting went on in the streets of Saigon, ... people were glued to their radios listening to the latest news. Suddenly I heard the Minister of Education on the radio calling for "the 71 university professors who had signed a petition for peace on January 16, 1968" to come to the ministry "for an urgent national matter." Then the speaker read all 71 names, including mine, not just once, but every half hour. My family urged me not to go, fearing that I would be shot. We had just seen on television Colonel Nguyen Ngoc Loan shooting a guerrilla he had caught. I was very afraid, but I thought that since the petition had been my idea, I had to take full responsibility and go.

[At the ministry, she was told that she was suspected of plotting the Tet Offensive with the communists and must retract her peace appeal. She refused and was then sent to the Minister of Education, who threatened her with immediate arrest and dismissal from her university post if she still refused to retract the peace declaration.]

I breathed deeply and said in a firm voice: "Sir, I came to you today because I knew that you were once a professor, my elder brother in teaching. When you speak in such a threatening way, it is impossible for us to have real communication. . . . Sir, I am like a bamboo shoot among university teachers. I am young, but my spirit may grow strong and beautiful. I spoke out frankly about the situation of the country, not for my own sake, but for the sake of the nation, even though prison may await me as a result. I appeal to your conscience as an elder brother to help me grow in this attitude, not to bow before coercion. Don't force me to go against my conscience. If I agree to sign your petition under threat of violence, then tonight if unknown men enter my house with guns and force me to sign a petition saying: 'Long live Mao Tse Tung,' must I not also sign that? If I sign under the threat of guns against my conscience and belief, who will be at fault? Do you really want to teach me that way of coercion?"

He looked embarrassed.... He let me go,... and the police
never came to arrest me. Apparently he protected me.

MADELEINE L'ENGLE

NEW YORK, CONTEMPORARY

*A gentle mystic and weaver of magical stories for children and adults, a
profound thinker and theologian, Madeleine L'Engle has published over
forty books, including the heartwarming best-sellers* A Live Coal in the Sea
and A Circle of Quiet, *and the children's classic* A Circle in Time *(which
has sold over two million copies). In fiction and nonfiction alike, ranging
from adventure stories and family dramas to an autobiography and religious
commentary, her Episcopalian faith and theology reach out to touch people
all over the world in a language everyone understands.*

*A course on the religious dimensions of Madeleine L'Engle's writing is
offered by Carole Chase, a Presbyterian minister and professor at Elon College in North Carolina; the author of* Madeleine L'Engle, Suncatcher; *
and co-editor of Madeleine's daybook,* Glimpses of Grace.

~♪

FROM "MARY SPEAKS"

[Like Michelangelo's blindingly beautiful *Pietà*, the following poem
honors Mary, the mother of Jesus, holding her dead son in her arms
after his crucifixion. It has been set to music, and an exquisite version is available on a Musical Heritage Society CD, *Trumpets
Sound, Voices Ring*, conducted by James Litton and performed by
the American Boy Choir and the Atlantic Brass Quintet.]

> O you who hold the world in your
> embrace, I carried you....
> And I, who with all others, you died for,
> Now I hold you.
> May I be faithful in this final test,
> In this last hour I hold my child, my son;

his body close enfolded to my breast:
the holder held, the bearer borne.
Mourning to joy, darkness to morn.
Open, my arms, your work is done.

CARING, ONE PERSON AT A TIME

We may be a global village, but instant communication often iso-
lates us from each other rather than uniting us. When I am bom-
barded on the evening news with earthquake, flood, fire, it is too
much for me. There is a mechanism, a safety valve, which cuts off
our response to overexposure to suffering.

But when a high-school student comes to me and cries because
the two- and three-year-olds on her block are becoming addicted to
hard drugs; when the gentle man who cleans the building in which
the Cathedral library is located talks to me about his family in
Guatemala, rejoicing that they are alive although their house has
been destroyed by earthquake; when a goddaughter of mine in
Luxembourg writes me about the hungry children of the Portuguese family with whom she is living, then in this particularity
my heart burns within me, and I am more able to learn what it is
that I can and ought to do, even if this seems, and is, inadequate.

But neither was Jesus adequate to the situation. He did not feed
all the poor, only a few. He did not heal all the lepers, or give sight
to all the blind, or drive out all the unclean spirits. Satan wanted
him to, but he didn't.

That helps me. If I felt that I had to conquer all the ills of the
world I'd likely sit back and do nothing at all. But if my job is to
feed one stranger, then the money I give to world relief will be dug
down deeper from my pocket than it would if I felt I had to succeed in feeding the entire world.

FROM *GLIMPSES OF GRACE*

FROM A CIRCLE OF QUIET

Una, a brilliant fifteen-year-old, a born writer who came to Harlem from Panama five years ago, and only then discovered the conflict between races, asked me out of the blue: "Mrs. Franklin, do you really and truly believe in God with no doubts at all?"

"Oh, Una, I really and truly believe in God with all kinds of doubts."

But I base my life on this belief.

ELIZABETH S. STRAHAN
CALIFORNIA, 1940–

Elizabeth Strahan is a Jungian psychoanalyst in private practice in Fuller-ton, California. A graduate of the C. G. Jung Institute in Los Angeles, she has served as chair of its certifying board and as president. She writes on the formerly taboo topic of menopause, noting that women at the turn of the twentieth century only lived to fifty while today life expectancy is closer to eighty. Menopause is no longer a bridge to death but instead an opening to a whole new era of life, the most numinous era, an exhilarating, highly charged time when a woman is invited and challenged to find renewal, to honor gods neglected in youth, letting go of what no longer fits, giving back to life in return for all that she has received.

~

WOMEN OF THAT CERTAIN AGE

I turned 50 this year. . . . Age had never mattered to me, except a mild crying spell at my 30th birthday lunch. I never thought about myself as a "middle-aged" woman, but 50 is bound to be somewhere near the middle. Along with the conceptual consciousness of aging was the very present physical reality of my body changing: gaining weight without eating more, crepeing skin, hot flashes, tiredness, heart palpitations, and so on. I also was finding myself crying often and deeply about very small things. This must be menopause, I thought.

What is the meaning of all of this change? What do the headaches, depressions, fears, and emptiness of women at this age suggest? What is life asking of us?....

The beginning of menopause is one of those very powerful in-between spaces in a lifetime: the woman is not a young woman anymore, nor is she one of the old wise ones. She is truly middle-aged. Such in-between spaces have great power: senses are heightened, emotions intensified, experiences peaked, both positively and negatively. Everything seems in stark relief....

This is a time for the return of the repressed. The repressed shadow creeps out around the corners of our existence: "nice" girls acting out in sexual frenzy, irritation at our mates with whom we have been too closely identified, bizarre spending patterns of frugal people, kleptomania in well-behaved middle-aged women who have given away too much. The neglected gods demand our attention.

Menopause invites our importune ghosts to come forward. It demands a more fundamental confrontation with our shadow. It is a neutral zone in which a woman might acknowledge the distance between her ideals and what is. She can acknowledge what in her is incomplete, fearful, and wounded. It is a time to weep the tears that are still unshed: the tears for what was, the tears for what might have been, and the tears for what will not be.

An encounter with Dionysus can break one out of the old structures of the appropriate and the expected. One woman dreamed that she was in a large, old fine building and the walls began to shake, and the thing crumbled around her, almost trapping her between some fallen, giant, heavy, wooden beams. She saw a small opening in the rubble and crawled through to bright light on the other side. She felt mysteriously "saved," and grateful to be able to begin again in a new place.

Such dreams point to the renewal that is possible through sacrifice, even when forced. The loss or the sacrifice removes the woman from the worn-out structures in her life: the rules, the "shoulds," the necessities, the established order. Through Dionysus, we learn to trust Nature. Dionysus brings a new kind of order: order by nature replaces the old order by principles. We are able to approach each situation with wonder, as if for the first time. We can encounter others with curiosity, noticing their part in the drama of reality, without preconceived notions of what they ought to be doing or not doing. At such times we can rest in a kind of quiet acceptance of what is, of the actual, no longer focusing on the potential. Such a way of life is rather anonymous, unstoried, plotless perhaps. It is not about accomplishment and visible success. It focuses on the holiness of the mundane and the familiar. Meaning and magic are found in the small ordinary events of the day. It can teach us to see the numinous in the everyday and the trivial.

JOAN CHITTISTER
PENNSYLVANIA, CONTEMPORARY

The name of Joan Chittister evokes respect and admiration throughout the Catholic Church and far beyond. A Benedictine sister trained in theology and spirituality, she is also a social psychologist and communications theorist deeply engaged in the struggle for social justice, peace, and equality in all areas of life, especially concerning the role of women in religious life. In 1992 she received the U.S. Catholic Award for her outstanding contribution to church and society. Two of Sister Joan's most beautiful books bring sixth-century Benedictine spirituality directly into the hearts of modern women and men: The Rule of Benedict: Insight for the Ages *and* Wisdom Distilled from the Daily. *She is also the author of* Womanstrength: Modern Church, Modern Women *and a charming book,* There Is a Season (*from which the following excerpt is taken*), *which refers to one of the Old Testament's most sublime and treasured writings, Ecclesiastes 3.1–8:*

> For everything there is a season,
> and a time for every matter under heaven,
> a time to be born, and a time to die,
> a time to sow, and a time to reap,
> a time to kill, and a time to build up;
> a time to weep, and a time to laugh,
> a time to mourn, and a time to dance....

~9

A TIME TO LAUGH

[There are some things, writes Sister Joan, that we must always laugh at.]

1. Laugh when people tell a joke. Otherwise you might make them feel bad.
2. Laugh when you look into a mirror. Otherwise *you* might feel bad.
3. Laugh when you make a mistake. If you don't, you're liable to forget how ultimately unimportant the whole thing really is, whatever it is.
4. Laugh with small children.... They laugh at mashed bananas on their faces, mud in their hair, a dog nuzzling their ears, the sight of their bottoms as bare as silk. It renews your perspective. Clearly nothing is as bad as it could be.
5. Laugh at situations that are out of your control. When the best man comes to the altar without the wedding ring, laugh. When the dog jumps through the window screen at the dinner guests on your doorstep, sit down and laugh awhile.
6. When you find yourself in public in mismatched shoes, laugh—as loudly as you can. Why collapse in mortal agony? There's nothing you can do to change things right now. Besides, it is funny. Ask me; I've done it.
7. Laugh at anything pompous. At anything that needs to puff its way through life in robes and titles.... Will Rogers laughed at all the public institutions of life. For instance, "You can't say civilization isn't advancing," he wrote. "In every war they kill you in a new way."...
8. Finally, laugh when all your carefully laid plans get changed; when the plane is late and the restaurant is closed and the last day's screening of the movie of the year was yesterday. You're free now to do something else, to be spontaneous,... to take a piece of life and treat it with outrageous abandon.

SHARON OLDS
CALIFORNIA, 1942–

Educated at Stanford University and Columbia University, Sharon Olds has published a number of prize-winning books of poetry. Her first book, Satan Says *(1980), won the inaugural San Francisco Poetry Center Award. The Guggenheim Foundation and the National Endowment for the Arts have awarded her fellowships, and her second book,* The Dead and the Living *(1983), won awards from the Academy of American Poets and from the National Book Critics Circle Award.*

~~9

NEW MOTHER

A week after our child was born,
you cornered me in the spare room
and we sank down on the bed.
You kissed me and kissed me, my milk undid its
burning slip-knot through my nipples,
soaking my shirt. All week I had smelled of milk,
fresh milk, sour. I began to throb:
my sex had been torn easily as cloth by the
crown of her head, I'd been cut with a knife and
sewn, the stitches pulling at my skin—
and the first time you're broken, you don't know you'll be
healed again, better than before.
I lay in fear and blood and milk
while you kissed and kissed me, your lips hot and swollen
as a teen-age boy's, your sex dry and big,
all of you so tender, you hung over me,
over the nest of stitches, over the
splitting and tearing, with the patience of someone who
finds a wounded animal in the woods
and stays with it, not leaving its side
until it is whole, until it can run again.

JULIA VINOGRAD
CALIFORNIA, 1943–

Julia Vinograd is a street poet in Berkeley, California. A graduate of the University of California at Berkeley, where she lived near historic People's Park and was an ardent political activist, she later received an MFA from the writer's workshop at the University of Iowa. In dozens of books of poetry she celebrates "the people who go by" and conversations overheard in bookstore cafés along Telegraph Avenue. Usually dressed in black with lots of multi-colored beads, a black and yellow velvet cap with a large button boasting "Weird and Proud," she sells her books on the streets of Berkeley and trades them with local vendors for holiday gifts.

BALLAD OF COLUMBINE
HIGH SCHOOL KILLINGS

Schoolboy, schoolboy, what did you learn in school today?
I learned to plant a potato in a jelly glass.
I learned to plant a child in a long-legged lass.
I learned to plant a bomb to blow up the class.
And that's what I learned in school today,
that's what I learned in school.

Schoolboy, schoolboy, what will you do now?
I'll take death to your wars, I'll make you proud.
I'll kill a frightened foreign crowd.
I'll graduate in a burning shroud.
And that's what I'll do now,
that's what I'll do now.

Schoolboy, schoolboy, who brought this to pass?
I see your face when I look in the glass.
Your countries send jets chanting "keep off the grass"
And who do you think teaches my class
Where I learn to lie under potatoes I plant?
Where I learn to lie so still.

MARILYN KRYSL

KANSAS, 1943–

A teacher of creative writing for over twenty-five years, Marilyn Krysl is the author of seven books of poetry and two volumes of short stories. Her latest books, Soulskin *and* Warscape with Lovers, *emphasize spiritual and psychological healing. Her magnificent poem "Grandmother" appeared in 1987 in* Prairie Schooner, *University of Nebraska Press.*

~ 9

GRANDMOTHER

I wasn't there when your body, signaling, woke you
When you sat, moving yourself to the edge, and stood
and knew July by its heat and wondered what time it was
and steadied yourself, sat down, and called out for my mother

When she came, her impatience visible in the air around her
because it was hot and something in a pot needed stirring
When she helped you into the slip worn thin by your patience
When she asked which dress you wanted to wear

and when you pulled on the stockings yourself, and the garters
and stepped into your shoes and looked down and knew
and did not tell my mother you knew
When you asked her please would she comb your hair

When you sat down to the meal with my mother and father
and my father asked *would you like some of this   and some of this*
When you lifted the glass and gazed through the water's prism
When you drank, swallow by swallow, all of the water

and opened the napkin but did not pick up the fork
When you folded the napkin and pushed back the plate,
pushed back the chair and stood with no help from anyone
and turned, saying nothing, and walked out of the room

When they called you   When you did not answer
When you shut the door and looked at your face in the mirror
Your face   that friend of long standing, that trustworthy sister
When you took this face in your hands to bid it goodbye

and when you said to them *I want to lie down now*
When they laid you down and covered you with a sheet
and you said *Go on now, go eat* and they did
because they had worked hard and were hungry and this had
    happened before

When you lay back in it to let it have you
knowing what you had waited for patiently and impatiently
what you had longed and hoped for and abandoned longing and
    hoping for
and prayed for and not received was finally here

When you lay back in it and let it have you
When you heard for the last time the clink of silver
and let go the sheet, let go light on earth
When your breath ceased to be a thing that belonged to you

I wasn't there
Forgive me
I wasn't there

ALICE WALKER

GEORGIA, 1944–

One of the most admired women of our times, Alice Walker is best known for her Pulitzer Prize–winning novel The Color Purple, *which was made into a movie directed by Steven Spielberg and featuring Oprah Winfrey. This moving and powerful story tells of poverty, abuse, and oppression in the African American community but also of the redemptive love and spiritual meaning found in black music, families, and spirituality.*

Born in Eatonton, Georgia, to sharecropper parents "wealthy of spirit and love," Alice Walker attended Spelman College in Atlanta and Sarah Lawrence College in New York, where her writing career began to take shape. Her young adult life centered in writing poetry and fiction and her participation in the civil rights movement. She has published poems, essays, short stories, and several critically acclaimed novels, including The Temple of My Familiar *and* Possessing the Secret of Joy. *She has received many honors, including an American Book Award and a Guggenheim Fellowship.*

A deeply committed practitioner of demanding Buddhist meditation practices such as Tonglen, a great admirer of Thich Nhat Hanh who often describes herself as a pagan Buddhist, she dedicated The Color Purple *"To the Spirit without whose assistance neither this book nor I would have been written." Her Buddhism includes a large measure of indigenous peoples' love of nature, closeness to the ancestors, and connection to the spirit world. She resides in northern California.*

～♪

FROM THE COLOR PURPLE

God ain't a he or a she.

Don't look like nothing, she say. It ain't a picture show. It ain't something you can look at apart from everything else, including yourself. I believe God is everything say Shug. Everything that is or ever was or ever will be. And when you can feel that, and be happy to feel that, you've found it.

Shug...look like a big rose.... She say, My first step from the old white man was trees. Then air. Then birds. Then other people. But one day when I was sitting quiet and feeling like a motherless child, which I was, it come to me: that feeling of being part of every-thing, not separate at all. I knew that if I cut a tree, my arm would bleed. And I laughed and cried and I run all around the house. I knew just what it was. In fact, when it happen, you can't miss it. It sort of like you know what, she say, grinning and rubbing high up on my thigh.

Shug! I say.

Oh, she say, God love all them feelings. That's some of the best stuff God did. And when you know God loves 'em, you enjoys 'em a lot more. You can just relax, go with everything that's going, and praise God by liking what you like.

'God don't think it dirty?' I ast.

Naw, she say. God made it. Listen. God love everything you love—and a mess of stuff you don't. But more than anything else, God love admiration.

You saying God vain? I ast.

Naw, she say. Not vain, just wanting to share a good thing. I think it pisses God off if you walk by the color purple in a field somewhere and don't notice it.

FROM THE UNIVERSE RESPONDS

What I have noticed in my small world is that if I praise the wild-flowers growing on the hill in front of my house, the following year they double in profusion and brilliance. If I admire the squirrel that swings from branch to branch outside my window, pretty soon I have three or four squirrels to admire. If I look into the eyes of a raccoon that has awakened me by noisily rummaging through the garbage at night, and acknowledge that it looks maddeningly like a mischievous person—paws on hips, masked eyes, a certain impudent stance, as it looks at me—I soon have a family of raccoons living in a tree a few yards off my deck. . . .

And then, too, there are the deer, who know they need never, ever fear me.

FROM THE TEMPLE OF MY FAMILIAR

HELPED are those born from love: They shall know joy equal to their suffering and they will lead multitudes into dancing and Peace.

HELPED are those too busy living to respond when they are wrongfully attacked: on their walks they shall find mysteries so intriguing as to distract them from every blow.

HELPED are those who find something in Creation to admire each and every hour. Their days will overflow with beauty and the darkest dungeon will offer gifts. . . .

HELPED are those who love the Earth, their mother, and who willingly suffer that she may not die; in their grief over her pain they will weep rivers of blood, and in their joy in her lively response to love, they will converse with trees. . . .

HELPED are those whose every act is a prayer for peace; on them depends the future of the world.

NAOMI RUTH LOWINSKY
CALIFORNIA, 1944–

A writer, poet, and Jungian analyst with a private practice in Berkeley, California, Naomi Lowinsky is a graduate of the Jungian Institute in San Francisco and received her doctorate in psychology from the Center for Psychological Studies. In her 1992 book, Stories from the Motherline: Reclaiming the Mother-Daughter Bond, *she names the generations of women related by genes and social history—a grandmother, mother, daughter, and great-granddaughter—as a "motherline." (She also discusses the male equivalent of this bond, the fatherline.) The author of many articles and poems, she recently published a collection of poetry,* Red Clay Is Talking, *in which the following poem appears. As part of her spiritual practice, she begins the day by writing poetry at home in a room overlooking San Francisco Bay.*

∼૭

INITIATE (AFTER H.D.)

White temple cut in gray rock
I have washed the stone floors
I have put the full blown
white peony
in amber glass
only Hecate knows the dark center

Through an arched window
blood red madrone stains the rocky slope
snake is sacred here
also mongoose

I await you
daughter of Isis
lover of the blood lord
sister of the frenzied one

climb the stony mountain in your bare feet
bring me your mouth and young breasts
white cave is the place I have prepared for you
hot flame of female word

ANNIE DILLARD

PENNSYLVANIA, 1945–

The author of the spiritual masterpiece Pilgrim at Tinker's Creek *and many other books, Annie Dillard is one of America's best-loved writers. She has the mystic's gift for finding awe and wonder in the most ordinary everyday event and transforming it into a parable or ritual.*

~ꝰ

THIS IS WHERE THE PEOPLE COME OUT

"Memoirs of a Cape Breton Doctor" describes, among many more dramatic incidents, the delivery of a transverse-presenting baby. "... I didn't time how long I was using mouth-to-mouth breathing, but I remember thinking during the last several minutes that it was hopeless. But I persisted, and I was finally rewarded when Anna McRae of Middle River, Victoria County, came to life." She came to life. There was a blue baby-shaped bunch of cells between the two hands of Dr. C. Lamont MacMillan, and then there was a person who had a name and a birthday, like the rest of us. Genetically she bore precisely one of the 8.4 possible mixes of her mother's and father's genes, like the rest of us. On December 1, 1931, Anna MacRae came to life. How many centuries would you have to live before this, and thousands of incidents like it every day, ceased to astound you?

Now it is a city hospital on a Monday morning. This is the obstetrical ward. The doctors and nurses wear scrubs of red, blue, or green and white running shoes. They are, according to the tags clipped to their pockets, obstetricians, gynecologists, pediatricians, pediatric nurse practitioners, and pediatric RNs. They consult one another on the hoof. They carry clipboards and vanish down corridors. They push numbered buttons on wall plaques, and doors open.

There might well be a rough angel guarding this ward, or a dragon, or an upwelling current that dashes boats on rocks. There might well be an old stone cairn in the hall by the elevators, or a well, or a ruined shrine wall where people still hear bells. Should we not remove our shoes, drink potions, take baths? For this is surely the wildest deep-sea vent on earth: This is where the people come out.

TEACHING A STONE TO TALK

The island where I live is all peopled with cranks like myself. In a cedar-shake shack on a cliff—but we all live like this—is a man in his thirties who lives alone with a stone he is trying to teach to talk. . . .

He keeps it on a shelf. Usually the stone lies protected by a square of untanned leather, like a canary asleep under its cloth. Larry removes the cover for the stone's lessons, or more accurately, I should say, for the ritual or rituals which they perform together several times a day.

No one knows what goes on at these sessions, least of all myself, for I know Larry but slightly, and that only owing to a mix-up in our mail. I assume that like any other meaningful effort, the ritual involves sacrifice, the suppression of self-consciousness, and a precise tilt of the will, so that the will becomes transparent and hollow, a channel for the work. I wish him well. It is a noble work, and beats, from any angle, selling shoes.

Reports differ on precisely what he expects or wants the stone to say. I do not think he wants the stone to speak as we do, and describe for us its life and many, or few, sensations. I think instead that he is trying to teach it to say a single word, such as "cup," or "uncle." For this purpose, he has not, as some have seriously suggested, carved the stone a little mouth, or furnished it in any way with a pocket of air which it might then expel. Rather—and I think he is wise in this—he plans to initiate his son, who is now an infant living with Larry's estranged wife, into the work, so that it may continue and bear fruit after his death.

LIKE A HOLE IN THE EARTH'S CRUST

A hole in the earth's crust releases clear water into the St. John's River of central Florida at the rate of one hundred million gallons a day. Saltwater issues from deep-sea mouths as very hot water and minerals. There iron and sulfur erupt into the sea from under the planet's crust, and there clays form black towers. In Safad, the kabbalist Isaac Luria began prayers by saying, "Open Thou my lips, O Lord, and my mouth shall show forth Thy praise."

RACHEL NAOMI REMEN, MD
NEW YORK, CONTEMPORARY

A medical doctor and author of wisdom books, Rachel Naomi Remen teaches health care professionals how to serve their patients by taking a relationship-centered approach to healing in which the accent is placed on compassion, understanding, and right communication. In public appearances and her many articles available free of charge on the Web, she talks about medicine's overemphasis on the body and loss of the soul in the centuries since Descartes split the human person into a thinking mind and material body. The work of the medical profession today, she believes, is to see the patient as a whole being whose soul and body are inseparable and to bring work and spirit together again, as in the premodern era. To this end, the feminine and masculine principles must be brought into balance. Health professionals need to have a personal spiritual practice, she says, and "to attend church."

Dr. Remen founded the Commonweal Cancer Help Program to bring a spiritual perspective to the treatment of people with cancer and their families. She has Crohn's disease and has been a patient of the medical system for some forty years, undergoing major surgery seven times, so her work reflects a blend of her profession as a psycho-oncologist and her personal experience with disease. She is the author of the beloved best-seller Kitchen Table Wisdom. *Her latest book is* My Grandfather's Stories.

~⁀

A ROOM WITH A VIEW

After completing the last treatment in a year of potent chemotherapy one of my clients went to San Francisco overnight with her husband to celebrate. Her oncologist had tried to discourage her from this. It had seemed rather pointless to him, as she was still far too weak to see the sights, go to a restaurant, or participate in any of the fabled activities of this rich and complex city. He couldn't imagine why she might want to go if she could not do these things, and he had suggested she wait a few months until she was stronger. But she and her husband had gone anyway and stayed in a nice hotel.

Afterwards, I asked her about it. "It was wonderful," she said. "First we ordered room service. They brought it in on a table with a cloth a half-inch thick. My first meal without a tray. It was so elegant, the wineglasses and the butter carved into little flowers. And the food! We sat in this lovely room overlooking a little park and ate real food that I could actually taste. In the nude. Then we made love. Then we took long, long hot baths and used up every single towel in the bathroom. Great big thick towels—there were twelve of them. And we used up all those delicious smelling things in the little bottles. And watched both movies. And ate most of what was in the little refrigerator. And sat outside on the terrace in our bathrobes and saw the moon rise over the city. We found all the pillows that they hide in the dresser drawers and slept in this king-sized bed with eight pillows. And saw the sunrise. We used it all up. It was glorious!" she said to me, a woman who spends most of her time in a hotel room asleep.

FROM *KITCHEN TABLE WISDOM*

THE RECOVERY OF THE SACRED: SOME THOUGHTS ON MEDICAL REFORM

We all know the power of the masculine principle, especially in health care. There are many people who would have died before today without the powerful, life-saving interventions of masculine-principle oriented medicine. I am one of them. So it's not about throwing away the masculine principle; it is about reclaiming wholeness, integrity. . . .

The imbalance in the medical system, the emphasis on masculine principles, approaches, and perceptions that pervades our entire culture, diminishes everybody. It cherishes the people who work within the system, and it diminishes the people who seek out the system for healing. When you leave the doctor's office, you may feel diminished, even though you may have been given the right diagnosis and the right pills. . . . If someone relates to you in a predominantly masculine-principle style, you experience their strength, their capacity. You get rescued, as it were, and you feel smaller.

What is it like then to relate to someone who is relating to you in a predominantly feminine style? . . . When someone relates to you from the feminine side of themselves, what you see reflected . . . is your own strength, your own capacity, your own uniqueness. What would the medical system be like if it could do that for us, as well as providing the right diagnosis, the right pills?

The yin is about comfort in the world of relationship, the world of connection, the interdependence of all things. We have had a disease-centered medical care. We have moved to a more patient-centered form of care. What we need is a medicine based on right relationship.

MICHELLE LYNN RYAN
CALIFORNIA, 1945–

Michelle Ryan is one of our most authentic mystical poets. As a young seeker, she traveled in over forty countries "following the fragments of an unknown teaching." She has gone alone on Hajj to Mecca and studied with spiritual teachers in Bhutan, Nepal, and Dharamsala, living and meditating for some time at Necluny Monastery. Having followed the mystical path all the way through supreme suffering to mystical love, she today devotes her life to deep prayer and meditation, writing sublime love poetry, offering spiritual guidance to seekers who appear at her door. A genuine recluse and renunciant with the capacity for affliction and joy that contemplation can birth, she lived until recently in a cabin with the companionship of a little blind dog.

Michelle's conversation and written work suggest long hours spent alone with the world's mystical legacy in Rumi, Rabia, and T. S. Eliot, to name but a few; in the world's sacred scriptures; in Buddha and Jesus. She has several academic degrees but thinks of her Sufi teacher, Irina Tweedie (see p. 183), as the most important influence in her life.

~⁹

MIDNIGHT OF THE SOUL
(FANA ANNIHILATION)

Beloved can You hear me,
Praying myself across this wilderness?
Why, Lord of all the worlds,
Have you brought me to this—
Dazzling Dark and foreboding place?
Here Love's combat will deny me
Yet another season.
For all too soon, falcon like,
You have torn my Heart—
And dropped me amid
The dead leaves of my pride!

I have sinned against myself,
But what Great Friend,
Have I done to You?
Have I squandered your Wealth,
And abandoned You to poverty?
Have I eaten Your daily bread
And left You Hungry?
Teacher of all Creations
Have I invented Thee?

I bow down to You
Mother of all the still stars,
And Golden Gates of Heaven.
I bow down to You,
Queen of the Flaming Doors of Hell.
Of my own free will,
I give You back my free will.
This infant Soul has no right to ask,
But at the hour when Angel Azrael comes,
Could You leave me just a little bit of me,
To play in Your Radiant Rose Garden—
And forever love You back?

MOUNTOLIVE—THE APOSTATE, CATACOMBS, 300 A.D.

Lord, again I sang the Litanies of the Cross.
Forty times have I watched the Holy Season
Come and also pass, celebrating the miracle
Of the child becoming father to the man once more.
But this year brings no joy,
Only relief that at last my ritual duties are done.
Forgive me, Lord, your devoted priest,
For I grow old, weak, and unworthy.

I must know, Lord, is it Your Holy Will
That I be hunted down like some mad dog,
Or dungeoned deep in these dark labyrinths.
Am I doomed to forever run before this devil's blind legions,
To forever flee the flashing swords of Julian?

FROM "UNDE MALUM?"

Old in this harbor to which I have come—
Older than all the days have been aware!
But I cannot linger here any longer,
Awaiting the friend who left
To find the fragrant isle of pines,
Nor for the friend departed on the open sea...

DIANA ECK
MONTANA, 1945–

Diana Eck looked surprised when a huge audience at the World Parliament of Religions in Chicago in 1993 received her keynote address with a thunderous standing ovation. The time was ripe for a woman to address the august gathering, and it was time for her message about pluralism and our pressing need for a worldwide, healing, interfaith dialogue based on the common ground of spiritual experience. The warm applause contrasted starkly with the cool reception given to Elizabeth Cady Stanton, who was not taken seriously when she spoke at the first World Parliament of Religions in 1893, one hundred years earlier, also in Chicago. Diana Eck urged her audience to work for worldwide interfaith dialogue to put an end to religious wars. (Over fifty religious wars were raging across the globe as she spoke.) Similarly, in her book Encountering God, *she calls for members of all religions to engage in community-building work, citing a persuasive statistic from the World Development Forum:*

> *If our world were a village of 1000 people, who would we be?... [T]here would be 329 Christians, 174 Muslims, 131 Hindus, 61*

Buddhists, 52 Animists, 3 Jews, 34 members of other religions, such as
Sikhs, Jains, Zoroastrians, and Baha'is, and 216 would be without any
religion. In this village, there would be 564 Asians, 210 Europeans, 86
Africans, 80 South Americans, and 60 North Americans. And in this
same village, 60 persons would have half the income, 500 would be
hungry, 600 would live in shantytowns, and 700 would be illiterate.

~~

ENCOUNTERING GOD IN OTHER TRADITIONS

Several years ago I spent an afternoon in Nairobi with the parents
of a Muslim colleague at Harvard. They were Sindhis (from the
part of the Indian subcontinent know as Sindh) and Ismaile Muslims, followers of the tradition of Islam led today by the Aga Khan.
We visited the large mosque and Islamic center in Nairobi and
enjoyed a meal at a Gujarati restaurant before they put me on the
evening train to Mombassa. Just as they were getting me settled in
my compartment, we heard the evening call to prayer. My friend's
father glanced at his watch and said to me, "It is time to remember God in prayer. Excuse us." We closed the compartment door
and he and his wife sat down to pray, I sat with them. "In the
name of God the Almighty, the Compassionate, the Merci-
ful. . ."—I recognized the first few lines of the Qur'an in Arabic. I
bowed my head and entered into the spirit of prayer with them,
although I did not know the words they spoke. Is our God the
same God? Frankly, the question did not occur to me then. I simply took it for granted.

What we take for granted in our experience is the very stuff of
theological reflection. What allowed me to feel so natural in entering into a spirit of prayer with my Muslim friends? When I
preached not long ago at a church on the green in Lexington
[Massachusetts], just across from the famous statue of the Minute-
man, I reflected on the matter. I spoke of the common monotheis-
tic tradition of Judaism, Christianity and Islam. Allah is not "the
Muslim God," I said, but simply the Arabic word for God. Allah is
none other than the one we know as God and is the name Arabic-
speaking Christians also use when they pray.

After the service [a parishioner insisted it was wrong to equate the Christian God, Father-Son-Spirit, with Allah]. As we discussed the matter together over coffee, the parishioner and I concluded that there were at least three alternatives. We both rejected the idea that there could be two Gods, the one we call God and the one Muslims call Allah, so the first possibility was that there could be one God, ours, with Allah being a false God. This would be a form of exclusivist thinking: our way of thinking about God excludes all others. That did not seem to account for the vibrant faith of the fifth of humankind who worship Allah.

The second alternative could be that we see God in God's fullness and that the Muslims see the same God less clearly. (Muslims no doubt would see it the other way around.) This would be an inclusivist view—our way of thinking includes the other, somewhat less adequate conception.

The third and perhaps most satisfactory alternative would be to insist that there is only one God whom Christians and Muslims understand only partially because God transcends our complete comprehension. As Muslims put it, "Allahu akbar!" It means not only "God is great," but "God is greater!" Greater than our understanding, greater than any human idea of God. This would leave room for the self-understanding of both Christian and Muslim and would be a pluralist view.

CHRISTIANE NORTHRUP, MD
MAINE, CONTEMPORARY

Christiane Northrop is a pioneer in women's health care. After graduation from Dartmouth Medical School in New Hampshire, while practicing as a gynecologist, she became deeply engaged in research on the biochemistry of health and illness, reaching the conclusion that the key to health lies in emotions. She believes that understanding the power of emotions in shaping our attitudes, perceptions, and daily thought patterns enables us to make behavioral changes, sometimes as simple as breathing, that promote health. Allowing the emotions to ebb and flow like ocean waves cleanses the body, she often says, and brings these strong energies into harmony. A widely sought lecturer and writer, one of our foremost experts on women's health, Dr. Northrup publishes a newsletter, and she also teaches women physicians how to set up medical practices by and for women.

~⁓

A ONE-SIZE-FITS-ALL PRESCRIPTION

It is easy to take the steps you need to change your perceptions and create health. You can start with everyday thoughts. So here's my one-size-fits-all prescription: When you have a thought that does not enhance your life, take a deep breath and keep breathing. Then, appreciate the situation for what it is. By this, I mean take responsibility for your thoughts and feelings, and be truthful, but do not blame others—or yourself—for an adversity you suffer. Try to feel your thoughts without judging them. Take these steps every time you have thoughts that disempower you and soon your body will begin to shift in response.

Now I don't mean for you to change your native temperament. It is not the same thing. But, you have within you the ability, through your own perceptions, to create your own health. . . . You should also pay attention to those things that bring you gratitude, joy, fun, and a feeling of well-being. Similarly, avoid people, places, and things that cause you stress. If you know that watching the news on TV is a stressor for you, turn it off. You may not have control over what happens in the world, or how events are portrayed on the evening news, [but you do have control over] your perception of those events.

. . . And the biochemical consequences of those perceptions are also completely up to you. Herein lies the big secret of the Health Wisdom for Women path: You are the only one who can create the balance necessary to put the maximum number of wisdom chips into your health bank account. In 20 years of medical practice, I can honestly say that emotions are the primary energy that tips the balance toward either illness or health in every situation. And, by the law of attraction—the law that states like is attracted to like—you will be able to create a life in which you're surrounded by those things that truly support you. I've seen this repeatedly and experience it on a daily basis myself. You can, too!

REGINA SARA RYAN
NEW YORK, 1945–

A former Roman Catholic sister, Regina Ryan has been searching for the feminine face of God for most of her adult life. She published her insights and understandings in 1998 in The Woman Awake: Feminine Wisdom for Spiritual Life, *which interweaves her own story with that of twenty-four women who inspired her, among them Irina Tweedie (see p. 183) and Hadewijch (see p. 80). Her other books include* No Child in My Life, The Fine Art of Recuperation, *and the* Wellness Workbook, *coauthored with John W. Travis, MD.*

~✌

THE WAY OF WAITING

When a woman knows how to wait, and is at peace in her waiting, I find it immensely compelling to be with her. When Susan is nursing her child, she rests in a way that I long for. When Lalitha works in the garden, her mood is overwhelming abundance and silence. When Tina sits at the bedside of her dying friend, holding her hand and stroking her head, I want to be there, too.

There is nothing weak about woman's ability to wait. Her surrender is not resignation, but rather a whole-hearted "Yes" to life as it shows up in both the joyous and excruciating details of everyday existence. When woman is attuned to her own body, she is resonant with and willing to serve the concrete reality of other human needs. And such service usually demands courageous waiting. Take, for example, the image of the women standing at the foot of the cross of Christ (and it was a group of women who stayed 'till the bitter end while the men-folk fled in fear of their lives). These courageous women endured the stripping away of all their hopes and expectations for what Christ was to be for the world.

THE WAY OF THE WARRIOR

The term "warrior" has a decidedly masculine connotation, and for many women engaged in spiritual life this notion of "warriorship" will be rejected as rigid or fearsome—too connected to a male dominance model which has suffocated them for too long. With that in mind, I offer the corresponding phrase "woman of power" to communicate the essence of this necessary quality, or state of being, which any serious spiritual practitioner will have to embody if she truly wants to progress in the vocation to personal integrity and selfless service or love, which is drawing her on.

Before abandoning the word "warrior," however, it may serve us to contemplate its meaning beyond our attachment to any feminine or masculine application. What are the qualities of one who goes to war, not necessarily against other human beings, but against injustice, against ignorance, against suffering? What are the qualities of the knight in the highest courtly tradition; the "peaceful warrior," if you will?...

A warrior is characterized by vigilance built by discipline and attention. From ancient Tibet comes the story of the scholarly young monk Saraha, who later became one of the most prominent "fathers" of Buddhism. One day, while passing through a village, the monk observed a woman sitting in front of her hut making arrows. He watched with amazement at the discipline, which showed up in the precision, lack of distraction, and elegance with which she approached her task. Immediately Saraha recognized a quality beyond the ordinary, and because he was an insightful monk, he assumed that such attention could only indicate a person of great spiritual achievement. He was right. Approaching her, the monk attempted to engage her by asking some trivial question. But the arrow-maker cut through his superficialities with her piercing words, telling him that "...The Buddha's meaning can be known through symbols and actions, not through words and books." Saraha was so astonished by this yogini's response that he put away his monastic robes and instead dedicated himself to her, taking her as his guru. The yogini proceeded to pass on great wisdom to him, and he in turn went on to carry out his destiny as one of the great teachers of the Tantric Buddhist tradition.

FROM *THE WOMAN AWAKE*

CYNTHIA BOURGEAULT
CANADA, 1945–

An Episcopal hermit priest, Cynthia Bourgeault is the author of an auto-biographical book concerned with an ancient idea of immense importance in Christian thought: the neglected topic of love after life. At fifty she met and fell in love with a seventy-year-old Benedictine monk named Rafael whom she recognized as an authentic spiritual master. Committed to a mostly solitary, silent life of prayer, work, and virtually nothing else, completely unaware of his rare spiritual attainment, a man who reflected on "Divine things" more than he reflected on himself, Rafe was unaccustomed to love relationships and eluded her for some time. But love emerged, uniting them for a few short years in a passionate bond abruptly cut off when Rafe died of a heart attack.

Crushed with grief, staggering under the weight of several monks' jealousy and resentment, Cynthia remained on the monastery grounds for a while, praying and wondering if love can continue after death. The answer to the greatest of all mysteries came to her in the experience related here, a crucial turning point that provided her with the title of her book: Love Is Stronger than Death: The Mystical Union of Two Souls. *What she called "post death encounters" with Rafe convinced her that he was still with her in "the pure essence of his presence and the immense energy of his love ... minus the physical body."*

Cynthia lives in British Columbia, dividing her time between solitude and her role as resident teacher for the Contemplative Society.

∼૭

THE MYSTICAL UNION OF TWO SOULS

"I'll meet you in the body of hope." Those strange words that came to me that night of the funeral wake! It was not a term Rafe and I had ever used, and for the first few weeks after his death I puzzled over what it might mean. Then one afternoon I suddenly found out.

In February, not quite two months after Rafe's death, I was walking up the road past the Stanley place [where she and Rafe used to meet to talk and drink coffee] when I was stopped in my tracks by what sounded like a sledgehammer pounding inside and a pile of debris accumulating out front in the snow.

"The monks are giving me this place for the summer," said the caretaker of the monastery's new retreat center, grinning, his face sweaty and smeared in dust. "I thought I'd open it up, get a little light in here."

Open it up—the place was gutted! It's hard to believe that a single human being in one afternoon's work could unleash such a whirlwind. Sheet rock and splintered cabinetry lay in a pile in what had once been the living room, along with smashed dishes and trampled foodstuffs that had gone flying in the melee. Electrical wiring hung loose from the ceiling beams, and a spigot dangling on a piece of copper tubing dripped the last hurrahs for the days of "hot and cold running water." The Stanley place was, as they say, history.

"I'll be back in the morning with a dump truck," he told me, then packed his tool bag and left. He never returned. Whether the monks called him off the project or he got overwhelmed by his own chaos, I don't know. It was like a ground strike, aimed precisely at that spot on earth where its demolition had to be accomplished. After he left, I stumbled around for awhile in the carcass of the Stanley. Like debris washed down in the spring torrents, little scraps of memory floated through the wreckage, strangely dislodged and incongruous—a barstool sticking out from the trash pile, Rafe's old pair of work gloves in the remains of a drawer. Still taped to a piece of splintered barnboard, once the living room wall, was the postcard from two Christmases ago bearing the reminder "Not to worry. All is swell." I went on the deck and dissolved in tears.

That's when it happened. As I wept out there in the snow, I began to notice a shift. Although I was still crying, the emotional sting started to lose force, and a new and tingling presence began to work its way up in me, literally starting from the tips of my toes. I felt like an empty glass slowly being filled with champagne.

In spite of myself, I was fascinated. A sparkling, bubbling life seemed to be pouring into me, filling me with such buoyancy that I could no longer sink into despair. And a moment came when the Stanley place simply fell away, like scales from my eyes, and I was able to look straight through all the relics and memories of love and simply see the love itself.

I got up and started dancing on the deck as in that final scene of *Zorba the Greek,* humming a little tune to the words that went, "When the building's built, you no longer need the scaffolding. . . ." I knew in that moment that I was sustained by an invisible and intensely joyous partner.

FROM *LOVE IS STRONGER THAN DEATH*

CAROL FLINDERS
OREGON, 1945–

In the 1960s, when Carol Flinders was working on a doctorate at Berkeley, she and some forty other students founded a spiritual community under the guidance of a beloved Fulbright professor of English, Eknath Easwaran. They raised funds to purchase a beautiful tract of land with a few abandoned buildings in California's golden hills, and settled into a modern version of the ancient monastic routine of prayer and work, meditating up to four hours each day. They also repaired leaky buildings, created organic gardens to grow their own food, and built a school to educate their children. Carol married Tim, a member of the community, and gave birth to a son, Ramesh, who is a college student. A wonderful writer, she co-authored the million-selling vegetarian cookbook Laurel's Kitchen *and authored* Enduring Grace: Living Portraits of Seven Women Mystics *and* At the Root of This Longing: Reconciling a Spiritual Hunger and a Feminist Thirst, *in which the following excerpt appears.*

OUR DAUGHTERS, OUR SELVES

[In *Sassafras, Cypress, and Indigo,* by novelist Ntozake Shange, twelve-year-old Indigo is visiting her good friend Sister Mary Louise when she feels a wave of intense emotion and realizes she has begun to bleed.]

"Speak, child," Sister Mary Louise shouts, "raise your voice that the Lord May Know You as the Woman You Are," and she springs into action.

> She gently took off Indigo's clothes, dropped them in a pail of cold water. She bathed Indigo in a hot tub filled with rose petals: white, red, and yellow floating around a new woman. She made Indigo a garland of flowers and motioned her to go into the backyard.
>
> "There in the garden, among God's other beauties, you should spend these first hours. . . . Take your blessing and let your blood flow among the roses. Squat like you will when you give birth. Smile like you will when God chooses to give you a woman's pleasure. Go now, like I say. Be not afraid of your nakedness."
>
> Then Sister Mary shut the door. Indigo sat bleeding among the roses, fragrant and filled with grace.

Here, puberty is presented as an awakening to a whole range of feelings and capacities, all at the same time: sexual desire and the capacity to give life and nurture it, but also, and unequivocally, spiritual power and spiritual hunger. Courage and joy. Sister Mary Louise invites her young friend to recognize all of these feelings in herself simultaneously and welcome them.

What to me is particularly interesting about the passage, moreover, is its explicitly religious language. Is there any way in the world Ntozake Shange could have conveyed the transformation of a girl into a woman with anything approaching the magnificence she does if she had not used words like *blessing, God,* and *grace*? If she had not called up that whole wretched biblical account of things explicitly and let Sister Mary Louise effectively rescind Eve's exile

from the Garden of Eden and revoke the curse God had laid on
Eve and Adam by telling Indigo not to be afraid of her own nakedness? In any other version, the result would have been less powerful. In effect, Shange makes of Sister Mary Louise a kind of high
priestess of a reinvented Western spirituality, reforging a connection between woman and the sacred feminine that four thousand
years of patriarchy has striven to keep severed, and in doing that
she gives us a tantalizing, heady glimpse of what life after patriarchy might actually feel like.

LAUREN ARTRESS
OHIO, 1945–

*In 1991, one of the most effective church leaders of our time, Lauren
Artress, reintroduced the ancient labyrinth walk as a powerful spiritual
practice for awakening and healing. After walking the stone labyrinth laid
eight hundred years ago in the floor of Chartres Cathedral in France, Lauren returned to her work as Canon for Special Ministries at Grace Episcopal Cathedral in San Francisco with a vision of installing the great
archetype at the cathedral. Encouraged by Alan Jones, the dean of Grace
Cathedral, she and many volunteers sewed heavy strips of canvas into a
portable labyrinth and painted the sacred design on it in purple. When the
forty-foot-wide pattern was opened to the public, participants reported
amazing bursts of energy, insights into a problem at work, tears cried in
grief and joy, uncommon calmness, joyful flights of imagination, forgiveness, the black velvety experience that many in the East name "God," and
much more. Lauren welcomed a person's sense of "chaos" with Nietzsche's
famous remark, "You need chaos in your soul to give birth to a dancing
star." In 1995, a permanent labyrinth made from terrazzo stone was laid
outdoors in the Interfaith Garden at Grace Cathedral, and in 1999, Lauren
organized a worldwide labyrinth walk for New Year's Eve to usher in the
new millennium with a massive collective experience of the Numinous.
Today she guides the transforming labyrinth process in worldwide workshops and retreats. She also holds a yearly event called "Let Us Walk with
Mary" at Chartres Cathedral to open the Divine Feminine in participants'*

lives. The selections below come from Lauren's 1995 book, Walking a Sacred Path: Rediscovering the Labyrinth as a Spiritual Tool.

~)

FROM WALKING A SACRED PATH

Much of our spiritual seeking is driven by the desire to manifest our unique and individual gifts in the world. Soren Kierkegaard said, "Every human being comes to earth with sealed orders." Many of us sense this. Something within us carries a deep, sometimes buried, sense that we have a special task. However, we need the tools to find our orders and decipher them. Many people find their way to the labyrinth in the process of searching for their own special talents. They come for insight into how their unique skills can serve the world. . . .

Walking the labyrinth is a body prayer. It is nonthreatening; all we are asked to do is walk. Even those of us with the deepest inner divisions can do that. Moving through the labyrinth, we can learn what it feels like to stand firm in the world. We sense our feet firmly planted on the ground; our legs, pelvis, torso, arms, and head flowing with energy and life. . . .

When we are grounded in our bodies, we are stabilized and can receive information more accurately. Much like fine-tuning a radio, if we are attuned to our bodies the static in the incoming messages and impulses is reduced. To reclaim the body is a sacred act. In doing so, we may discover a path to the Divine. Dancing, skipping, crawling, or solemnly walking are all encouraged on the labyrinth. The more free and spontaneous we are in the labyrinth, the more energy we bring into our lives. . . .

Sacred space can be anywhere, is everywhere, especially when we are able to remain in an open, receptive consciousness. Friends told me about making a labyrinth in the sand at the beach north of San Francisco. They played in it with their children and walked it ritually. As they left that day, they saw cloud formations that appeared to them as a great bird they felt blessing them on their way. This is sacred play.

LINDA HOGAN

CHICKASAW PEOPLE, 1947–

Linda Hogan is a Pulitzer Prize finalist, a poet, novelist, and essayist with wide-sweeping mystical vision. A foundational voice in the evolution of Native American writing, she intuitively sees beyond dualism to the sacred oneness of reality and insists that all beings, from the tiniest wounded bird to the worst human being, deserve compassionate care and love. Throughout her writing, sensuality and spirituality are mirror images showing how the physical union of two people parallels the soul's most intimate moments with God. Among her books are two novels, Mean Spirit *and* Solar Storms, *and various volumes of poetry, including* The Book of Medicines.

In the paragraphs that introduce this passage, Linda is preparing for the sacred Native American ritual of the sweat lodge and has made fifty prayer ties, which will hang inside the hutlike structure during the ritual. Each prayer tie has a prayer in it and is made from a four-inch square of cloth that is filled with tobacco then shaped into a pouch and tied with a string. The day before the sweat lodge, an eagle is seen flying overhead, which is interpreted as a good sign. Perhaps the participants will emerge from their enclosure feeling renewed and whole, the broken pieces of self and world put back together again in right relationship.

∽）

THE SWEAT LODGE

In the background, the sweat lodge structure stands. Birds are on it. It is still skeletal. A woman and a man are beginning to place old rugs and blankets over the bent cottonwood frame. A great fire is already burning and the lava stones that will be the source of the heat for the sweat are already being fired in it. . . .

By later afternoon we are ready, one by one, to enter the enclosure. The hot lava stones are placed inside. They remind us of earth's fiery core, and of the spark inside all life. After the flap, which serves as a door, is closed, water is poured over the stones and the hot steam rises around us. In a sweat lodge ceremony, the

entire world is brought inside the enclosure. The soft odor of smok-
ing cedar accompanies this arrival of everything. It is all called in.
The animals come from the warm and sunny distances. Water from
dark lakes is there. Wind. Young, lithe willow bent overhead remember their lives rooted in ground, the sun their leaves took in. They
remember that minerals and water rose up their trunks, and that
birds nested in their leaves, and that planets turned above their
brief, slender lives. The thunder clouds travel in from far regions of
earth. Winds arrive from the four directions. It has moved through
caves and breathed through our bodies. It is the same air elk have
inhaled, air that passed through the lungs of a grizzly bear. The sky
is there, with all the stars whose lights we see long after the stars
themselves have gone back to nothing. It is a place grown intense
and holy. It is a place of immense community and of humbled solitude; we sit together in our aloneness and speak, one at a time, our
deepest language of need, hope, loss, and survival. We remember
that all things are connected.

Remembering this is the purpose of the ceremony. It is part of a
healing and restoration. It is the mending of a broken connection
between us and the rest. The participants in the ceremony say the
words "All my relations," before and after we pray; those words create a relationship with other people, with animals, with the land.
To have health, it is necessary to keep all these relations in mind.

LUISAH TEISH
LOUISIANA, 1948–

*A priestess of Oshun in the Yoruba Lucumi tradition of Africa, "Teish" is
a large and handsome woman with tremendous warrior presence who
dresses in striking gold and orange robes, a high turban, and heavy strands
of multicolored beads. She spends her enormous resources of inner
power—a resonant deep voice, commanding presence, passion, and knowledge—in the interest of empowering other women. As a priestess in an
African tradition, she leads worship services and rites of passage marking
transitional eras in a woman's life cycle, for example, a three-day rite of*

initiation of twelve-year-old girls into womanhood. For this particular passage, Teish puts the girls through every arduous ordeal she can think of to test their readiness for the sacred transition to womanhood. Those who persevere (most do) are welcomed into the new stage of life in a public ceremony with their grandmothers sitting in front of them, their mothers standing behind them, very proud. Each elder shares with her grandchild three aspects of a woman's life that are wonderful and three aspects that are hard, and the ritual concludes with the ecstatically happy "women" going out into the audience with baskets of gifts that they have prepared for participants.

One of Teish's most important teachings concerns ancestor reverence, which honors the genetic continuity of humankind from generation to generation in our bodies and personalities as well as the continuing existence of the ancestors in the spirit world and their ability to influence human life. She recommends when a loved one dies to create an altar covered with a piece of a garment (preferably white) owned by this person. Fraying the garment's edges will provide symbolic nerve endings, an energy field where the living connect with the "new ancestor."

The author of Jumbalaya: The Natural Woman's Book of Personal Charms and Practical Rituals, *excerpted below, she lectures and leads workshops and classes on women's rites of passage, the African religion of the Mother, African rituals and goddesses, shamanism, and related subjects.*

~⁀⁀

ANCESTOR REVERENCE

[E]gun is the Yoruba word used to describe those souls or intelligences who have moved beyond the physical body. The eguns who are existing at another level within the creative energy are treated with *loving reverence.* They, like the Egyptian ancestors, are given an honorable burial and they are provided with the tools they need to conduct meaningful work in the spirit world. They receive offerings of food. Special dishes are cooked for the ancestors, sometimes elaborate, sometimes simple, depending on the descendant's means. Beautiful songs and undulating dances are done in their honor. They are well spoken of, respected. It is important in African society to remember the names and deeds of one's ancestors. Children are named after them, of course. They hold a place of affection in the hearts of their descendants. Elaborate annual rites are held in their honor, which the whole village attends. People dress up in costumes and reenact the stories of their ancestors, using carved masks, special props, and musical instruments. The ancestors are subjects of African theater. In exchange for this loving reverence, they offer protection, wisdom, and assistance to those who revere them. . . .

The first step in communicating with your ancestors is building a shrine. . . . Here everyone's artistic ability comes out. People mold, carve, arrange, and combine [ingredients] until they have an altar that is useful and pleasing.

Here are some suggestions [for yours]:

1. The earth pot. . . . containing earth from your place of birth and as many places as you can get earth from . . .
2. A rock basket . . . rocks from various places
3. Collected waters . . . from various places
4. A bowl of grains . . .
5. An herb pot . . .
6. A vessel of shells . . .
7. A collection of feathers . . .

STARHAWK

CALIFORNIA, CONTEMPORARY

Starhawk is a self-declared witch whose Wiccan community in San Francisco, Reclaiming, has taken leadership in making the Pagan tradition known in the modern world. A teacher, workshop leader, counselor, and political activist, Starhawk is the author of the influential best-selling book The Spiral Dance: A Rebirth of the Ancient Religion of the Great Goddess, *which for many years has been a principal source of the rituals used by women's spirituality circles in the United States. Among her other books is* Dreaming the Dark: Magic, Sex, and Politics, *from which the passage below is excerpted. One of her favorite sayings from the Wiccan tradition is "Where there is fear, there is power."*

~♪

POWER-OVER AND
POWER-FROM-WITHIN

[I write] about the calling forth of power, a power based on a principle very different from power-over, from domination. For power-over is, ultimately, the power of the gun and the bomb, the power of annihilation that backs up all the institutions of domination.

There are many names for power-from-within, none of them entirely satisfying. It can be called *spirit*—but that name implies that it is separate from matter, and that false split . . . is the foundation of the institutions of domination. It could be called *God*—but the God of patriarchal religions has been the ultimate source of power-over. I have called it *immanence,* a term that is truthful but somewhat cold and intellectual. And I have called it *Goddess* because the ancient images, symbols and myths of the Goddess as birthgiver, weaver, earth and growing plant, wind and ocean, flame, web, moon and milk, all speak to me of the powers of connectedness, sustenance, healing, creating.

The word *Goddess* makes many people who would define themselves as "political" uneasy. It implies religion, secularism, and can be mistaken for the worship of an external being. "Goddess" also makes people who would define themselves as "spiritual" or "religious" uneasy; it smacks of Paganism, of blood, darkness, and sexuality, of lower powers.

Yet power-from-within *is* the power of the low, the dark, the earth; the power that arises from our blood, and our lives, and our passionate desire for each other's living flesh. And the political issues of our time are also issues of spirit, conflicts between paradigms or underlying principles. If we are to survive, the question becomes: how do we overthrow, not those presently in power, but the principle of power-over? How do we shape a society based on the principle of power-from-within?

CAROLYN MYSS

ILLINOIS, CONTEMPORARY

Carolyn Myss is a pioneer in the area of energy medicine and human con-sciousness. A medical intuitive, she is able to diagnose disease by "seeing" it in the patient's body without using any of the customary medical tools of diagnosis. Through her best-selling book, Anatomy of the Spirit, *she became one of the first authors in the West to incorporate the seven chakras (bodily energy centers) into a health care system, comparing their healing power to the seven sacraments in the Roman Catholic Church.*

One of the most sought-after lecturers in the United States, Carolyn Myss appears regularly on educational television and is heard on audiotapes such as Why People Don't Heal, Energy Anatomy, *and others. She has released a videotape,* Energy Anatomy and Self-Diagnosis, *and coauthored a book with Norman Shealy, MD, titled* The Creation of Health: Merging Traditional Medicine with Intuitive Diagnosis. *Carolyn has a master's degree in spirituality and a doctorate in theology. The selection here comes from her 1997 book,* Why People Don't Heal and How They Can.

~⁀

ON HEALING

Our thoughts powerfully influence the health of our minds and bodies, and delving into our inner selves is essential to the healing process. Yet negative patterns are not always at the root of illness, and a failure to heal should not always be blamed on negative past experiences or on negative beliefs buried deep in the unconscious mind.... Sometimes illness is the result of a complex of causes and it can be futile to try to fix the cause on a single, simple factor. Life is just not that simple. Some illnesses develop, for example, because of our increasingly toxic environment as well as exposure to germs, bacteria, and viruses. Others are the result of exposure to contaminated water or parasites. Still others are the result of genet-ics that may just be impossible to outrun. And some...can be a form of spiritual guidance. In our quest to become physically and spiritually strong, we have forgotten that our emotional journey is relatively new and that our physical bodies are still subject to powerful dominance by our environment and by the rapidly changing, unsettling patterns in our society.

Healing from illness would be better served if we investigated our past for positive patterns as well as negative ones. Even as we seek out all that can contribute to our weaknesses, we need to bring into focus the strong and enduring parts of our personalities. When people focus only on their negative patterns, all that is good about them and their lives can be eclipsed. . . .

Support programs should not only help people recover from their wounds but also celebrate their strengths. The human spirit does not go to sleep within us because of negative life patterns, nor are most people's lives only a series of tragedies. Unearthing the positive is as effective a healing process as is clearing out the negative parts of our history.

KATHLEEN NORRIS

SOUTH DAKOTA, 1950–

Kathleen Norris has received many awards and widespread praise for three heart-warming, best-selling books published in rapid succession in the 1990s: Dakota: A Spiritual Geography, The Cloister Walk, *and* Amazing Grace. *A Midwestern Protestant poet with a longing to understand the ancient ways and the allure of monasticism, she spent two nine-month retreats with the Benedictines of St. John's Abbey in Minnesota, whom she found to be natural, kind, and wise, not given to "that kind of holy talk that can make me feel like a lower life form." In* The Cloister Walk, *her revelations about the beauty in the flow of the liturgical year have enchanted the hearts of religious people, kindling spiritual longings and hope.*

For ten years, Kathleen Norris has been an oblate of Assumption Abbey in North Dakota. Oblates strive to live by the Rule of St. Benedict without pronouncing religious vows. She is married to the poet David Dwyer.

FROM DAKOTA

"When my third snail died," the little girl writes, sitting half way in, half way out of her desk, one leg swinging in the air, "I said, I'm through with snails." She sits up to let me pass down the aisle, the visiting poet with the third grade: in this dying school, in this dying town, we are writing about our lives. I'm hungry, looking forward to the lefse I bought for lunch at the Norwegian Food Festival sponsored by the Senior Citizen Center, one of the few busy places on Main Street. That and the empty post office, the café, the grocery. The other buildings are empty.

The teacher's writing too. Yesterday she told me that when I asked the kids to make silence and the room was suddenly quiet, she thought of her mother. "She's been dead for years," she said, adding almost apologetically, "I don't know why I thought of her. But then I just had to write." She told me about the smells, how this time of year the lingering scent of pickling spices in the house would gradually give way to cinnamon, peppermint, cloves, the smells of Christmas baking. . . .

The sunsets here have been extraordinary, blazing up like distant fire in the window of the old boarding house where the school has put me. Last night I was reading when the light changed: I looked up and gasped at the intensity of color, a slash of gold and scarlet on the long scribble of horizon.

I was reading one of the old ones who said, "One who keeps death before his eyes conquers despair." The little girl calls me, holding up her paper for me to read:

> When my third snail died, I said,
> 'I'm through with snails.'
> But I didn't mean it.

MAKING SILENCE

Over the years when I worked as an artist in elementary schools, I devised an exercise for the children regarding noise and silence. I'll make a deal with you, I said, first you get to make noise, and then you'll make silence....

What interests me most about my experiment is the way in which making silence liberated the imagination of so many children. Very few wrote with any originality about making noise. Most of their images were clichés, such as "we sound like a herd of elephants." But silence was another matter; here, their images often had a depth and maturity that was unlike anything else they wrote. One boy came up with an image of strength as being "as slow and silent as a tree," another wrote that "silence is me sleeping waiting to wake up." "Silence is a tree spreading its branches in the sun." In a parochial school one third grader's poem turned into a prayer: "Silence is spiders spinning their webs, it's like a silkworm making its silk. Lord help me to know when to be silent." And in a tiny town of western North Dakota a little girl offered a gem of spiritual wisdom that I find myself returning to when my life becomes too noisy and distractions overwhelm me: "Silence reminds me to take my soul with me wherever I go."

FROM *AMAZING GRACE*

FEASTING WITH THE
BENEDICTINE SISTERS

God, the laughter. I hear it as soon as I enter the dorm. Women are cooking, chopping vegetables, washing paring knives and serving spoons, transforming the homely little communal kitchen into a place of feast. My offerings, homemade bread and a magnum of champagne, are accepted with joyful exclamation. One of the grad students pokes his head in the door and says, "My, Sister Julie, you're looking sultry tonight." Julie, a high spirited and pretty young woman, replies with mock confusion, "Sultry? Why? Is my face broken out?" as she good-naturedly shoos the young man out.

At dinner, discussion turns to something I've noticed the Benedictines seldom talk about, that is, the angelic nature of their calling. Their Liturgy of the Hours is, at root, a symbolic act, an emulation of and a joining with the choirs in heaven who sing the praise of God unceasingly. To most people even to think of such things seems foolish. . . .

But one of the Australian sisters insists that Benedictines be willing to admit the angelic charism. "The best thing we can do," she says, "is to praise." I tell the story of a monk I know who dreamed one night that armed men in uniform had entered the abbey church, and when he tried to stop them from approaching the altar, they shot him. As he lay by the altar, he saw Christ before him. "Am I dead?" the monk asked him, and Christ nodded and answered, gravely, "Yes." "Well, what do I do now?" the monk inquired, and Christ shrugged and said, "I guess you should go back to choir."

The laughter comes as blessing: women, youthful and aged, with nubile limbs and thick, unsteady ankles, graceful, busy hands and gnarled fingers slowed by arthritis, making a joyful noise.

FROM *THE CLOISTER WALK*

NITA PENFOLD

NEW YORK, 1950–

A writer who has published over three hundred poems, whose work has appeared in some twenty anthologies, Nita (Bonnie) Penfold offers workshops on the topic "Writing from the Soul." She is director of religious education at the First Parish Church in Milton, Massachusetts (Unitarian Universalist), and is a candidate for a doctor of ministry degree at the University of Creation Spirituality. Pudding House Press published her chapbook The Woman with the Wild-Grown Hair, *and will be publishing her next chapbook,* Mile-High Blue Sky Pie, *in 2002. (A chapbook is a relatively small collection of poems printed in a limited number.) Nita is the mother of two young daughters.*

THE WOMAN WITH THE WILD-GROWN HAIR
RELAXES AFTER ANOTHER LONG DAY

After she drives her younger daughter to school, struggling
to get the wheelchair out without running over her foot and
the car stalls for the fifth time as she leaves because of
the cracked distributor cap;

after she meets the new cashier's stare over her food stamps
at the Star Market going to buy soda crackers and soup and
gingerale for another daughter who is home sick after
throwing up her entire dinner in the middle of the night;

after she exchanges babysitting for their rent in the main house
downstairs with the sweet fat/baby and blonde sister who owns
nine Little Ponies in their pink castle and a Pig-faced Doll
with its very own brass bed;

after she lugs out the deep steel pot to catch the rain dripping
from the skylight and kills the horde of fungus/gnats in the
bathroom with their thin wings splayed against the white walls
like Christmas miniatures of squashed angels;

after she spends an hour with the child psychologist explaining
why she thinks her marriage failed and how it has affected
the children's lives and she wonders aloud if she can take
much more of this and still be able to write poems;

after the dishes, the laundry, the second daughter's throwing up,
after trying to scrub the permanent ring out of the clawfoot tub
    and fixing the
cabinet door so it won't scrape the wall when
it opens;

after all of this, she soaks in bubbled bathwater and thinks of
Job's unnamed wife, caught between a righteous husband and his
war between God and Satan—how that woman must have tried to

smother the heavenly fire with her mantle as it destroyed their
sheep and servants, and—fiercely—dug at the stones that killed
her ten children when the great wind breathed from the wilderness
to topple their home, how she tended Job's sores, washing him
    gently
with cool water, soothing the flame of Satan's tongue,
comforting him, and how she stood alone while he debated his
faith with God, proved himself again worthy to give his wife
another ten children to raise.

As she rubs her tight thighs with a worn washcloth, she thinks
about the faith of women creating foundations out of their flesh,
becoming the anonymous survivors of daily battles,
that never seem to win the war.

KAREN MCCARTHY BROWN

NEW YORK, CONTEMPORARY

In an impressive book called Mama Lola: A Vodou Priestess in Brooklyn, *religion scholar Karen McCarthy Brown tells the story of a remarkable Haitian woman who has emerged as an important spiritual and moral leader among Haitian immigrants in New York City. A priestess in the Vodou religion as well as a healer with immense gifts for restoring well-being to the ill and suffering, Mama Lola (whose name is Marie Thérèse Alourdes Macena Margaux Kowalski) was born in Haiti to descendants of African slaves who also served the community as Vodou priests. After a difficult marriage and a brief career as a singer, she immigrated to the United States in her twenties. In New York she discovered her true vocation as a healer and returned to Haiti to undergo initiation in the religion of her childhood. Today her practice, like that of aboriginal healers throughout the world, blends the arts of medicine, psychotherapy, and social work with deeply held religious beliefs. Widely respected both for her healing and priestly skills and for her refusal to take adequate pay for her work, she has been called to many places in the United States, Canada, the Caribbean, and Central America to work cures where others have failed. Her prayers and rituals combine Haiti's African, Creole, and Roman Catholic traditions.*

About six times a year, on Roman Catholic saints' days, Mama Lola pre-
sides over religious rituals in the basement of her Brooklyn home, where
altars said to be stunning are covered with burning candles; vials of roots
and herbs; stones resting in oil; bottles of perfume, syrup, and rum; perhaps
a crucifix or picture of a Catholic saint or an image of Ezili, as Haitians
name the Vodou Spirit of Love: Mary the mother of Jesus. During the
sacred rite, participants pray and sing until Mama Lola falls into a trance
state, possessed by an ancestral spirit who intermingles with the community,
healing physical and moral problems, conflicts, and miscommunications,
softening loss and suffering, strengthening and knitting people into a faith
community.

Karen McCarthy Brown emphasizes that "there is no Vodou ritual,
small or large, individual or communal, which is not a healing rite." She
attributes unfair negative stereotypes surrounding the Vodou religion to the
humanness of the spirits who behave and misbehave like Greek and Roman
gods, gods in many other cultures, and like women and men. Karen empha-
sizes the injustice of such stereotypes and treats Mama Lola's faith with the
respect it deserves. She has undergone Vodou initiation herself.

~ɔ

FROM MAMA LOLA: A VODOU PRIESTESS
IN BROOKLYN

[In a private session with Mama Lola, Karen Brown seeks the
counsel of the Vodou spirit Papa Ogou. Karen calls the priestess
"Alourdes":]

She anchored the small white candle on the edge of her work
table and settled herself on a low stool next to the table. I was
asked to reach into Ogou's altar cabinet for a bottle of rum. She
poured a dollop or two of the amber liquid onto a red metal plate
and then dropped matches on the thin film of rum until it ignited.
Alourdes sat staring into the fire while tipping the plate from side
to side to keep the blue flames dancing across its surface.... Nar-
rowing her eyes, Alourdes sought the focused state of mind that
creates a portal through which ordinary consciousness slips away.

For a *manbo* [priestess] as accomplished as Alourdes, the struggle that marks the onset of trance is usually pro forma.... When Alourdes does not have the energy and support of a crowd to push her along, this process can be slower, as it was on this night.

As she concentrated on the slippery blue flame, a light tremor passed through her body from time to time, and she squeezed her eyes shut. Once, she jerked her left hand away from her forehead and shook it vigorously as if it had gone numb. But like a restless sleeper, Alourdes seemed to wake with a start each time she dipped below the surface of the waters of unconsciousness. At one point, her body shook so much I was sure the spirit had come. But the crisis passed.

Alourdes sighed and reached for the rum bottle to refuel her small fire. Again, there was intense concentration, and this time it worked. Barely perceptible tremors became intense shaking, and then the energy shot out her arms and legs, making them do a stiff, staccato dance in the air. When the shaking stopped, Alourdes's body was drawn up straight, and keen black eyes were staring at me with interest. Papa Ogou had arrived.

AMY TAN
CALIFORNIA, 1952–

The best-selling author of The Kitchen God's Wife *and* The Joy Luck Club, *which was made into a popular movie, Amy Tan was born in Oakland, California, and grew up in the San Francisco Bay Area. She completed high school in Montreux, Switzerland, and received a master's degree in linguistics from San Jose State University in California. Among her other books are* The Hundred Secret Senses *and such children's books as* The Moon Lady *and* The Chinese Siamese Cat.

The following scene from The Joy Luck Club *suggests the miraculous birth of spirit in the heart of a fifteen-year-old girl virtually enslaved to her mother-in-law and husband. The road to independence opens as she begins to think for herself.*

FROM THE JOY LUCK CLUB

"Teach her to wash rice properly so that the water runs clear. Her husband cannot eat muddy rice," she'd say to a cook servant.

Another time, she told a servant to show me how to clean a chamber pot: "Make her put her own nose to the barrel to make sure it's clean." That was how I learned to be an obedient wife. I learned to cook so well that I could smell if the meat stuffing was too salty before I even tasted it. I could sew such small stitches it looked as if the embroidery had been painted on. And even Huang Taitai complained in a pretend manner that she could scarcely throw a dirty blouse on the floor before it was cleaned and on her back once again, causing her to wear the same clothes every day.

After a while, I hurt so much I didn't feel any difference. What was happier than seeing everybody gobble down the shiny mushrooms and bamboo shoots I had helped to prepare that day? What was more satisfying than having Huang Taitai nod and pat my head when I had finished combing her hair one hundred strokes? How much happier could I be after seeing Tyan-yu [her husband] eat a whole bowl of noodles without once complaining about its taste or my looks? It's like those ladies you see on American TV these days, the ones who are so happy they have washed out a stain so the clothes look better than new.

Can you see how the Huangs almost washed their thinking into my skin? I came to think of Tyan-yu as a god, someone whose opinions were worth much more than my own life. I came to think of Huang Taitai as my real mother, someone I wanted to please, someone I should follow and obey without question.

FRAN PEAVEY
UNITED STATES, CONTEMPORARY

A writer and environmental activist, Fran Peavey is perhaps best known for undertaking the monumental task of cleaning up the Ganges River in India and for her efforts to help women in such war-ravaged areas as Bosnia and Croatia. She traveled to Zagreb to bring messages of caring and support for women victims of war in the former Yugoslavia.

She is the author of Heart Politics, By Life's Grace: Musings on the Essence of Social Change, *and* A Shallow Pool of Tears.

~⁹

THE CHIMPANZEE AT STANFORD

One day I was walking through the Stanford University campus with a friend when I saw a crowd of people with cameras and video equipment on a little hillside. They were clustered around a pair of chimpanzees—a male running loose and a female on a chain about twenty-five feet long. It turned out the male was from Marine World and the female was being studied for something or other at Stanford. The spectators were scientists and publicity people trying to get them to mate.

The male was eager. He grunted and grabbed the female's chain and tugged. She whimpered and backed away. He pulled again. She pulled back. Watching the chimps' faces, I began to feel sympathy for the female.

Suddenly the female chimp yanked her chain out of the male's grasp. To my amazement, she walked through the crowd, straight over to me, and took my hand. Then she led me across the circle to the only other two women in the crowd, and she joined hands with one of them. The three of us stood together in a circle. I remember the feeling of that rough palm against mine. The little chimp had recognized us and reached out across all the years of evolution to form her own support group.

FROM *HEART POLITICS*

DOMINIQUE MAZEAUD
UNITED STATES, CONTEMPORARY

Dominique Mazeaud, an artist who lives in Santa Fe, brought attention to the plight of polluted, potentially dying rivers through a unique "art project" that she undertook in the 1980s. The project, more like a sacred ritual

than a work of art meant to hang on a museum wall, entailed the consecra-
tion of a designated day each month to the removal of debris from the Rio
Grande. Sometimes accompanied by one or two friends, Dominique would
go to the river with big black plastic garbage bags donated by the local gov-
ernment and spend the next twelve to fourteen hours removing cans, spoiled
food, discarded clothing, even money from the dying river. She regarded the
long day's work as a prayer, and she filled journals with reflections and
poems that she called "riveries."

~ ⁹

THE GREAT CLEANSING OF
THE RIO GRANDE

Nov. 19, 1987
Yes, I see what I am doing is a way of praying.

> Picking up a can
> From the river
> And then another
> On and on
> It's like a devotee
> Doing countless rosaries.

Nov. 24
Visitors stop by my door and look down at a group of objects laid
down on a strip of fabric. "What is this?" they ask. "These are some
of the treasures I have collected from the river." "You found this little girl's shoes?" "Yes," I reply, "even the two $5 bills.". . .

Dec. 2
Why in all religions is water such a sacred symbol? How much
longer is it going to take us to see the trouble of our waters? How
many more dead fish floating on the Rhine River . . . ? How many
kinds of toxic waste dumpings? When are we going to turn our
malady of separateness around? Most of the glass we find is broken, but even so, the two of us picked up 103 lbs. in the 14 hours of
work we put in that day.

How many times did I wonder about the persons who hurl the beer bottles down the rocks. . . .

March 1988

> I can't get away from you river,
> In the middle of the night
> I feel you on my back
> In my throat, in my heart. . . .

We decide to clean the dumping area. . . . It's soiled rabbit litters, crates filled with rotting fruit scattered all over, and more. Some of it is encrusted in the ice, some of it has been burnt. As soon as we start stirring, the offensive smell of the decaying fruit hits us and the ashes soil the water. . . . [W]hat a mess, but we get to it "faces down," so to speak.

July 14

I went to the block where, back in November, I not only saw the suffering of the river but the death of the river. Just as I could no longer walk on trashed riverbanks without doing something about it, I could no longer be there without transposing my witnessing into some form that people could share. That day I started my "riveries."

July 20

All alone in the river, I pray and pick up, pick up and pray.

TIRZAH FIRESTONE
UNITED STATES, 1954–

Tirzah Firestone grew up in a middle-class Orthodox Jewish family, where her parents raised her and her five siblings "with an iron hand, not only in religious doctrine" but in their rigid and harsh treatment of their children. Tirzah rebelled against what she knew of Jewish tradition, robbed of the inherent joy and goodness to be found there. After an adventurous and sometimes dangerous journey through Eastern religion, seventies-style hippie culture, healing practices, Jungian analysis, and several lovers, she married a Christian minister in an interfaith ceremony and found personal happiness. Still on a spiritual quest, she met Rabbi Zalman Schacter-Shalomi, a Jewish Renewal teacher and in that return to her roots found a spiritual home. As a result of her studies with Reb Zalman, she courageously made the decision, in the face of strong opposition from some religious leaders, to become ordained as a rabbi in Boulder, Colorado, where she now teaches, lectures, counsels, and provides spiritual leadership in her congregation. She is the author of a 1998 book, With Roots in Heaven.

~～

FROM WITH ROOTS IN HEAVEN

I believe that this is what God most wants of us: to discover and offer our true selves. According to the teachings of our Chasidic masters, each of us has a portion of God implanted within us as our truest nature. But this *chelek Eloha mima'al*—our divine portion—requires nurturing and development. In a very real sense, we are duty-bound to become who we were meant to be in this world, so that we can offer our unique gifts back to the world.

Like a dream that builds like a tide and forces itself over the threshold of our consciousness, the call arrives one day to each of us, if we are listening. It rushes to us from the Self in a completely unfiltered manner, delivering its message without bowing to our personalities. When we hear this voice, we know it. It vibrates with the other world, setting our bowels to water or our heads into a fever. For a split second, we are able to see with all of our soul's clarity why we are here and where we must go in this lifetime. Thank God for such moments!

There is a striking passage from the Talmud: *"Eyn makom panui l'lo Shechinah"*: "Wherever there is an empty space, there the presence of God is found."

A teaching popped into my mind which a Chasidic master had taught in relation to breaking the middle *matzoh*, the unleavened ritual bread at the Passover seder: *There is no whole heart but a broken heart.* If your own suffering does not serve to unite you with the suffering of others, if your own imprisonment does not join you with others in prison, if you in your smallness remain alone, then your pain will have been for naught.

GURUMAYI CHIDVILASANANDA
INDIA, 1955–

One of the few women spiritual leaders whose teaching has reached around the world, a woman of riveting speech and commanding presence whose every word conveys an authority and depth born of lifelong spiritual practice and discipline, Gurumayi Chidvilasananda virtually grew up in the ashram of Swami Muktananda in Ganeshpuri, India, where she received a rigorous training in meditation practices and a broad education in the theology and spirituality of Kashmir Saivism. Recognizing her mystical and intellectual gifts, her strength of will and potential for leadership when she was still a child (named Malti), Swami Muktananda personally oversaw her training and deemed her ready for initiation at the age of only fourteen. That same year, 1969, he said of her, "That girl Malti is a blazing fire. One day she will light up the entire world."

In 1975, she began to serve as Muktananda's translator for English-speaking audiences on his world tours. One evening he surprised her by suddenly announcing to the audience that she would give the talk. She immediately stood up and said, "He wants me to speak. Yet what's the use of lighting a lamp when the sun is shining? What's the use of offering a handful of water to the ocean?" She then extemporized a powerful talk on the Siva Sutras, (a foundational text in Kashmir Saivism) that surprised many and thrilled everyone, revealing powers of intellect, delivery, passion, and leadership.

In 1982, after some twenty years of training and testing according to the East's traditional, often painful ways of cutting through the ego to release God-consciousness, she was initiated as a swami, receiving the name of Chidvilasananda, and a few months later was consecrated successor to Muktananda (who passed away in October 1983). Today Gurumayi guides ashrams in India, the Middle East, Australia, Europe, and the Americas, inspiring people of all ages to meditate, to participate in all-day chants, to read and study, to practice mantra repetition, hatha yoga, and other spiritual disciplines. Among her books are Courage and Contentment, Kindle My Heart, and the Yoga of Discipline. A superb book on her movement is titled Meditation Revolution: A History and Theology of the Siddha Yoga Lineage.

~

WAKE UP!

[R]ecognize that you have the courage within you to fulfill the purpose of your birth. Summon forth the power of your inner courage and live the life of your dreams. Do you step lightly upon the earth or heavily? On the whole, are the things that come before you full of smiles or frowns? What about your possessions? Do they bring you happiness or unhappiness? Are the people in your life helping you to make greater progress or inhibiting your growth? How much of that is up to you? More than you think! Whether you feel you are winning or losing ultimately depends on the way you approach things and the way you let them approach you.

Courage is not just a response to crisis; it is not just a sudden act of bravery in a fire or war. And contentment is not merely the sense of satisfaction that comes after you get everything you want. Whatever happens in your life is for your own upliftment. Fragrant, delicious fruit is hidden within every occurrence of every kind. Have the courage to find the best outcome in every situation. Wake up to your inner courage and become steeped in divine contentment.

Whatever the adventures or challenges of life may be, you are the one who has the power to decide how you want to look at things, which way you want to turn your head. Even the best news in the world can bring you down if you insist on it. Your own being in its totality approves or disapproves of your existence on this planet. You hold the reins. You have a choice.

Courage is such a simple word, and yet at the same time it is multifaceted. It holds many other great qualities within itself. Strength, generosity, kindness, hope, love, learning, acceptance of life, and gratitude—these are all a part of courage.

True courage must stem from the depth of your being. It is yours. Courage is the very membrane that shields your heart. Courage is what fends off negativity and transforms adversity into growth. Its undaunted power can pierce through the distracting pull of the senses and make a miracle happen. In fact, courage attracts miracles. Truly, a life of courage is filled with miracles.

Is courage always easy to feel? Easy to spot? Not really. Sometimes courage is invisible. Yet courage is an inherent part of you; it is natural to you. It is really you—you are courage. Courage is you. However, just to wake up to the presence of courage inside you takes tremendous courage. It's not like waking up after a nap or a good night's sleep. Waking up to your own courage is actually a matter of waking up to the light of the Truth, to the light of supreme Consciousness within you. An awakening like that demands your firm determination and the touch of grace. . . .

Even when you just repeat these words to yourself, "Have courage," you dive into the ocean of your own inner Self and emerge as a new being, dazzling with light. To express the dauntless spirit of inner courage takes a whole new language, and it is good to see this quality in a new light. With this new language and new vision, allow every moment of your life to pulsate with courage and contentment. . . .

Courage is not about breaking the rules to prove to others that you can do exactly what you want. It is not about inviting suffering into your life either, just so everyone can see your unflinching devotion to God. Having courage is not a question of accepting everything that happens passively. To have courage does not mean shrugging your shoulders or sighing, "What can I do? It's my karma."

On the contrary, having courage means engaging in every single situation as a blessing from God, as a loving gesture of nature. Courage means rising to meet the demands of each moment with total delight, knowing you are equal to it. Courage means having faith that within you is an innate force whose essence is never depleted by external events. Live your life courageously, dharmically, knowing that whatever you are faced with is not stronger than you are. You are equal to each other. Your problem is not greater than you are, nor is it smaller. This approach is a dharmic way of living. This is courage. You look at your problem as your equal. And therefore, you can rise to the demands of each moment. With great delight you are able to face and accept whatever comes your way.

Everywhere you look, throughout the history of the world, you find wonderful, heartrending stories about courage. You come across stupendous tales and incredible anecdotes. They fill you with the desire to live courageously. They "en-courage" you. What's more, the same sorts of events that are written in those tales are also taking place right now. At this very moment there are people who are revealing their vast inner reserves of courage. They are saving the world in both large and small ways. Their benevolent thoughts are full of the light of courage, and this makes their resolutions firm. They have become beacons of courage for others. Right now, all this is happening.

Recognize your inner courage. You have it. You may already be a living hymn to courage. And this is as it should be. The infinite light of the Truth must definitely be translated into everyday life.

ADRIANA DIAZ
CALIFORNIA, 1955–

An educator, artist, writer, justice worker, and professional coach, Adriana Diaz is the author of a celebrated book on creativity that has been featured for ten years in museum stores across the country: Freeing the Creative Spirit: Drawing on the Power of Art to Release the Magic and Wisdom Within. *The recipient of a masters degree in spirituality, she teaches courses in the Bay Area on painting as a sacred art and on related topics, and she works as a coach whose guidance is much sought in both the United States and Argentina. Adriana is also a prize-winning tango dancer who was recently awarded a trip to Buenos Aires for taking first place in a dance competition. Her essay "Tantric Tango" portrays dancing as a mystical art that can bring partners into union with each other and with God.*

TANTRIC TANGO

Heat rises from the ball of my foot caressing the floor through a thin leather sole. It moves up my legs and into the first, then second chakras in ascending pleasure. A sheer veil of perspiration breaks across my skin as the pulse of my partner encircles me and we begin.

You think, perhaps, that I will continue from there to guide you through every steamy inch of an ecstatic, and certainly mystical, Tantric sexual encounter. But that passage is not about sex. It is, rather, the account of the beginning of the most erotically mystical experience I've ever had... dancing tango in Buenos Aires, Argentina, in a place appropriately named La Ideal.

I had been studying the dance, the discipline, culture, and spirit of Argentine Tango for six years when a partner took me onto the dance floor and taught me what none of the others had: the mystical dimension of Divine Eros present in the tango experience.

Tango demands commitment and perseverance. I learned quickly that spiritual practice and meditation are excellent training grounds for tango studies, as the best tango students are those who are willing to check their ego at the studio door. Maintaining a Beginner's Mind attitude is essential, and an alert, responsive, but relaxed awareness must be practiced.

After some years of this study, after one has learned to master *caminada, ocho, mordida, barrida, corte,* and *quebradas,* the tango practice opens a door to a completely unexpected experience: the spiritually ecstatic state. What begins as a dance becomes The Dance. Tango becomes a study of the seven chakras from the inside out, all pulsating with Divine energy. It teaches all there is to know about Yin and Yang. It is, as in Herman Hesse's *Siddhartha,* the full metaphor: the river, the boat, *and* the boatman.

The world gossips about tango with words like "sexy," "steamy," or "torrid," but those who dedicate themselves to it will tell you that it can be one of the deepest, most spiritually compelling experiences in life. The difficulty is, that state can only be reached occasionally, and with the "right" partner, and we never can know who that partner will be. Amazingly, it is seldom one's soul mate or spouse: It is more likely to be a stranger. Tango removes us from everything except the body and soul in which we live. It is the beating heart, the throbbing pulse. One meets the Divine presence within one's partner, and hand in hand, heart to heart, the two feel the pulse of life as a thrilling gift. It is a sacred profane experience that many people achieve through sex. But with tango, the ecstasy rises in a three-and-a-half-minute wave. The music ends, the dancers return to their seats, to their significant others, and to the sacred memory cherished in the body.

Wrapping me in a humid embrace, he sweeps me across the floor like an ocean wave. I am buoyant yet guided by his lead. Joyfully, I go where he places me as, step by complex step, we paint our tango across the marble floor until the music brings us to a stop.

Waiting for the next tango to begin, he does not release me, and I feel our hearts beat in my chest and the rhythm of our coupled pulse continue like that of a single dancer. Slowly I open my eyes to see the throbbing in his throat, and I realize that this is not his pulse nor mine, but the rhythmic beating of Divinity that dances through the universe.

I am reminded of the words of Thomas Merton: Art allows us to find ourselves and lose ourselves simultaneously. If I didn't know better I would swear that Merton had learned that from dancing tango at La Ideal.

LOUISE ERDRICH
NORTH DAKOTA, 1955–

Louise Erdrich is a mixed blood who is enrolled in the Turtle Mountain Band of Ojibwe, a consummate wordsmith, a writer's writer, a brilliant and passionate woman who has won many awards for her novels and short fiction. She received the National Book Critics' Circle Award for her novel Love Medicine *and is the author of children's stories, poetry, six other novels, and a memoir of early motherhood,* The Blue Jay's Dance.

Her just-published book, The Last Report on the Miracles at Little No Horse, *belongs to a series of novels set on the same reservation that has generated such a complex genealogy of characters that the lineage is now diagrammed on the inside cover of the book. Her short fiction was selected for the O. Henry and Best American collections and has also won the National Magazine Award. Louise Erdrich lives in Minnesota with her children, who help her run a small bookstore, the Birchbark. Her mother was her consultant in Catholicism during the writing of* The Last Report of the Miracles at Little No Horse. *Her grandfather was tribal chair of the Turtle Mountain Band of the Ojibwe.*

~ ⌒

FROM THE LAST REPORT ON
THE MIRACLES AT LITTLE NO HORSE

If you know about the buffalo hunts, you perhaps know that the one I describe, now many generations past, was one of the last. Directly after that hunt, in fact, before which Father LaCombe made a great act of contrition and the whirlwind destruction, lasting twenty minutes, left twelve hundred animals dead, the rest of the herd did not bolt away but behaved in a chilling fashion.

As many witnesses told it, the surviving buffalo milled at the outskirts of the carnage, not grazing but watching with an insane intensity, as one by one, swiftly and painstakingly, each carcass was dismantled. Even through the night, the buffalo stayed, and were seen by the uneasy hunters and their families the next dawn to have remained standing quietly as though mourning their young and their dead, all their relatives that lay before them more or less unjointed, detongued, legless, headless, skinned. At noon the flies descended. The buzzing was horrendous. The sky went black. It was then at the sun's zenith, the light shredded by scarves of moving black insects, that the buffalo began to make a sound.

It was a sound never heard before; no buffalo had ever made this sound. No one knew what the sound meant, except that one old toughened hunter sucked his breath in when he heard it, and as the sound increased he attempted not to cry out. Tears ran over his cheeks and down his throat, anyway, wetting his shoulders, for the sound gathered power until everyone was lost in the immensity. That sound was heard once and never to be heard again, that

sound made the body ache, the mind pinch shut. An unmistakable
and violent grief, it was as though the earth was sobbing.

NANCY DIAMANTE BONAZZOLI
MASSACHUSETTS, 1957–

*Nancy Bonazzoli is a mystical poet in the tradition of Mirabai who
reached intimacy with the Divine Beloved through ordeal and daily deep
prayer and meditation. Her spiritual practice has enabled her to live graciously with prolonged and serious illness.*

LYING WITH THE BELOVED

There is no need
to knock, my love.
I have left the door open.
A small blue candle
stands on the oiled bench,
its flame erect,
and waiting
to dance Your shadow
throughout
my living
room.

I have perfumed the air
with incense,
and whispered the sweet nothings
whose passion once carved
curled letters
in the polished banister,
rooted at the stairway
of my Becoming.

I lie here naked,
hungry for the sound
of Your footsteps
in my hall.
My flushed skin
shimmering
with the heat.

The mind
can be
a fickle thing
How precious my remembrance
of You
inside me.

How often I forget.

MARJORIE CROCOMBE

COOK ISLANDS, CONTEMPORARY

Marjorie Crocombe, a writer virtually unknown in the West, has a master's degree in Pacific history and works at the University of the South Pacific as coordinator of its extension program. She comes from the Cook Islands, an independent state formerly part of Oceania (Polynesia, Micronesia, and Melanesia). While her story "The Healer" is fictional, it accurately describes how aboriginal healers often cure the incurable through their wisdom, faith, and love.

~

FROM "THE HEALER"

Mata was known as the "ghost-maker," for she had power to call on her own special spirit, Ka'u Mango, or Ka'u the Shark. Because of this she was both feared and respected, especially by children.

Mata, it seems, knew everything that went on in the spirit world, but of course she kept up to date on what went on in the real world too. Keeping abreast of gossip and scandal was part of her stock in trade, and the spiritual answers usually reflected the material realities.

The screeching of wagon wheels on the sandy road and the whoa-ing of the driver soon brought Piri [Mata's husband] back to the present. "That coming here?" Mata asked. "Oi—oi," she was answered from outside, as if the visitors had heard her question. . . .

[Outside] a young boy was lying on a pillow in a wagon. "Take him into the other house," Mata called to Piri. "I'll come in after them." Mata picked up the knife and finished prising the chestnuts out of their shells, carefully placing them on a tin plate. . . .

Inside the separate sleeping house, the leader of the party was telling Piri why they had come. . . . "My grandson here we took him to hospital. The doctor, a European, he tap him here; he tap him there; he listen to his chest and took a picture—aue—where was it, Mere?" She turned to her daughter [who tried] to pick up the thread. "Ae—ae—a picture of the chest, but he find nothing. They give us a big bottle of white medicine, but he drank it all up quick, nothing happen to him. Still the boy not well. The Maori doctor friend he say—'Ae, try our own medicine at the ta'unga. Maybe she can fix him.'"

Mata said nothing for a while. Nor did she examine the patient. She seemed to withdraw into herself and her eyes became glazed. Her body trembled and her mouth twitched as she fell into a trance. At last she asked Mere: "Where is the boy's father?"

"Dead."

"Where?"

"Makatea island, digging phosphate."

"He write to you? He send you things?"

"Yes, every ship from there bring something."

"You write back?"

There was silence. The mother wept, blowing her nose. The spluttering of the candlenut lamp cast eerie shadows in the house and the smell of the nut was very strong. The sick boy wanted so much to cough, but he was too scared to break the silence. Mata stared towards the entrance of the house as if she was willing something to enter. Piri, the two women and the boy looked towards the door, wondering. It was getting late now. Then the silence was broken by a distant voice that immediately stopped the boy's weeping. The voice came from the direction of Mata.

'E Mere! Can you hear? You know who it is—don't you? Listen carefully to me. Don't waste time weeping. My sweat—I wasted it in the mines working—to earn money for the European house you wanted. I sent you the money—the plates— the glasses—the linen—and—and perfume—yet you lie to me—I didn't know you lie so much. My friend had a letter— from his wife. She say who you live with—that news made me angry. My gang was working that night—I fell from the top— top of the cliff. And I want—want my son—to—aaaah!

"Aue, aue," wept the mother of the sick child. "It's true! It's true what you say."

Mata did not move anymore. She sat as if in a deep sleep. Then her eyes twitched and slowly opened. Still no one spoke. When she was fully awake, she said: "I make some medicine for him to drink." Piri got up and went out to gather the stalk of the red sugar cane, a few leaves of a plant which grew by the creek, and some green guava leaves. Then Mata said, "I think your son has cried for his father—he wants to die like his father. He doesn't like his new father. Ask him at home if that is true. You and he can help each other sort out what to do. Then come again next week."

On the way home, the young boy, Tei, thought about Mata's words. Indeed he had cried for his father to come and take him away. For he hated to see the new man around the place who would not even help his mother in the tomato plot, who wouldn't even cut the grass around the place. All he seemed to do was to get drunk on the weekends and sleep off the effects of his three-day bout for the rest of the week. Once he had thrashed Tei for answering back, and that day Tei had decided to die like his father. It had been his secret until this day, but as Mata knew, it was a common "way out" among her people.

"Mamma," he whispered to his mother after everyone had gone to bed, "I did call Papa to come and get me. I wanted to die very much."

"Why?"

Tei told his mother the secret. As his mother held him in the dark, Tei felt for the first time that maybe he didn't want to die after all.

And Mere made up her mind to send away her lover.

SHARON LEBELL

CALIFORNIA, 1957–

Sharon Lebell is a writer, musician, and mother of four children living in northern California. She is married to the writer and editor John Loudon. Among her books are Naming Ourselves, Naming Our Children *and* A Manual for Living: Epictetus, A New Interpretation, *from which the selection that appears here is excerpted. Her brilliant rendering of Epictetus' masterpiece, which is as sacred to the West as the Dhammapada is to the East, brings the great philosopher and former slave vibrantly to life again, a little more grown-up and whole this time, with the gentle touch of a woman's wisdom added to his own.*

Her summary of his timeless "prescription for the good life" revolves around three central points: mastering one's desires, performing one's duties, and learning to think clearly about oneself and one's relationships in the context of humankind.

Sharon Lebell is working on a major new book on moral philosophy, tentatively called The Best Possible Life. *It is expected to appear in 2003.*

~)

CONDUCT YOURSELF WITH DIGNITY

No matter where you find yourself, comport yourself as if you were a distinguished person.

While the behavior of many people is dictated by what is going on around them, hold yourself to a higher standard.... [R]emain rooted in your own purposes and ideals.

FROM *A MANUAL FOR LIVING*

SELF-MASTERY IS THE TARGET THAT THE DIVINE WILL WISHES US TO AIM AT

Evil does not naturally dwell in the world, in events, or in people. Evil is a by-product of forgetfulness, laziness, or distraction: it arises when we lose sight of our true aim in life.

When we remember that our aim is spiritual progress, we return to striving to be our best selves. This is how happiness is won.

FROM *A MANUAL FOR LIVING*

TREASURE YOUR MIND, CHERISH YOUR REASON, HOLD TO YOUR PURPOSE

Don't surrender your mind.

If someone were to casually give your body away to any old passerby, you would naturally be furious.

Why then do you feel no shame in giving your precious mind over to any person who might wish to influence you? Think twice before you give up your own mind to someone who may revile you, leaving you confused and upset.

FROM *A MANUAL FOR LIVING*

EVA WONG

HONG KONG, CONTEMPORARY

Dr. Eva Wong is a Chinese philosopher, monastic, and teacher of Taoism, the ancient wisdom tradition practiced by her family in China. The predominant spiritual tradition of China, also called "the yin-yang school," Taoism originated in the seventh century B.C.E. with Lao Tzu, whose masterpiece, the Tao Te Ching, *has exercised enormous influence in the West since translations began appearing in the 1960s. In this same era, monks from Hong Kong brought Taoism and the Taoist arts—such as tai ji, qi gong, and Taoist chanting and dancing—to the United States. The* I Ching *is also Taoist in origin.*

Now living in Colorado, Eva Wong is a member of the Fung Loy Kok
Institute of Taoism in Denver, where she considers herself "a keeper of the
tradition." She has a doctorate and is the translator of Cultivating Stillness,
Seven Taoist Masters *and* Lieh-Tzu: A Taoist Guide to Practical Living.
The following is part of an interview taken from A Gathering of Cranes
by Solala Towler.

~)

TAOIST CHANT AND DANCE

My particular lineage views chanting as a *qi gong* practice, because
the sounds resonate within the body and enhance circulation. The
five notes of the songs of the chants also resonate with the five
internal organs. Also, on a more physical level, chanting actually
loosens up blockages, because there are major acupuncture points
in the area of the jaws. Also, the two meridians, the governing and
functioning meridians, meet at the palate, in the mouth. A lot of
the chanting is designed to connect these two meridians. Once we
get into a more advanced level of chanting it becomes a breathing
exercise, a form of *qi gong.* The fast and the slow pace coincide
with the hot and the slow fires, and this is really a way of transforming the internal....

[We chant] two basic categories of liturgies. Liturgies are sometimes encoded forms of instruction, like how to experience the
spiritual world: It describes the internal environment.... Another
kind of liturgy we do is purely sound. Mantra is probably the closest way you can describe it. That is where the Hindu influence
comes in. We have Sanskrit sounds that we chant and those are
also designed to vibrate inside the body and also facilitate the flow
of internal energy....

There are several forms of dancing. Many of the Taoist rituals
have footwork associated with them. They can be performed outdoors or indoors. In our big sacred festivals the participants in the
ceremony walk in a certain pattern that mimics the celestial movements of the stars, the sun, moon and so on. That is one form of
dancing. Another form of dancing is what we call using the dance
to induce a trance, so that the practitioner is taken to another

world. In other words the dance is a kind of shamanic journey to another realm to learn from the powers of that realm.

MARIA CRISTINA GONZALEZ
TEXAS, 1957–

A deeply spiritual intellectual who is also a poet and ritual leader, especially of rituals to the Divine Mother, Cristina Gonzalez comes from a family with two-hundred-year-old roots in Mexico. She is the first woman in the family to live alone and have no children, preferring to direct her maternal energies toward the healing of the world. Cristina spent two years on a Fulbright scholarship living and teaching in Mexico and today serves on the faculty of Arizona State University in the School of Communication, where she teaches cultural ethnography. The recipient of both doctor of ministry and doctor of philosophy degrees, she is also a member of the adjunct faculty at the University of Creation Spirituality in Oakland, California. Cristina is the author of many scholarly articles, poems, and performance pieces. In the mythology of her Aztec ancestors, the circumstances surrounding her birth under a full moon on the day of March 15 hold rich symbolic meaning and life guidance.

The following essay, a starkly beautiful celebration of ariditas, *dryness, provides a unique correction to the West's overemphasis on* viriditas, *greenness, as the enlivening power in nature and the soul.*

~✎

THE NURTURING OF
THE DESERT MOTHER: ARIDITAS

I come from a genetic and cultural history of people of the desert. My ancestors are Apache, Raramuri, Comanche, Mexican, Spanish, Sephardic and Basque. We are people of rough terrains, people who have stumbled on many a dusty road and managed to get up repeatedly, knowing the comfort of a beautiful desert night. It is uncanny to many in this society whose spirituality is heavily influenced by the mythology of the forested lands that I would find comfort in the dry, that heat would stir in my soul the sense of being at home.

The language of spirituality that we inherit from our European cultural ancestors tells us that the desert is something we want to avoid—that at best, it is the place for retreat, and never a place one would stay. This view of the desert imposes upon those of us who have grown and lived in the desert for many generations the sense that we must go elsewhere—that truly thriving spiritual lives are evidenced by verdant pastures and richly wooded forests. The desert is equated with a "test," and a "test" with perhaps not yet having earned the right to return to that eternally looming mythical *garden*.

I grew up calling trees simply "trees." I knew there were names for the trees, but there was no pragmatic purpose for those names in my general experience as a young child. The names of trees were poetic, the language of stories and romance—beacons of a garden paradise that was never anything like the land I considered home. On the other hand, I could tell you what was an ocotillo, a cholla, a lechuguilla, a nopal or a saguaro. But the literature of the divine I was given to study over a lifetime did not mention these friends of mine.

In my search for the divine feminine, the nurturing Mother, I looked for a mother who was voluptuous as the woods, who resonated with the Celtic myths, or who was humid and moist as the jungles of Africa. She did not look like me. I am a woman who has not given birth to a child. I am a "barren" woman, from a "barren" land. The language for my land and for my body implies there is no life. No Mother. Ahhhh, but it is not true.

The Mother of the desert does not come wearing garlands of leaves and flowers. No—she comes in the prickly red fruit of a cactus, in the fluorescent hues of desert flowers, surrounded by protective thorns and with petals resistant to our human desire to pick them. Her gifts are the wisdom that comes from moving slowly. It is foolish to move too rapidly in the desert. By day, rapid movement ensures overheating and possible death. By night, one can stumble into an unfriendly thorned bush or interrupt the evening outing of a rattlesnake or two. The ground is hard and rough in the desert. There are sharp thorns everywhere. And getting pricked reminds us of our thin skins.

Ariditas—that is what I call the spirit of this desert Mother. She gives to me by knowing my resilience, my inner fortitude and strength. She gives by making me aware of the fountains of water that live within my soul. I believe the words of the Jewish rabbi carpenter we call Jesus make a lot more sense if we remember he lived in the desert...and so did his mother Miriam. We desert folk understand the yearning of the deer for water—can appreciate small amounts of the Divine as evidence of the larger reality. We are externally people of scarce resources, because our resources are inside us, like the water in the tall saguaro cactus or the succulent prickly pear.

It is said that the Mexica (meh-*shee*-kah) people who are my ancestors, as a mestiza with grandparents from Mexico (and otherwise called *Aztec* by many), looked to the blood red fruit of the prickly pear as evidence of the divinity in a woman's blood. A woman gives life by providing fruit that is sweet and can comfort the parched soul. That is the gift of the barren mother, the spirit of *Ariditas*, the blessing of my beautiful life. *Ariditas* has taught me the wisdom of harsh experience, the ecstasy of small comforts like a slight shade provided by a passing cloud. *Ariditas* is the spirit of stillness that fills the dark night when millions of stars remind us that there is light. She teaches that night brings comfort to those who are weary of being scorched by the glaring light.

I am a woman of the desert, and I walk with many peoples of the wooded and watery lands. From them, I learn to honor abundance and *viriditas,* the greening. But my Mother nurtures me with a little bit of salt and a little bit of water. She pricks me as she feeds me and never lets me forget that I am alive by the grace of an all-providing Creator. When I love, I will require very little, but the *ariditas* Mother in me will save your life if you dare to be pricked a time or two in search of the fruit.

PAULA KANE ROBINSON ARAI
UNITED STATES, CONTEMPORARY

Born to a Japanese Buddhist mother and an American Christian father, Paula Arai found herself drawn to Buddhism and in 1987 she journeyed to Bodh Gaya in India to visit the place where the Buddha attained enlightenment.

There she met a Japanese nun, Kito Sensei, who seemed a true embodiment of Buddhist teachings and who introduced her to a moving book written by her abbess, On Becoming a Beautiful Person. *Touched deeply, Paula traveled to the Zen monastery for women in Nagoya, Japan, to live with the nuns and undergo for an extended period of time the rigorous training that a Zen novice receives. From the moment she set foot in Nagoya, she was told that nuns are highly respected in Japan. Even the taxi driver who took her to the monastery when she first arrived mentioned that "monastic women are among the finest people in Japan."*

Paula immediately began adhering to the nuns' surprisingly strict routine, rising at 4:00 A.M., sitting zazen (meditating) until 5:00, chanting till 6:00, cleaning the monastery until 7:30, then at last eating a meager breakfast. Then classes for four hours, a modest vegetarian lunch, three hours of work, more chanting, cleaning, and study, a small supper, and lights out at 9:00 P.M. This grueling daily schedule quickly taught her that a monastery is not the place to go for rest. "Even the mere sound of the footsteps of someone you currently are upset with," she confesses, "can raise your ire." At one point she conspired on the phone with a friend in the U.S. to help her quit the project and return home. Fortunately, the abbess thwarted the plan. Paula has a doctorate in Buddhist Studies from Harvard University.

～つ

TO BECOME LIKE A PLUM BLOSSOM:
(NOT AS EASY AS IT SOUNDS)

I became increasingly aware that I was not alone in feeling defeated and frustrated at not being able to do all the necessary actions. I ventured out into the hallway after lights out and discovered that this is the time senior teachers informally apply the healing balm of understanding that they themselves nurtured through their own experiences. One teacher in particular, Kito Shunko Sensei, was commonly sought out for the compassion of her wisdom. She would instruct novices to let their feelings flow like water, because if they let problems or tensions build up, they would clog or begin to sour. Frequently she drew images from nature to encourage the discouraged. I was not the only one who benefited from her stopping to point to the gnarled old gingko tree out back that had weathered countless seasons. She exclaimed at the sight of the tree aflame with brilliant yellow leaves and explained the natural development of strength over time, the need for each season.

... Kito Sensei [taught us to focus] on disciplined actions, rather than being consumed with self-indulgent thoughts and mindless actions.

LORI ARVISO ALVORD, MD
NEW MEXICO, 1959–

Lori Arviso is the first Navajo woman surgeon in history. Raised on a Navajo reservation in New Mexico, where grandmothers transmitted sacred stories and medicine men chanted and danced and prescribed natural remedies, she relearned as a surgeon what she had been taught in childhood: that illness means something is out of balance, and songs have healing power. At sixteen, Lori Arviso won a scholarship to Dartmouth College, where a thriving program in Native American studies helped her cope with loneliness and "white people's ways." She then trained for ten years in general surgery at Stanford Medical School, choosing instead of a lucrative career in a wealthy community to return to the reservation to help her own Navajo people. Observing that her relationship with her patients and even the degree of tension in the operating room affected the outcome of surgery, she devised ways to communicate respect for her patients, to maintain calmness in the operating room, and to foster Navajo wisdom as a complement to Western medicine. The following passage comes from her 1999 book, The Scalpel and the Silver Bear: The First Navajo Woman Surgeon Combines Western Medicine and Traditional Healing.

~2

A NAVAJO MEDICINE MAN BLESSES THE ICU

One day the ICU nurses called all the doctors at the hospital to the new ICU. When I got there, I saw why. One of the nurses' relatives was a medicine man, and the nurses had invited him to perform a blessing ceremony over the new ICU—a Navajo blessing, over a place where Navajos came when they were very, very sick. Many had died in that room, so the blessing was very important and would abolish any lingering *ch'iindis* [harmful spirits].

The *hataalii* [medicine man] stood next to his wife. They were both dressed in traditional clothing. Inside, patients lay in their beds in various states of consciousness, some of them glancing over, a tiny bit curious about what was about to happen. Some had suffered strokes. Others had cancer. Still others had illnesses associated with alcoholism like acute pancreatitis and kidney disease. In his hand the *hataalii* held a feather and a bowl of sacred water. He began to sing.

Amid the brand-new computers with their readouts of heart tracings, the oxygen equipment that fed patients vital gases, and the IV bags that dripped nourishment and medicine into patients' veins, among the new, special ICU beds and the most high-tech equipment in the whole hospital, the ancient man walked. He stepped over to the row of doctors and waved an eagle feather. Over each of our bodies, he twirled the feather and then sprinkled us with water. His voice rang out, rhythmic and atonal, that familiar sound of Navajo chant, a series of glottal stops and resonating notes that seemed to come from deep inside. I remembered this healing sound from the furthest reaches of my childhood. This ceremony medicine could make it possible for Navajo patients to feel safe being treated in the new ICU. I shut my eyes and let the rattle and hum of his voice enter my bones.

RIGOBERTA MENCHÚ

GUATEMALA, 1959–

A leader in the fight for human rights in Guatemala since her twenties, a recipient of the Nobel Peace Prize at the age of thirty-three, Rigoberta Menchú found her inspiration in the biblical story of Judith (see p. 21), a Jewish freedom fighter who like herself is a model for women of courageous political engagement and self-defense. Fortified by deep religious faith, she began her revolutionary work as a Catholic catechist and soon was risking her life in struggles with governmental and military enemies of indigenous communities in Guatemala. Even as she fought to preserve Indian culture and lives, even as wealthy tourists flocked to Guatemala's ancient pyramids and sunny resorts, in remote villages the military was committing genocide, practicing a scorched-earth policy, slaughtering men, women, children, animals, everything alive and growing, then burning down entire villages until nothing remained but blackened earth.

When Rigoberta was nineteen her parents and one of her brothers were murdered in separate atrocities, and many more family members and friends, like literally millions of other Guatemalans, are desaparecidos: *missing and presumed dead. Mass graves have been found with tens of thousands of* desaparecidos, *often too late to identify victims. The horror of their plight was publicized in a documentary made for educational television featuring the politically engaged singer Sting. Sting invited hundreds of grieving mothers of* desaparecidos *to appear with him, and over the course of the evening, he danced for a minute or two with each one of them as though he were her missing son given a chance to say goodbye.*

In 1983 Rigoberta told her story in I, Rigoberta Menchú, an Indian Woman in Guatemala. *Today she continues her fight by lecturing around the world on the ongoing misery of the poor in Guatemala and the rest of Latin America. When she addressed the World Parliament of Religions in Chicago in 1993, a small woman wearing the colorful blouse, skirt, and apron of her people, she told her story in a quiet, sad voice reminiscent of Elie Wiesel's when he talks about the Holocaust.*

In the following passage from her autobiography, Rigoberta tells about one of the sacred beliefs she has fought so hard to save. Handed down orally for many generations by her tribal ancestors, the simple belief contains power and implications for the entire lifetime of the people.

~⁀)

FROM I, RIGOBERTA MENCHÚ, AN INDIAN WOMAN IN GUATEMALA

Every baby is born with its own nahual. This is a spirit, like your shadow, that protects you and stays with you for your entire life. Your nahual is a representative of the earth, the animal kingdom, the sun, and the water. A child communicates with nature through its nahual. Your nahual is your double, and that is very important to our people. We create an image for our nahual that is usually an animal. Children are taught that that they must not kill an animal, because the animal's human double will be very angry. You must not ever take someone's nahual.... And if you harm a human, you also harm their nahual.

My people have a nahual for every day. So days are grouped as dogs, cats, bulls, birds and so on. If you were born on a Wednesday, you have a sheep for a nahual.... And every Wednesday is special for you. The parents know the day a baby is born how it will behave. A Tuesday baby grows up to be unpleasant, so Tuesday is not a good day to be born. That happens because the nahual for Tuesday is a bull, who is generally angry.

We have 10 sacred days in the year, like our ancestors. And these days have a nahual too. They can be dogs, cats, horses, bulls, or they can be wild animals like lions. There are trees selected by our ancestors many years ago that can be nahuals, too....

For my people, a day only has meaning if a baby is born on that day. If no baby is born on a certain Tuesday, that Tuesday is not important for anyone. There is no celebration. It often happens that we love our nahual before our parents tell us what it is. We love everything in the natural world, but maybe we are more attracted to one kind of animal than to all the other kinds. We grow up loving it. Then one day we are told that it is our nahual.

The animal kingdom and all the other kingdoms are related to human beings. A human is part of nature. There is not one world for animals and another world for humans. We are all part of one world where we live side by side. You can see this in our last names. Many of our last names are the names of animals, like Quej. That means horse.

We Indians must hide our identity. We do not tell our secrets. That is why people are prejudiced against us. We do not reveal much about ourselves. We have to conceal a lot to preserve our Indian culture and keep it from being taken away from us. So I have told you only vague things about the nahual. I cannot tell you what my nahual is because that is a secret.

ORIAH MOUNTAIN DREAMER

CANADA, 1960–

A spiritual teacher, poet, and writer, Oriah Mountain Dreamer is the author of the best-selling book The Invitation *and a new book titled* The Dance: Moving to the Rhythms of Your True Self. *She gives inspirational speeches and leads vibrant workshops, ceremonies, and retreats throughout the United States and Canada, distilling wisdom and power for daily life.*

~)

THE INVITATION

IT DOESN'T INTEREST ME WHAT YOU DO FOR A LIVING. I want to know what you ache for, and if you dare to dream of meeting your heart's longing.

It doesn't interest me how old you are. I want to know if you will risk looking like a fool for love, for your dream, for the adventure of being alive.

It doesn't interest me what planets are squaring your moon. I want to know if you have touched the center of your own sorrow, if you have been opened by life's betrayals or have become shriveled and closed from fear of further pain. I want to know if you can sit with pain, mine or your own, without moving to hide it or fade it or fix it.

I want to know if you can be with joy, mine or your own, if you can dance with wildness and let the ecstasy fill you to the tips of your fingers and toes without cautioning us to be careful, to be realistic, to remember the limitations of being human.

It doesn't interest me if the story you are telling me is true. I want to know if you can disappoint another to be true to yourself; if you can bear the accusation of betrayal and not betray your own soul; if you can be faithless and therefore trustworthy.

I want to know if you can see beauty, even when it's not pretty, every day, and if you can source your own life from its presence.

I want to know if you can live with failure, yours and mine, and still stand on the edge of the lake and shout to the silver of the full moon, "Yes!"

It doesn't interest me to know where you live or how much money you have. I want to know if you can get up, after the night of grief and despair, weary and bruised to the bone, and do what needs to be done to feed the children.

It doesn't interest me who you know or how you came to be here. I want to know if you will stand in the center of the fire with me and not shrink back.

It doesn't interest me where or what or with whom you have studied. I want to know what sustains you, from the inside, when all else falls away.

I want to know if you can be alone with yourself and if you truly like the company you keep in the empty moments.

JACKIE JOYNER-KERSEE
ILLINOIS, 1962–

In an interview with Time *magazine a few years ago, Jackie Joyner-Kersee remarked, "I don't think being an athlete is unfeminine. I think of it as a kind of grace." A living example of that grace, she has been called the World's Greatest Female Athlete, Superwoman, and the First Lady of Sports. Bruce Jenner, 1976 Olympic decathlon champion, called her "the best who's ever lived." She is an outstanding example of the feminine spirit prevailing over nearly insurmountable obstacles—poverty, racism, the early loss of her beloved mother, many athletic injuries, and life-threatening asthma—while earning six Olympic medals. Jackie has held the world record in the long jump and the heptathlon (the seven-event women's version of the decathlon), and she has met unfair accusations and criticism of her marriage to coach Bob Kersee with a devout spirituality of optimism, courage, and hope. Through personal appearances and her philanthropic foundation, Jackie continues to inspire and teach young athletes, women and men alike.*

BEING AN ATHLETE IS A KIND OF GRACE

For me, the joy of athletics has never resided in winning. Don't get me wrong, I love every one of those high school championships, gold medals and world records. But I derive as much happiness from the process as from the results. I don't mind losing as long as I see improvement or I feel I've done as well as I possibly could. If I lose, I just go back to the track and work some more.

There has been within me a driving force to be the best I could be, to run faster, jump higher, leap farther, for as long as I can remember. When I started long jumping, nothing was better than the feeling of flying farther and farther down the pit and watching my coach's tape measure get longer and longer as he measured my jumps.

As for what or who is truly beautiful and glamorous, I look beyond the superficial. I see beauty, elegance and grace in every female athlete. Selfishly speaking, I believe there's something especially beautiful about the ability to perform seven distinct athletic skills well. I consider heptathletes the Renaissance women of track and field. In my mind, ours is the most glamorous competition of all.

[At the 1996 Olympics in Atlanta, where Jackie Joyner-Kersee competed despite painful injuries, she won the bronze medal in the long jump.]

While the national anthem of Nigeria played in honor of the gold medalist, Chioma Ajunwa, I realized that the essential lesson of athletics has also been the essential lesson of my life. The strength for that sixth jump came from my assorted heartbreaks over the years—the loss of my mother, the disappointing performances, the unfounded accusations, the slights, the insults and the injuries. I'd collected all my pains and turned them into one mighty performance. And I had, indeed, been uplifted by the result. I showed the world that the little girl from East St. Louis had made something of herself. She was a woman, an athlete, with character, heart and courage.

TRACY COCHRAN

NEW YORK, CONTEMPORARY

A writer, journalist, and editor, Tracy Cochran is a contributing editor to Tricycle: The Buddhist Review *and to* New Age Journal *and is coauthor of* Transformations: Awakening to the Sacred in Ourselves. *Her work was selected for the anthology* The Best Spiritual Writing, 1999, *edited by Philip Zaleski, and she is a regular contributor to such publications as* Tricycle *and* Parabola. *She lives in New York with her husband and their precocious ten-year-old daughter, Alexandra.*

~୨

ALEXANDRA'S FIRST RETREAT

[The author has taken her daughter to a retreat led by the world-famous Buddhist monk, Thich Nhat Hanh.]

One day, during walking meditation, I began to get an inkling of what it is to find my true home. Every day the children, who left the dharma talk after the first twenty or thirty minutes, were invited to meet up with Thich Nhat Hahn and the grown-up students as they flowed out of the dharma hall to walk toward the lake. On one beautiful azure day in late October, those of us who were with the children watched Thich Nhat Hahn walking toward us from the dharma tent, leading his multitude: 1200 tall Americans dressed in bright Polartec colors following a small figure in brown.

No sooner had Alexandra and several other children joined to walk up front with Thay than she split off to scamper to the top of a leaf-carpeted hill.

"I'm going to roll down this hill!" she shouted to another girl. "Come on!"

It actually awed me that she was so unselfconscious about shattering the silence. Alexandra rolled down the hill, sounding like a bear crashing through the forest.

I dropped my head and trudged along. Suddenly, I noticed Thich Nhat Hahn gliding along, like a mountain on rails, almost next to me. His face looked calm and fresh, while mine ached like a clenched fist. Alex had raced ahead to the water's edge, where she stood waving and smiling at me. I felt a pang of love for her and really experienced how the voice of my heart was being drowned out by a welter of negative thoughts that seemed to come from somewhere in my brain that didn't even feel organic—more like a robot, a split-off part of me mechanically repeating bits of old programming.

Aware as I now felt, I was haranguing myself that really good mothers didn't get swamped by nasty reactions. Good mothers, my mind chided, were capable of unconditional love.

The bell calling for mindfulness sounded. I knelt down in the warm sand. The bell rang again, and a third time. I picked up my head to see an old man's hand gently stroking a familiar head of thick ash-blond hair. Thich Nhat Hanh and my daughter were sitting side by side. It slowly dawned on me that it was Alexandra who had just rung the bell calling the rest of us back to our true homes. Thay had been inspired to pick Alexandra, the loudest kid there that particular day, to sound, or "invite," the bell that called everyone else to silence.

FROM "PLAYING WITH GOD: A CHILD'S RESPONSE TO RELIGION"

When I was a little girl, there was a game I played when I couldn't sleep. Although I never thought of it as a prayer or used these words, it was my way of seeking God. I would peel off my blankets and slip down to the cold hardwood floor (I remember doing this mostly in the winter). The first few moments on the floor were my leap of faith. Freezing and feeling utterly exposed and alone, I thought of all the other people and other beings who had no beds, no blankets, no shelter at all. These thoughts were a ritual that always made me feel gratitude or a stab of empathy. They made me feel connected to the rest of the world. I would also feel brave in a special way, as if I were daring to venture out on my own. I was not only dipping into dangerously big subjects, I was risking being seen by the unknown.

As I lay there, a shift always took place. The labels I had about "cold" and "hard" gave way. I noticed that the polished hardwood was soft in its own way, more giving than stone or steel. As I listened to the wind blowing outside my bedroom window (the winter temperatures in Watertown, New York, often hit twenty and even thirty below zero), I imagined what it was like outside, and truly valued that I was in a warm, life-saving shelter. As I broke through the isolation of my thoughts and sank into the experience of my body, I began to sense that everything in the world had emerged from mystery. Why was there a world and not nothing? As a child I couldn't help but ask the question with my whole being, and as I asked it I felt vibrantly alive and present in a living world.

I would scramble back up to my bed and experience its incredible softness, wondering how I could have been numb to it before. I would pull up the sheet, savoring its smoothness. I would pull up the blankets and quilt one at a time, feeling unimaginably rich and relaxed and provided for. Even the air that touched my face was luxurious. I felt cradled in a benevolent, listening silence, and I knew without words that I had drawn closer to God by going deep within myself.

TONI BOEHM

UNITED STATES, CONTEMPORARY

Toni Boehm is an ordained minister and the dean of administration at Unity School for Religious Studies, where she also teaches seminars and writes books. Unity is the nondenominational Christian organization co-founded by Myrtle Fillmore (see p. 135), headquartered in Unity Village, Missouri, a suburb of Kansas City. A former nurse who has a master's degree in nursing and has served at the world headquarters of the American Nurse's Association, Toni Boehm also offers retreats and workshops on such topics as prayer, forgiveness, and the power of choice. She has a special interest in the Black Madonna and has led pilgrimages to European shrines to the Black Madonna. The excerpt is taken from her book The Spiritual Intrepreneur.

DIAGNOSIS

Finally—the test was over. They helped me to a sitting position and, [because I had asked the doctor to tell me the truth, holding nothing back], the doctor began to explain what had been found. These words rang in my ears: "You have what appears to be a large tumor, 3–4 inches long and approximately 2 inches wide, in your abdominal cavity. I will need to look more closely at the x-ray, then I will call your doctor. You can call him tomorrow. I don't have any further information." He and the nurse then turned and left, leaving me alone with my thoughts.

Suddenly I was numb, but somehow I managed to get dressed. I walked into the hallway, when it hit me—FEAR. It all happened so quickly. The fear began to grip me, "Oh my god, I have a tumor. I could die." I began to tremble. I looked up and there on the wall was a phone. My first thought was to call the prayer line of Silent Unity. I picked up the phone and made the call. I spoke to a sweet voice on the other end and asked her to hold me in prayer, to hold the "high watch" for me. We then prayed and I hung up the phone.

In the very next moment the "still small voice" boomed loudly within me and said, "This is your moment of Truth! Do you believe that there is only One Presence and One Power?"

In the midst of feeling like I was going to faint, another feeling began to surface. This one was from the depths of my Being. It was a sense of deep Faith, abiding Peace, and a new understanding of my relationship to Divine Life. In that moment I knew that I knew, that no matter what the outcome, nothing would change the reality of my Being. . . . From somewhere deep within me I said, "Yes! There is only One Presence and One Power and I am one with it.". . .

That moment of knowing left me with the gift of an assurance of eternal life. Divine life goes on without end, and my responsibility is to remain centered in that belief, thus allowing The Presence within me to live and work through me. From that moment in the hallway, until the time of surgery, I did not have one more anxious thought take hold of me. I came through the surgery (a benign tumor) holding to the promise of John 8.32:

"You shall know the Truth and the Truth shall set you free."

Yes, knowing the Truth did set me free. Free from anxiety, concern, and worry ... and free to experience the fullness of God's gifts, no matter how they are wrapped!

MALIA DOMINICA WONG
HAWAII, 1964–

A Dominican sister who was born in Hawaii and has been stationed in the Philippines and Hawaii, Malia Dominica Wong is a college teacher, writer, poet, dancer, and artist whose hobbies include sacred hula and the culinary arts. She recently completed a doctor of ministry degree, writing her dissertation on "The Gastronomics of Learning from Each Other: Recipes for Anyone Hungry on the Spiritual Path." In a forthcoming book based on the dissertation, Sister Malia shows how mealtime and great meals can be reminders to connect with the sacred all day long. To "dish out" fresh spirituality, she advises, try using beautiful prayers and practices from all over the world throughout the day. Christian, Sufi, Buddhist, Taoist, and other traditions' practices combine like the fresh ingredients "in a good Asian stir-fry, Mexican fajita, or Mediterranean vegetable grill." "Seasonings vary," she adds, but "essentials are the same." Moreover, everything lost to TV dinners is recovered; communication, community, shared work, and fun. Even a person in danger of becoming a jar of vinegar can be transformed into a "juicy, full-stem strawberry."

~෴

RECIPES FOR ANYONE HUNGRY
ON THE SPIRITUAL PATH

Another beautiful day in Hawai'i. It was about 11:30 A.M. when I arrived at Ku'ulima—Turtle Bay Resort, having just completed the fifty-minute drive from the west side of the island to the north shore past the majestic wind-swaying sugar cane fields, glistening lush green coffee plantations, trademark pineapples galore, and the mesmerizing hum of waves breaking along the seacoast. Such a feast for the eyes, ears, nose, and soul!

"Today's lunch, hmmm . . . ," I mumbled to myself while unloading the van and checking my delivery list. "Chicken and pork *adobo* (vinegared and spiced meat that's boiled until extra tender), deep fried *lumpia* (spring rolls), *mongo* beans (mung beans prepared in a stew), *bibingka* (butter mochi-glutinous rice dessert), and . . . of course the most important element, "steamed white rice," all accounted for. Perfect timing, too, as I could see the faint outlines of black and white emerging over the hilltop. No, not a group of penguins, but a group of nuns—with their black veils flapping on the breath of refreshing trade winds.

"Last night's dinner was too rich and too starchy. What kind of a meal is pasta, anyway?" I overheard one nun say. "Too oily and the portions were too big," another one chimed in. "How do they expect us to have a good retreat on that kind of food?" a third exclaimed. "No rice!" a group of them chorused.

All complaints! My ears were shocked. My mouth gaped. We had decided before the retreat that breakfast would be on their own, lunch would be brought in, and dinner would be at the resort restaurant. It was a financial move, and also a sacrifice on my part to make the long drive every day. But, I was happy to "feed the hungry"—up until that moment.

As they dug into the food I brought and cleared the pans, I felt that something else must be devouring them—some other hunger beyond the food . . . something really ravenous in their appetites. What it was, I didn't know. All I knew was that I was hurt, upset, and felt that I was wasting my time feeding an unappreciative crowd. As a missionary myself, I could hear a voice within saying that I knew how it was to be in a foreign land and to eat things unheard of or unseen before. I also knew what it was to feel gratitude for any edible morsel, because sometimes all I was offered was a scoop of rice as a meal. On other occasions, there was nothing available to satiate the hunger pangs. Not even a grain of rice.

I called my spiritual director that evening and asked her insights into the situation. She listened and then suggested that it was probably because they were in need of nourishment that they were griping. "Imagine," she said, "it's just been two days since they finished another academic year of teaching. They are probably drained and tired. Add to that having to pack up and move on to a six day retreat—the very thing they need—and yet, because of the new environment, faces, and food, they are complaining because they are out of their comfort zone. They need their comfort food. They need their rice, like a security blanket. And, because you are tired and stressed, also in need of nourishment with no one giving it to you, all you think you're getting is 'scraps from the Master's table.'"...

Lunchtime is a good time to pause a moment and reflect. At the time when the sun is directly overhead, all of life is in clear illumination. Lunchtime also marks that half of our working day has passed, a half of our day's life. St. Ignatius offers a few questions for examining our consciousness: "What have I done for Christ? What am I doing for Christ? What will I do for Christ?" In work-related terms, we might ask: "What have I done so far with this day—how many smiles have I engendered? What am I doing right now to nourish myself? What will I do to foster peace and harmony after work, when I get home?" Traditionally, in the Divine Office (Liturgy of the Hours), all parts of the day were consecrated with times appointed to pray and "re-member," put back together, what may have become scattered as we moved from activity to activity. Going back to the tradition of Midday Prayer, *Salat Al-Zuhr* (Islamic midday prayer), remembering the Sun Dance (Native American tradition), or repeating the Buddhist *paramis* (virtues) throughout the day can serve to enhance our moment-to-moment living. It may be the pause we need to sustain us as evening draws near.

LUNCHTIME RECIPE: CHICKEN ADOBO

3 pounds chicken, cut up or pieces
$\frac{1}{2}$ cup vinegar
$\frac{1}{4}$ cup soy sauce
2 cloves of garlic, crushed
$\frac{1}{4}$ teaspoon peppercorns, crushed
pinch of salt
1 bay leaf
achuette for coloring (optional)

Clean chicken if needed. Combine all ingredients in a large pot. Bring to a boil; reduce heat and simmer for 45 minutes or more, or until liquid evaporates and chicken is golden brown. Serves 6.

JOAN DUNCAN OLIVER

KENTUCKY, CONTEMPORARY

The author of a beautiful book entitled Contemplative Living, *Joan Duncan Oliver has covered transformative events, ideas, and people for such publications as* Health, Self, *the* New York Times, *and* New Age *Journal. A former editor-in-chief of* New Age Journal *and editorial director of* One Spirit Book Club, *she is a regular contributor to* O: The Oprah Magazine *and* My Generation *and is a lecturer at Omega Institute. Her work draws on twenty-five years' study of meditation, mysticism, psychology, and a variety of spiritual, esoteric, and mind-body teachings.*

~)

MOVING WITH SPIRIT

Can't sit still? Prefer movement to words? Don't worry. That won't keep you off the contemplative path. In fact, some of history's most devout mystics have moved and shaken their way to God. The mystery schools of the East included music and movement in their menu of sacred practices. The great cathedrals of the Middle Ages rocked with song and dance in praise of the divine—a tradition of celebration that maverick theologians like Matthew Fox are reviving today. And seekers in every culture continue the age-old, spirit-renewing ritual of pilgrimage. If you can walk, you can meditate. If you can dance, you can pray. Anyone, no matter how restless or rebellious, can find a way to connect with the divine.

THE SPIRIT OF EXERCISE

You've no doubt heard of runner's high. It's more than just a physiological phenomenon, a release of endorphins that lifts your mood. Long-distance running is how many people leave behind everyday worries and obsessive thinking, and get in touch with something outside themselves, Whether you call it "being in the zone" or "making a soul connection," the feeling is the same.

In Tibet there are monks known as *lung-gompas,* who perform super-human feats, running hundreds of miles at a stretch. How do they do it? Their motto is: Aim for a faraway star—and keep your eyes at your feet. Like any form of repetitive physical activity, including swimming and cycling, running is not only an excellent concentration practice but also a metaphor for living consciously. It asks you to take a long view—to set a distant and challenging goal—then bring your attention to the here and now, and experience each step, each moment, as fully and mindfully as possible.

One practice you can do when you're running—or walking, for that matter—is to tune your senses to your surroundings. Listen carefully to the sounds in the environment; try to identify everything you hear, whether bird calls, traffic noise, sirens, or the surf. Look around you; be aware of the images and colors you see—a child's stroller, an old woman in a red hat, blue sky, pine trees. Inhale and take in smells—flowering shrubs, newly cut grass, swamp grass, fresh bread wafting from a bakery. Notice how the air feels against your skin—hot or cool, damp or dry, the caress of a soft breeze or the slap of a winter gale. Stay open to whatever you experience, without judging it good or bad, pretty or ugly, pleasing or distasteful.

TARA GRABOWSKY, MD
MEXICO, 1970–

Tara Grabowsky is a third-year resident in a Boston hospital where desperately ill people come for treatment. In addition to the difficult medical and ethical pressures doctors face every day, and the painful challenge of incurable suffering and unpreventable death, young residents are on call every third night. This means that they work all day, starting at 6 A.M., continuing all night long and all the next day, going home if possible around 6 P.M., thirty-six sleepless hours after their work "day" began. Nevertheless, studies show that American residents, who have the world's most demanding schedule, can go directly from an on-call night to board exams and perform splendidly, better than well-rested residents in other countries.

Tara is a graduate of Dartmouth College and Stanford Medical School, a writer and concert singer as well as a scientist. She began publishing in high school and is the author of medical books, articles, fiction, and poetry. The selection that appears here suggests how the medical profession is recovering today ancient knowledge lost for some fifty years. Doctors are rediscovering that relating to the patient's soul (while using the best of modern science and technology) releases healing power for both the patient and the physician. (One young doctor dreamed that she was accompanied on hospital rounds by an iridescent blue-green hummingbird that placed a tiny seed in the hand of each patient she visited.) See also other physicians' writings in Sacred Voices—Rachel Naomi Remen *(see p. 253) and Christiane Northrup (see p. 260).*

~⁏

FURY AND LOVE

Ms. Grady was on a breathing machine. She was one of the ones we didn't have to sedate into sleep. She could let the tube in her throat breathe for her, forcing air into her lungs at predetermined intervals. She was always awake, somehow tolerating that tube down her throat. She wasn't my patient, actually, but I knew the basics from our team's morning rounds. "Eighty-six-year-old woman with Klebsiella pneumonia" we heard each day as we approached her room in the intensive care unit. "Hospital day number sixteen, ventilator day number four, this time." She had failed to stay off the breathing machine when we took the tube out five days ago. "A turn for the worse," we called it. I had never spent much time with her; there had been no need. She had been stable every third night when I was on call in the unit, and most call nights there isn't time to do anything but keep people alive. So I knew what I needed to know.

I knew her numbers: "five of pressure support, five of positive end expiratory pressure." I took care of her numbers.

When I arrived at work one day at 6:30 A.M. to prepare for rounds, I looked in on my patient, Mrs. Newcombe, in the corner room next to Ms. Grady. She had come in after a devastating stroke. All she had left of her life was a heartbeat. She was no better that day, and I knew that my role that afternoon would be to help the family come to terms. As I was washing my hands before I moved on to my next patient, I found myself furious—furious over my powerlessness. Fury had become my constant companion that year; it was often the only emotion I could feel through the fatigue.

En route to my next patient, I was thinking about my hand on Mrs. Newcombe's forehead, stroking her hair, wondering if she had felt anything. I passed Ms. Grady's room. Just as I walked by, the hose connecting her breathing tube to the machine hissed loudly, popped, and disconnected. I veered off my course to reconnect the hose, not thinking much of it. These things happen all the time with this equipment; the alarm would have sounded if I hadn't been right there. Ms. Grady would have been without air for no more than thirty seconds.

As I reached across her to grab the tube, I looked down at her face for the first time. She looked up at me with a gaze that still, one year later, fills me with a sense of the wisdom, grace, and dignity of elderhood. The terror on her face softened into love. Love for me, simply because I happened to be in the right place at the right time. Though she couldn't talk with the breathing tube in, she puckered her lips around it and managed to blow me a kiss. The tears that had formed in her eyes receded. I put my hand on her forehead, and for a few minutes the fury, the fatigue, the powerlessness went away.

JULIA BUTTERFLY HILL

ARKANSAS, 1975–

Julia Butterfly Hill lived for two years 180 feet off the ground in a giant redwood tree named Luna. The thousand-year-old tree was slated for destruction by a logging firm in northern California when Julia began her famous tree-sit, living on a tiny platform in the tree's branches without ever once coming down despite howling storms and snow that gave her frostbite, terrifying threats from loggers who once buzzed her in a helicopter and at another time cut off her meager food supplies, no entertainment, possessions, or distractions—more than enough stress to threaten one's sanity. Pushed to the limits of endurance, like a renunciant monk in a cave, forced to fall back on her own resources, she found heroic stores of courage, faith, and prayer. "When I almost died in that mother of all storms," she wrote, "my fear of dying died, too. Letting go of that freed me, like the butterfly frees itself of its cocoon. I began to live each day, moment by moment, breath by breath, and prayer by prayer."

Eventually, long after the tree-sit caught national media attention, the logging company signed a complex legal agreement promising perpetual protection of Luna, and at the age of twenty-five, Julia climbed down and embraced a new life working in ecological issues, helping to create the Circle of Life Foundation. Retaliation occurred the following year when unidentified forest terrorists sawed two-thirds of the way through Luna's ancient trunk, assuring the tree's death.

Julia tells her gripping story in a book published in 2000: The Legacy of Luna: The Story of a Tree, A Woman, and the Struggle to Save the Redwoods.

~⁀

THE STORM

The moment the storm hit, I couldn't have climbed down if I had wanted to. To climb you have to be able to move, and my hands were frozen. Massive amounts of rain, sleet, and hail mixed together, and the winds blew so hard I might have been ripped off a branch.

The storm was every bit as strong as they said it would be. Actually, up here, it was even stronger. When a gust would come through, it would flip the platform up into the air, bucking me all over the place.

"Boy! Whoahhh! Ooh! Whoa!"

The gust rolled me all the way up to the hammock. Only the rope that cuts an angle underneath it prevented me from slipping through the gap in the platform.

"I'm really ready for this storm to chill out. I'm duly impressed," I decided. "I've bowed and cowered once again before the great almighty gods of wind and rain and storm. I've paid my respects—and my dues—and I'd appreciate it if they got the heck out of here."

My thoughts seemed to anger the storm spirits.

"Whoa! Whoa!" I cried, as the raging wind flung my platform, straining the ropes that attached it.

"This is getting really intense! Oh, my God! Oh, my God! Okay, never mind, I take it back! Whoaaaah!"

The biggest gust threw me close to three feet. I grabbed onto the branch of Luna that comes through the middle of the platform, and I prayed.

"I want to be strong for you, Luna. I want to be strong for the forest. I don't want to die, because I want to help make a difference. I want to be strong for the movement, but I can't even be strong for myself."

It seemed like it took all my will to stay alive. I was trying to hold onto life so hard that my teeth were clenched, my jaws were clenched, my muscles were clenched, my fists were clenched, everything in my body was clenched completely and totally tight.

I knew I was going to die.

The wind howled. It sounded like wild banshees, *rrahhh,* while the tarps added to the crazy cacophony of noise, *flap, flap, flap, bap, bap, flap, bap!* Had I remained tensed for the sixteen hours that the storm raged, I would have snapped. Instead, I grabbed onto Luna, hugging the branch that comes up through the platform, and prayed to her.

"I don't know what's happening here. I don't want to go down, because I made a pact with you. But I can't be strong now. I'm frightened out of my mind, Luna, I'm losing it. I'm going crazy!"

Maybe I was, maybe I wasn't, but in that moment I heard the voice of Luna speak to me.

"Julia, think of the trees in the storm."

And as I started to picture the trees in the storm, the answer began to dawn on me.

"The trees in the storm don't try to stand up straight and tall and erect. They allow themselves to bend and be blown with the wind. They understand the power of letting go," continued the voice. "Those trees and those branches that try too hard to stand up strong and straight are the ones that break. Now is not the time for you to be strong, Julia, or you, too, will break. Learn the power of the trees. Let it flow. Let it go. That is the way you are going to make it through this storm. And that is the way to make it through the storms of life."

I suddenly understood.

FROM *THE LEGACY OF LUNA*

MIRANDA SHAW

UNITED STATES, CONTEMPORARY

Miranda Shaw published a groundbreaking book in 1994 that forever changed our notion of women's role in Tantric Buddhism: Passionate Enlightenment. *Winner of a coveted prize from the American Historical Association, the* Tricycle *prize for Buddhist scholarship, and other awards, the book meticulously disproves the long-held belief that in Tantra, a spiritual practice that uses sexuality as a means to enlightenment, women participants were exploited victims or prostitutes, or at the very least marginalized, while enlightenment was only for men. Miranda found texts and documents in the East that were discounted until she delved into them, and for the first time brought forth a woman's perspective and interpretations. She showed convincingly that women were equal partners of men in the creation of Tantra and were taken seriously as candidates for enlightenment. A typical text said: "One should honor women. Women are Buddha, women are religious community, women are the perfection of wisdom."*

The second selection below appeared in Buddhist Women on the Edge, *by Marianne Dresser.*

FROM PASSIONATE ENLIGHTENMENT

Anyone who reads a Tantric text or enters a Tantric temple immediately encounters a dazzling array of striking female imagery. One discovers a pantheon of female Buddhas and a host of female enlighteners known as *dakinis*. The *dakinis* leap and fly, unfettered by clothing, encircled by billowing hair, their bodies curved in sinuous dance poses. Their eyes blaze with passion, ecstasy, and ferocious intensity. One can almost hear the soft clacking of their intricate bone jewelry and feel the wind stirred by their rainbow-colored scarves as they soar through the Tantric Buddhist landscape. These unrestrained damsels appear to revel in freedom of every kind. . . . Tantric literature describe *yoginis* who can . . . spark a direct experience of reality with a precisely aimed word or gesture.

These female figures . . . communicate a sense of mastery and spiritual power.

Since women mastered every level of Tantric Buddhist practice and realization, it follows that women would assume roles of leadership and authority as enlightened teachers and initiating gurus. In this unrestrictive religious setting, there were no institutional barriers to the leadership of women, such as a priestly hierarchy of clerics seeking to exclude women from their ranks, wealth, and prestige. Religious authority was based on personal realization and timely displays of supernatural powers or religious insight. These qualifications represented no disadvantage for women. For the duration of the movement in India, women claimed authority and undertook religious guidance of others on the same basis as men—their wisdom, magical powers, and religious expertise.

WILD, WISE, PASSIONATE: DAKINIS IN AMERICA

Archetypal images of female wholeness are indispensable as a source of positive self-understanding that a woman can cultivate in any environment. They provide an antidote to the poisonously destructive female imagery that pervades our culture, destroying our ability to nurture, appreciate, and value one another and ourselves. Meditating on images like these can inspire a woman to reenliven her body and spirit, awaken her divine potentialities, and rekindle the passion that can be directed to her spiritual practice and the fulfillment of her life's purpose.

It is crucial that women receive initiation and instruction in female deities from women. This has always been the case. In an initiation ceremony, the guru embodies the deity into which he or she is conferring initiation, literally channeling the deity's energy to the initiates. The word that we translate into English as "initiation" is more literally translated as "empowerment." The purpose of initiation is to empower the initiate to do successful practice upon that deity and to awaken the enlightened qualities of the deity within herself. In the case of a female deity, it is deeply meaningful for women when the initiation comes from a woman. A female guru can provide what a male guru cannot—namely, the presence of a female deity manifesting in a female mind and body.

When a woman experiences that power emanating from another woman, she is encouraged to discover the same enlightened essence within herself. Further, when the energy of a female deity is transmitted through a woman, there is no implicit suggestion that a male must be present at any point to mediate, legitimate, or authenticate this process. An initiation received from a male teacher can be sublime, but the process takes on another dimension when it comes from that woman. It makes the extraordinarily empowering statement that women can tap directly into the ultimate source of power, energy, and truth in female form. It powerfully communicates the sufficiency of female embodiment as a vehicle of total freedom.

SARA SVIRI

ENGLAND, CONTEMPORARY

A deeply spiritual academic with a specialty in the Naqshbandi Sufi path, Sara Sviri received a doctorate in Arabic and Islamic studies from the Hebrew University of Jerusalem, where she later taught in the Arabic department. Today she holds a lectureship in medieval studies at University College, London, and writes on Sufism and other topics, especially depth psychology and dreams, from a Sufi perspective. She also lectures extensively on Sufism in the United States and Europe. Sara is the author of an exquisite 1997 book on Sufism, The Taste of Hidden Things, *which echoes with lyrical passion the living beauty of the Sufi way. Combining her scholarly knowledge with learning from her own Sufi journey, she builds on the teachings transmitted by the great Irina Tweedie (see p. 183) from Sai Bahib.* The Taste of Hidden Things *was published at the Golden Sufi Center in Inverness, California.*

~♪

BLACK LIGHT

Black light, a contradiction in terms. This is one the deepest of mystical experiences. At the core of our separate existences as individual human beings, as well as at the core of Existence as such, there is a void, a black point of nothingness. This is the edge of knowing, this is the edge of consciousness, the edge of experiencing. And yet, in some mysterious way, it is experienced. It does become known, and it has been reported and documented by many mystics of different affiliations. But at the moment of experiencing it, its totality takes over, and in the face of the black light everything perishes; the black light alone exists.

KHIDR, THE "GREEN MAN"

[Khidr is an archetypal image that appears in myths, legends, stories, and seekers' dreams when an ultimate turning point is met.]

One's sense of achievement must die so that the Sacred can radiate within the heart. The point of death for the *nafs* [ego] is the point of revival for the soul. At this point Khidr is waiting. He is both the undertaker and the midwife. He shatters illusions and delusions, and then gives meaning and direction to the soul's search. If, like Moses, Alexander, and Gilgamesh, the seeker vows to keep up the journey even if it takes a lifetime, even though he has to retrace his steps many times, then, at the right place and time, he will encounter Khidr who will guide him from station to station.

Khidr lives on a green island by the source of the Water of Immortality. He is the life force behind all natural phenomena. Nothing can be alive and vital without Khidr's touch or presence. When a seeker goes through times of emptiness and depression, in an inner wilderness where nothing seems to grow, he has seemingly lost touch with Khidr. Khidr has veiled himself. But he is there, hiding behind the thorny, barren branches, or in the empty water-holes. When friends gather and there is no feeling of intimacy and empathy, when words sound empty and meaningless, Khidr seems to be absent; he keeps himself in hiding. When things become mechanical, repetitive, unconscious, then, too, Khidr is veiled. But if companions gather with a sense of purpose, if there is something meaningful in their lives that has brought them together, here, now, and if that which happens in that "here and now" has vitality, then they know: This is the imprint of Khidr. When the eyes glimmer and shine, when Eros is in the air, then Khidr is around.

RASHANI

BIRTHPLACE UNKNOWN, CONTEMPORARY

Rashani is the spiritual name of a Sufi poet who lives as a solitary in a remote hermitage. She gave her poem to Michelle Lynn Ryan (see p. 256), who gave it to the editor of Sacred Voices. *We have no other information about this great soul.*

~

THERE IS A BROKENNESS

There is a brokenness
out of which comes the unbroken,
a shatteredness out
of which blooms the unshatterable.

There is a sorrow
beyond all grief which leads to joy
and a fragility
out of whose depths emerges strength.

There is a hollow space
too vast for words
through which we pass with each loss,
out of whose darkness
we are sanctioned into being.

There is a cry deeper than all sound
whose serrated edges cut the heart
as we break open
to the place inside which is unbreakable
and whole,
while learning to sing.

KOEI HOSHINO
JAPAN, CONTEMPORARY

Abbess Koei Hoshino is head of Jushokusan, a beautiful wooden temple on the outskirts of Tokyo that dates to the fourteenth century (although the original building burned down and the present one was constructed in 1934). Trained at the chief temple of the Rinzai sect of Buddhism in Kyoto, she is also a sensei, *or master teacher, in the art of Zen cooking* (shojin ryori)*. The word* shojin *is composed of two Chinese characters meaning "spirit" and "to prepare" and denotes an art of vegetarian cooking that features the use of simple, natural ingredients to foster the practice of meditation in monasteries.*

The Zen cook selects ingredients according to the four seasons, always avoiding anything that results from the killing of animals. She or he must heed "the three qualities"—lightness and softness, cleanliness and freshness, precision and thoroughness—and the six flavors of bitter, sour, sweet, hot, salty, and delicate. There are also five colors and methods of cooking that are maintained in balance. Most important, Zen identifies a special taste for which there is no word in English, tanmi; *it describes a delicate "aftertaste," a gentle, quiet state that one feels after a meal has been eaten mindfully. Central to the spirituality of cooking, the gentle feeling of* tanmi *would not be possible if one were angry or anxious during the meal.*

THE ZEN ART OF COOKING

As the process of preparing food takes over, there is *mu* (nothingness). The mind enters a state in which it is not caught up in anything.... So if you are thinking, "Let's prepare this well for others" or "Let's offer our affectionate heart in preparing this food," you will know your practice is still shallow. When you are doing your best, you get to the point where you are just doing your best, not thinking of it....

Let us use [as an example] the dish called sesame tofu. It is a difficult dish, made from ground sesame, water, and arrowroot. It must be stirred for a very long time, and it is hard work. When you are stirring and stirring with all your might, enough of the heavy batter for fifty people, it's so hard that you want to give up being a human being! But in the midst of the stirring you are not thinking of anything. All your attention is on the sesame. You just keep stirring and watching until the heat begins to soften the mixture and it becomes elastic. You just keep looking into the pan and stirring until the sesame tofu tells you what to do. It gets heavy again and then soft again until suddenly the surface swells up and leaps forward making a clear sound. It tells you that it's ready. Then as you quickly respond and remove it from the heat, a wonderful delicious aroma comes floating up and you know with your whole body that the sesame tofu is done....

If your attention wanders even a little, if your mind jumps to something else for even a moment, the sesame will burn. So you put everything you've got into it. You are completely one-pointed on what you are doing.

MERCY AMBA ODUYOYE

GHANA, CONTEMPORARY

The former deputy general secretary of the World Council of Churches in Geneva, Mercy Oduyoye is a prominent leader in the African women's movement. She writes and lectures all over the world about her experience of domination and hope of freeing all women from the spirit of submission. Motivated by deep Christian beliefs, she says that her faith has taught her to speak her truth. Among her books are Hearing and Knowing, The Will to Arise, *and the recent* Daughters of Anowa: African Women and Patriarchy, *which has been widely acclaimed as the birth of an African women's liberation theology and ethics.*

~୨

WOMAN WITH BEADS

I am Woman
I am African
My beads mark my presence
Beads of wisdom, beads of sweat
I am Woman
I am Bota
The precious black bead
Skillfully crafted from black stone
I do not speak much
But I am not without a voice
The authentic black bead does not rattle noisily
I am an African woman, wearing beads ground
by Anowa and from the womb of Anowa
Other beads I have which do not belong to her
They have come from over the seas
They are glass and easily shattered
Created by humans they can be ground
Back to powder and remodelled.

I am Woman
I am African
Here I sit—not idle
But busy stringing my beads
I wear them in my hair
I wear them in my ears
They go round my neck, my arms
My wrist, my calves and my ankles
Around my waist will go the
Most precious of them all
And from this hidden strength
Will burst forth the New Me—for
I am in the process of giving birth
To myself—recreating Me
Of being, the Me that God sees.
I am Woman
I am African
My beads mark my presence
And when I am gone
My beads
will remain.

CLARISSA PINKOLA ESTÉS
UNITED STATES, CONTEMPORARY

A prophetic voice whose messages are both timeless and fifty years ahead of their time, Clarissa Pinkola Estés is one of our finest poets, a Jungian analyst, the Founding Director of a charitable society devoted to Our Lady of Guadalupe, and the author of the twentieth-century classic Women Who Run With the Wolves. *This book was on the* New York Times *best-seller list for more than 150 weeks. She is also a* cantadora, *a keeper of the stories in the Latina tradition. Her work is charged with the sacred mission of transmitting wisdom and life guidance to the next generation.*

Clarissa Pinkola Estés lectures and teaches extensively both here and abroad while working for justice at every level of life. She has been a post-trauma specialist at Columbine High School ever since the massacre. She resides in Colorado, is married and is both mother and grandmother.

The following poem, like a crystal sphere in the sun, reflects and radiates outward in all directions the light and beauty of a great soul.

~ɔ

FATHER EARTH

There's a two-million year old man
no one knows.
They cut into his rivers,
peeled wide pieces of hide
from his legs,
left scorch marks
on his buttocks.
He did not cry out.
No matter what they did,
he held firm.
Now he raises his stabbed hands
and whispers that we can heal him yet.
We begin the bandages,
the rolls of gauze,
the unguents, the gut,
the needle, the grafts.

We slowly,
carefully, turn
his body
face up,
and under him,
his lifelong lover, the old woman,
is perfect and unmarked.
He has lain upon
his two-million year
old woman
all this time, protecting her
with his old back, his old scarred back.
And the soil beneath her
is black with her tears.

INDEX OF AUTHORS AND SOURCES

Akhmatova, Anna / 167

Alacoque, Margaret Mary / 111

Alvord, Lori Arviso / 307

Anandamayi Ma / 173

Angela of Foligno / 74

Anonymous Hymn in Praise of
Inanna / 9

Anonymous Lament (from
Mesopotamia) / 22

Anonymous Lament of Mary / 38

Anonymous Love Song (from
Egypt) / 13

Anonymous Love Song (from
Spain) / 53

Anonymous Pawnee Chant / 108

Arai, Paula Kane Robinson / 305

Artress, Lauren / 268

Ashanti Women / 121

Baring, Anne / 220

Beatrice of Nazareth / 68

Boehm, Toni / 316

Bonazzoli, Nancy Diamante / 296

The Book of Ruth / 20

Boorstein, Sylvia / 232

Bourgeault, Cynthia / 264

Bradstreet, Anne / 109

Brown, Karen McCarthy / 281

Buckland, Clare / 196

Cabrera de Armida, Concepción
(Conchita) / 141

Canda / 16

Catherine of Genoa / 99

Catherine of Siena / 84

Chan Khong / 236

Chidvilasananda, Gurumayi / 289

Chittister, Joan / 242

Chödrön, Pema / 233

Christina of Markyate / 54

Christine de Pisan / 94

Clare of Assisi / 65

Clifton, Lucille / 231

Cochran, Tracy / 314

Coleman, Anita Scott / 171

Colette, Sidonie-Gabrielle / 154

A Court Record / 30

Cowdery, Mae V. / 190

Crocombe, Marjorie / 297

Day, Dorothy / 179

de Gasztold, Carmen Bernos / 205

de la Cruz, Sor Juana Inés / 113

Devi, Sarada / 139

Dhuodana / 46

Diaz, Adriana / 292

Dickinson, Emily / 129

Dillard, Annie / 251

Douglas, Diana / 196

Duncan, Isadora / 159
Eck, Diana / 258
Egeria / 32
Elizabeth of the Trinity / 146
Erdrich, Louise / 294
Eskimo Prayer / 125
Estés, Clarissa Pinkola / 336
Eulogia, Irene / 82
Fillmore, Myrtle / 135
Firestone, Tirzah / 287
Flinders, Carol / 266
Frontier Women / 137
Galgani, Gemma / 144
Gertrude the Great / 76
Gidlow, Elsa / 183
Gonzalez, Maria Cristina / 303
Goodall, Jane / 227
The Gospel of Mary / 24
Grabowsky, Tara / 322
Hadewijch / 80
Hadley, Leila / 207
Hall, Eliza Calvert / 147
Hashepsowe / 11
Hayati, Bibi / 123
Heloise / 56
Hildegard of Bingen / 58
Hill, Julia Butterfly / 325
Hobday, José / 209
Hogan, Linda / 270
A Hopi Creation Story / 125
Hoshino, Koei / 332
Hypatia / 36
Jackson, Mahalia / 195
Jacobs, Harriet A. / 126
Joyner-Kersee, Jackie / 312
Judith / 21
Julian of Norwich / 91
Kasa, Lady / 39
Kempe, Margery / 96

Khema, Ayya / 203
Krysl, Marilyn / 246
Laksmi, Bhiksuni / 52
Lalleshwari / 87
Lane, Mary Mercedes / 152
Lebell, Sharon / 300
Lee, Ann / 116
LeGuin, Ursula K. / 217
L'Engle, Madeleine / 238
Lorde, Audre / 226
Lowinsky, Naomi Ruth / 250
Macy, Joanna / 216
Mahadevi / 63
Mandarava of Zahor / 43
Mary the Mother of Jesus / 23
Mazeaud, Dominique / 285
Mechthild of Magdeburg / 70
Menchú, Rigoberta / 308
Mettika / 18
Mirabai / 101
Mistral, Gabriela / 169
Morrison, Toni / 223
The Mother / 157
Mother Teresa / 192
Mountain Dreamer, Oriah / 311
Muktabai / 73
Myodo, Satomi / 176
Myss, Carolyn / 275
Nightingale, Florence / 128
Nitsch, Twylah / 202
Norris, Kathleen / 276
Northrup, Christiane / 260
O'Brien, Thea / 219
Oduyoye, Mercy Amba / 334
O'Keeffe, Georgia / 163
Olds, Sharon / 244
Oliver, Mary / 230
Oliver, Joan Duncan / 321
Osage Chant / 143

Patacara / 15
Peavey, Fran / 284
Penfold, Nita / 279
Perpetua / 26
Porete, Marguerite / 78
Praxilla / 19
A Priestess of Inanna / 10
Pygmy Women / 120
Rabia Al-Adawiyya / 40
Radha, Sivananda / 194
Rashani / 331
Ratushinskaia, Irina / 151
Rayhana / 45
Remen, Rachel Naomi / 253
Richards, Mary Caroline / 199
Rose of Lima / 107
Rwala Bedouin Women / 115
Ryan, Michelle Lynn / 256
Ryan, Regina Sara / 262
Sappho / 13
Shaw, Miranda / 327
Starhawk / 273

Strahan, Elizabeth / 240
Sumangalamata / 18
Sun Bu-er / 62
Sviri, Sara / 329
Tan, Amy / 283
Teish, Luisah / 271
Teresa of Avila / 104
Truth, Sojourner / 118
Tweedie, Irina / 183
Umm Abdallah / 49
Underhill, Evelyn / 155
Valtorta, Maria / 178
Vinograd, Julia / 245
Walker, Alice / 247
Walters, Dorothy / 211
Weil, Simone / 187
Wong, Eva / 301
Wong, Malia Dominica / 318
Woodman, Marion / 214
Woolf, Virginia / 161
Yamatohime / 39

INDEX

OF TITLES

About Painting Desert Bones / 164

After Great Pain / 131

Alexandra's First Retreat / 314

All Shall Be Well / 94

Ancestor Reverence / 272

Anointing with Sacred Ointment / 109

Antiphon for Divine Wisdom / 61

The Archbishop Puts Her in Chains / 97

Ar'n't I a Woman? / 119

At Last Free! / 19

The Babushki's Trousseau / 151

Ballad of Columbine High School
   Killings / 245

Be a Candle / 192

Be a Gardener / 92

A "Beggar's" Gift: A Low-Budget
   Affair / 210

Being an Athlete Is a Kind of
   Grace / 313

Black Light / 330

The Black Madonna / 220

Bridegroom, beloved of my heart / 10

The Bridge: God Speaks to the
   Soul / 86

Caring, One Person at a Time / 239

Chant for a Sick Child / 121

The Chimpanzee at Stanford / 285

Circulation of Light in the Body / 184

The City Seeks Its Lord / 103

Commitment / 100

Conduct Yourself with Dignity / 300

Conscious Dying / 197

Contemplation / 66

Cover Me with the Night / 123

The Crone / 215

Cucumbers, Apples, and Pears / 20

Cut brambles long enough / 63

Cutting Through the Six Forests / 90

Dancers: You Are Priests and
   Priestesses / 214

The Dark One Is Here Inside / 103

The Delight of Old Age / 219

Diagnosis / 317

Digging a Hole Big Enough to Sit
   In / 202

Divine Birth in the Soul / 77

Divine Love in the Midst of
   Affliction / 189

A Dream of Love / 190

A Dream (Rabia) / 41

A Dream (The Mother) / 158

Electronic Communications / 153

The Empty Mirror / 79

Encountering God in Other
   Traditions / 259

The Erotic as Sacred / 226

An Experience of Oneness / 74

Father Earth / 336

Feasting with the Benedictine
Sisters / 278

Fire in My Mind / 73

From A Circle of Quiet / 240

From A Journey with Elsa Cloud / 208

From A Letter on Women's Stagnation
in the Nineteenth Century / 128

From A Letter to Abelard / 57

From A Letter to Anita, 1929 / 166

From A Letter to Anita, October
1916 / 166

From A Letter to Anita, September
1916 / 166

From A Letter to Anita Pollitzer, January
1916 / 165

From A Manual for William / 47

From Antiphon for the Angels / 61

From Antiphon for the Holy Spirit / 62

From A Room of One's Own / 162

From A Vision of the Divine
Heart / 112

From Be an Island / 203

From Beloved / 223

From "Chains of Fire" / 183

From (Conchita's) Diary / 142

From Dakota / 277

From Incidents in the Life of a Slave
Girl / 127

From I, Rigoberta Menchú, an Indian
Woman in Guatemala / 309

From Mama Lola: A Vodou Priestess in
Brooklyn / 282

From "Mary Speaks" / 238

From Movin' On Up / 195

From Mrs. Dalloway / 162

From Passionate Enlightenment / 328

From Perpetua's Diary / 27

From "Playing with God: A Child's
Response to Religion" / 315

From "Prayer" / 169

From (Rabia Al-Adawiyya's)
Biography / 42

From Start Where You Are / 234

From The Chant to Accompany Her
Fasting Practice / 53

From The Color Purple / 248

From The Gospel of Mary: The
Sacredness of Mary Magdalen to
Jesus / 25

From "The Healer" / 297

From The Joy Luck Club / 284

From The Last Report on the Miracles at
Little No Horse / 295

From The Menstrual Rite of
Passage / 122

From The Temple of My Familiar / 249

From The Universe Responds / 249

From The "Way" of Saint Clare / 67

From "Those Who Do Not Dance" / 171

From (Toni Morrison's) Nobel Lecture,
December 7, 1993 / 225

From To the Lighthouse / 162

From "Unde Malum?" / 258

From Waiting for God / 188

From Walking a Sacred Path / 269

From When Things Fall Apart / 235

From With Roots in Heaven / 288

From World As Lover, World As
Self / 216

Fury and Love / 323

Gently, Gently, I Trained My Mind / 90

The Goal of the Mystical Journey / 156

Go Beyond Experience / 89

God Be With You, Dear Friend / 81

God Does Not Punish / 136

God Is Our Mother / 93

God Speaks to Mary During
    Creation / 178
Go Forward Securely / 66
Grandmother / 246
The Great Cleansing of the Rio
    Grande / 286
Hail King . . . Female Sun! / 12
The Hazelnut / 91
Hidden in My Body / 90
Holy Night / 231
How a Wise Woman, in the Year 1405,
    Works for Peace / 95
How Can We Teach Love? / 201
How I See Our Souls in God / 145
I Am Going to Stay Right Here and
    Stand the Fire! / 119
I Am Watching All the Roads / 65
I Cannot Dance, O Lord / 71
I Dreamed I Held a Sword / 39
If I Desire Something / 81
I Find All My Joy in You / 78
I, God, Am in Your Midst / 62
I Had Been Hungry All the Years / 130
I Live in My Body / 160
In Defense of Eve / 119
In Desperation of Grief / 123
Initiate (After H. D.) / 250
In Praise of Judith's Courage / 21
In the War Zone / 237
In the Womb of Earth-Mother / 126
The Invitation / 311
I Put Bells on My Ankles / 104
I Saw No Way / 131
Is this darkness the night of
    power? / 124
I've Done What I Was Taught / 16
I Was Lost / 17
I Wear the Morning Light / 64
Jail / 181

Journey to Jerusalem / 33
Khidr, the "Green Man" / 330
A Kundalini Awakening / 213
Lament of Mary for Her Son / 38
Lament of the Flutes for Tammuz / 23
Leave Crete / 14
The Leave-Taking / 44
Let One Remain / 122
Letter Concerning Her Pink
    Cactus / 155
A Letter to Mrs. J. G. Holland / 133
A Letter to Susan Dickinson
    Gilbert / 134
A Liberating Experience / 177
Like a Hole in the Earth's Crust / 253
Live in the Soul! / 89
Lord, Now I Am Naked / 72
The Lord of the Dance / 117
Lord, You Are My Lover / 72
Love Has Subjugated Me / 81
Lying with the Beloved / 296
The Magnificat / 24
Making Silence / 278
Midnight of the Soul (Fana
    Annihilation) / 256
The Mind Can Never Understand / 82
Moonlight Full of Knowledge / 89
Mosquitoes in Praise / 108
Mountolive—The Apostate, Catacombs,
    300 A.D. / 257
Moving with Spirit / 321
My Hand Is in Your Hand / 13
My Joy / 42
Mystical Burning / 145
The Mystical Union of Two Souls / 264
A Navajo Medicine Man Blesses the
    ICU / 307
New Mother / 244
No. 60 in Ward 400 / 171

The Nurturing of the Desert Mother: Ariditas / 303

O Friend, Understand / 104

O Friends, I Am Mad / 103

O Mother of Rain, Rain Upon Us! / 115

O My Beloved Star / 146

On Corruption in the Fourteenth-Century Church / 87

A One-Size-Fits-All Prescription / 261

On Healing / 275

On Saying What She Wanted To / 165

On the Burning of Our House, July 10, 1666 / 110

On the Wideness and Wonder of the World / 165

Others May Forget You / 39

Other Teachings / 136

Our Daughters, Our Selves / 267

Our Sensuality / 92

Owl, Coyote, Soul / 218

A Page from the Diary of Catherine Haun / 138

Piecin' a Quilt's like Livin' a Life / 148

Planting Chant / 144

Powerful Against the Poor, 1928 / 170

Power-Over and Power-from-Within / 274

A Prayer of Praise / 86

Prayer of the Bee / 206

Prayer of the Butterfly / 206

Prayer of the Cat / 205

Prayer to the Sacred Heart / 112

Praying in the Spirit / 86

Psalm / 18

Recipes for Anyone Hungry on the Spiritual Path / 318

Recovery of the Sacred: Some Thoughts on Medical Reform / 255

Right Effort: "Remember, Be Happy" / 232

A Room with a View / 254

The Runaway / 212

Sayings and Advice / 174

The Second Dream / 50

Seeing with the Inner Eye / 200

Selections (from Anna Akhmatova) / 167

Selections (from Sor Juana Inés de la Cruz) / 114

Selections on Working with Chimpanzees / 228

Self-Mastery Is the Target That the Divine Will Wishes Us to Aim At / 301

She Made the Night Come Forth like the Moonlight / 9

So Much Loving / 54

A Soul Rises Up / 85

The Soul Speaks to the Beloved / 80

The Spirit of Exercise / 322

Stars Are Shining / 40

The Storm / 325

Such Are My Gods! / 38

The Sweat Lodge / 270

Tantric Tango / 293

Taoist Chant and Dance / 302

Teaching a Stone to Talk / 252

Teachings on Daily Spiritual Life / 140

Teachings on Prayer / 42

Thanks for the Birth of a Baby Girl / 125

Thank You, My Dear / 14

That Prayer Has the Greatest Power / 71

There Is a Brokenness / 351

The Third Dream / 51

A Thirteenth-Century Search for Spiritual Guidance / 83

This Is a Promise, and I Will Keep
    It / 186
This Is Where the People Come
    Out / 251
Thoughts / 132
Three Teachings / 100
Through a Desert Without a Path / 77
A Time to Laugh / 243
'Tis the Gift to Be Simple / 117
To Become like a Plum Blossom (Not as
    Easy as It Sounds) / 306
Transparency / 100
Travels That Kindle Spirit / 221
Treasure Your Mind, Cherish Your
    Reason, Hold to Your Purpose / 301
The Trial and Sentencing of Agape,
    Chione, Irene, and Four of Their
    Friends / 31
Two Fountains, Two Ways of Prayer / 106
A Vision of Mary / 178
A Vision of the Living Light / 61
A Vision of the Sacred Feminine / 60
Vision of the Shadow of the Living
    Light / 60
Vision of the World as a Wheel / 69
Voluntary Poverty / 180
Waiting / 213
Wake Up! / 290
A Waterfall of Ineffable Delight / 68
The Way of the Warrior / 263
The Way of Waiting / 262

A Wedding Sermon of the Reverend
    Senior Pulliam / 224
Where Should I Turn for
    Guidance? / 222
Where the Eyes See Nothing / 73
Where You Go Will I Go / 20
Who Are the Poor? / 193
The Whole Forest Is You / 64
Why / 212
Why Lalla Stopped Wearing
    Clothes / 88
Why Mira Can't Go Back / 102
Why Practice Yoga? / 194
Wild Geese / 230
Wild Longing / 88
Wild Nights—Wild Nights! / 131
Wild, Wise, Passionate: Dakinis in
    America / 328
Without You / 41
The Woman with the Wild-Grown
    Hair Relaxes After Another Long
    Day / 280
Women of That Certain Age / 240
Woman with Beads / 334
Women's Morning Song / 120
Would You Know My Meaning? / 72
You Are My Longing / 45
You Are Sufficient / 41
You Cannot Make Me Forget / 55
The Zen Art of Cooking / 333

FOR FURTHER READING

Anderson, Sarah, editor, *Heaven's Face Thinly Veiled: A Book of Spiritual Writings by Women*. Boston: Shambhala Publications, 1998.

Brock, Sebastian P., and Susan Ashbrook Havey, translators, *Holy Women of the Syrian Orient*. Berkeley, CA: University of California Press, 1987.

Buerkle, Susanne. *Literatur im Kloster: Historische Funktion und rethorische Legimitation frauenmystischer Texte des 14*. Jahrhunderts, Tuebingen, Germany: Francke, 1999.

Cahill, Susan, editor, *Writing Women's Lives: An Anthology of Autobiographical Narratives by 20th Century American Women Writers*. New York: HarperPerennial, 1994.

———, editor, *Wise Women: Over 2000 Years of Spiritual Writing by Women*. New York: W. W. Norton and Co., 1996.

Carmichael, Alexander, editor, *Carmina Gadelica*, 5 vols. Edinburgh, Scotland: Scottish Academic Press, 1900–1954.

Chonam, Lama, and Sangye Khandro, translators, *The Lives and Liberation of Princess Mandarava, The Indian Consort of Padmasambhava*. Somerville, MA: Wisdom Publications, 1998.

Cottrell, Leonard. *Queens of the Pharaohs*. London: Evans Brothers Limited, 1966.

Dresser, Marianne. *Buddhist Women on the Edge: Contemporary Perspectives from the Western Frontier*. Berkeley, CA: North Atlantic Books, 1996.

Dronke, Peter. *Women Writers of the Middle Ages: A Critical Study of Texts from Perpetua (d. 203) to Marguerite Porete (d. 1310)*. New York: Cambridge University Press, 1984.

Dzielska, Maria (translated by F. Lyra), *Hypatia of Alexandria*. Cambridge, MA: Harvard University Press, 1995.

Elder, Jo-Anne, and Colin O'Connell, editors, *Voices and Echoes: Canadian Women's Spirituality*. Waterloo, Ontario, Canada: Wilfrid Laurier University Press, 1997.

Fox, Matthew. *Breakthrough: Meister Eckhart's Creation Spirituality in New Translation*. New York: Image Books, 1980.

———. *A Spirituality Named Compassion*. San Francisco: HarperSanFrancisco, 1979.

———. *The Coming of the Cosmic Christ*. San Francisco: HarperSanFrancisco, 1988.

Fremantle, Ann Jackson, editor, *The Protestant Mystics*. Boston: Little, Brown, 1964.

Hanut, Eryk. *The Road to Guadalupe: A Modern Pilgrimage to the Virgin of the Americas*. New York: Jeremy P. Tarcher/Putnam, 2001.

Harvey, Andrew. *The Return of the Mother*. Berkeley, CA: Frog, Ltd., 1995.

——— (with illustrations by Eryk Hanut), *Son of Man: The Mystical Path to Christ*. New York: Jeremy P. Tarcher/Putnam, 1998.

———, editor, *The Essential Mystics: The Soul's Journey into Truth*. San Francisco: HarperSanFrancisco, 1996.

——— with Eryk Hanut, *Mary's Vineyard*. Wheaton, IL: Quest Books, 1996.

Haskins, Susan. *Mary Magdalen: Myth and Metaphor*. New York: Harcourt Brace, 1994.

Hirshfield, Jane, editor, *Women in Praise of the Sacred: 43 Centuries of Spiritual Poetry by Women*. San Francisco: HarperSanFrancisco, 1994.

Hogan, Linda, Deena Metzger, and Brenda Peterson, editors, *Intimate Nature: The Bond Between Women and Animals*. New York: Fawcett Columbine, 1998.

Hollywood, Amy M. *The Soul as Virgin Wife: Mechthild of Magdeburg, Marguerite Porete and Meister Eckhart*. Notre Dame, IN: University of Notre Dame Press, 1995.

Howell, Alice O. *The Beejum Book*. Monterey, MA: Rosecroft, 2002.

Johnson, Thomas S., *When the Iron Eagle Flies: Buddhism for the West*. London and New York: Arkana, 1991.

——— , editor, *Emily Dickinson: Selected Letters*. Cambridge, MA: Harvard University Press, 1998.

Laporte, Denise. *The Role of Women in Early Christianity*. New York: Edwin Mellen Press, 1986.

Leslie, Julia, editor, *Roles and Rituals for Hindu Women*. Rutherford, NJ: Fairleigh Dickinson University Press, 1991.

Lewis, I. M. *Ecstatic Religion: A Study of Shamanism and Spiritual Possession*. London and New York: Routledge & Kegan Paul, 1989.

MacHaffie, Barbara. *Her Story: Women in Christian Tradition*. Philadelphia, PA: Fortress Press, 1986.

Mallasz, Gitta. *Dialogues avec l'Ange (traduit du Hongrois par Helene Boyer et Gitta Mallasz)*. Paris: Editions Aubier, 1990.

Mayeski, Marie Anne. *Women Models of Liberation*. Kansas City, MO: Sheed and Ward, 1900.

Medwick, Cathleen. *Theresa of Avila: The Progress of a Soul*. New York: Alfred A. Knopf, 1999.

Migne, J.-P. *Patrologia cursus completus. Series latina. Supplementum, accurante Adalberto Hamman*. Paris: Garnier, 1958.

———, *Patrologia cursus completus. Series graeca, Supplementum Cavallera, Ferdinand*. Paris: Garnier, 1912.

Miller, Beth, editor, *Women in Hispanic Literature*. Berkeley and Los Angeles, CA: University of California Press, 1983.

Miller, Catherine M. *Marguerite Porete et Marguerite d'Oingt de l'autre cote du miroir*. New York: P. Lang, 1999.

Miller, Kamae A. *Wisdom Comes Dancing: Selected Writings of Ruth St. Denis on Dance, Spirituality, and the Body*. Seattle, WA: Peace Works, 1997.

Oden, Amy, editor, *In Her Words: Women's Writings in the History of Christian Thought*. Nashville, TN: Abingdon Press, 1994.

Pritchard, James B., editor, *Ancient Near Eastern Texts: An Anthology of Texts and Pictures*. Princeton, NJ: Princeton University Press, 1955.

Renard, John, editor, *Windows on the House of Islam*. Berkeley, CA: University of California Press, 1998.

Sewell, Marilyn, *Cries of the Spirit: A Celebration of Women's Spirituality*. Boston: Beacon Press, 1991.

Sherma, Ram Padarth. *Women in Hindu Literature*. New Delhi, India: Gyan Publishing House, 1995.

Smith, Margaret. *Rabia: The Life and Work of Rabia and Other Women Mystics in Islam*. New York: Oxford One World, 1994.

Towler, Solala. *A Gathering of Cranes: Bringing the Tao to the West*. Eugene, OR: The Abode of the Eternal Tao, 1996.

Tsomo, Karma Kekshe. *Innovative Buddhist Women: Swimming Against the Stream*. Richmond, VA: Curzon, 2000.

Umansky, Ellen U., and Diane Ashton, editors, *Four Centuries of Jewish Women's Spirituality: A Sourcebook*. Boston: Beacon Press, 1992.

Wendt, Albert. *Lali: A Pacific Anthology*. Auckland, New Zealand: Longman Paul Ltd., 1980.

Willis, Janice D. *Feminine Ground: Essays on Women and Tibet*. London: HarperCollins, 1983.

Wilson-Kastner, Patricia, et al, translators, *A Lost Tradition: Women Writers of the Early Church*. Washington, DC: University Press of America, 1981.

Wolkstein, Diane, and Samuel Noah Kramer. *Innana, Queen of Heaven and Earth: Her Stories and Hymns from Sumer*. New York: Harper and Row, 1983.

PERMISSIONS AND ACKNOWLEDGMENTS

Alba House, New York, for excerpts from *A Mother's Spiritual Diary* by Concepción (Conchita) Cabrera de Armida, translation copyright © 1978 by A. J. Owen.

Arkana, Penguin Books Ltd., London, United Kingdom, for an excerpt from *The Myth of the Goddess: Evolution of an Image* by Anne Baring and Jules Cashford, copyright © 1991 by Anne Baring and Jules Cashford.

Bantam Books, New York, NY, for an excerpt from *The Feminine Face of God: The Unfolding of the Sacred in Women* by Sherry Ruth Anderson and Patricia Hopkins, copyright © 1991 by Sherry Ruth Anderson and Patricia Hopkins; and from *The Scalpel and the Silver Bear* by Lori Arviso Alvord, MD, copyright © 1991 by Lori Arviso Alvord.

Beacon Press, Boston, MA, for an excerpt from *Encountering God: A Spiritual Journey from Bozeman to Banaras* by Diana Eck, copyright © 1993 by Diana Eck.

Becoming Books, Vancouver, BC, Canada, for excerpts from *Always Becoming— Forever! A Journal of Conscious Living/Conscious Dying* by Clare Buckland and Diana Douglas, copyright © 1999 by Clare M. Buckland and Diana C. Douglas. Reprinted by permission of the authors.

Black Opals 1 (June 1928): pp. 6–8, "A Dream of Love," by Mae Cowdery.

Boni and Liveright, New York, for an excerpt from *My Life* by Isadora Duncan, copyright © 1927 by Isadora Duncan.

Casa de las Americas, Havana, Cuba, for excerpts from *Me llamo Rigoberta Menchú (I, Rigoberta Menchú, an Indian Woman in Guatemala)* by Rigoberta Menchú, ed. Elizabeth Burgo-Debray, copyright © 1983 by Rigoberta Menchú.

Curtis Brown Ltd., New York, NY, for excerpts from *Two-Headed Woman* by Lucille Clifton, first published by The University of Massachusetts Press, copyright © 1980 by Lucille Clifton; now appears in *Good Woman: Poems and a Memoir 1969–1980,* published by BOA Editions, Ltd., copyright © 1987 by Lucille Clifton. Reprinted by permission of Curtis Brown, Ltd.

Dell Publishing, Random House, Inc., New York, NY, for excerpts from *Contemplative Living* by Joan Duncan Oliver, copyright © 2000 by The Omega Institute.

Dorrance Publishing Co., Pittsburgh, PA, for an excerpt from *The Spiritual Intrepreneur: Awakening the Power and Potential Within You* by Toni Boehm, copyright © 1996 by Toni Boehm.

Clarissa Pinkola Estés, PhD, for "Father Earth," copyright © 1995 by Clarissa Pinkola Estés. All rights reserved including but not limited to performance, derivative, adaptation, oral, musical, audio and recording, illustrative, theatrical, film, pictorial, reprint and electronic. Reprinted by kind permission of Dr. Estés.

Fawcett Columbine, The Ballantine Publishing Group, New York, NY, for an excerpt from *Intimate Nature: The Bond Between Women and Animals* by Fran Peavy, copyright © 1998 by Fran Peavy.

The Fountain Press, New York, NY, for an excerpt from *A Room of One's Own* by Virginia Woolf, copyright © 1929 by Virginia Woolf.

The Golden Sufi Center Publishing, Inverness, CA, for excerpts from *Daughter of Fire: A Diary of a Spiritual Training with a Sufi Master* by Irina Tweedie, copyright © 1986 by The Golden Sufi Center UK Charitable Trust; and for excerpts from *The Taste of Hidden Things* by Sara Sviri, copyright © 1997 by The Golden Sufi Center UK Charitable Trust. Reprinted by permission of the publisher.

Grove/Atlantic, Inc., New York, NY, for an excerpt from *Dream Work* by Mary Oliver, copyright © 1986 by Mary Oliver. Reprinted by permission of the publisher.

T. K. Hall, Boston, MA, for excerpts from *The Color Purple* by Alice Walker, copyright © 1982 by Alice Walker.

Hampton Roads, Charlotteville, VA, for selections from *Naming a Rose: An Account of a Kundalini Awakening* by Dorothy Walters, copyright © 2002 by Dorothy Walters. Reprinted with permission by the author.

Harcourt Brace Jovanovich, New York, NY, for an excerpt from *Mrs. Dalloway* by Virginia Woolf, copyright © 1925 by Virginia Woolf and for an excerpt from *To the Lighthouse* by Virginia Woolf, copyright © 1925 by Virginia Woolf.

HarperCollins Publishers, Inc, New York, NY, for "Cut brambles long enough" by Sun Bu-er, "Is this darkness the night of power?" by Bibi Hayati, "Bridegroom, beloved of my heart" by Shu-Sin's Ritual Bride, a Priestess of Innana, and "Leave Crete" by Sappho from *Women in Praise of the Sacred: 43 Centuries of Spiritual Poetry by Women,* edited by Jane Hirshfield, copyright © 1994 by Jane Hirshfield; for "The Invitation" from *The Invitation* by Oriah Mountain Dreamer, copyright © 1999 by Oriah Mountain Dreamer; for an excerpt from *The Legacy of Luna: The Story of a Tree, a Woman, and the Struggle to Save the Redwoods* by Julia Butterfly Hill, copyright © 2000 by Julia Hill; for an excerpt from *Jumbalaya: The Natural Woman's Book of Personal Charms and Practical Rituals* by Luisah Teish, copyright © 1985 by Luisah Teish; for an excerpt from *The Long Loneliness,* copyright © 1952 by Harper & Row, Publishers, Inc. copyright renewed © 1980 by Tamar Teresa Hennessey. Reprinted with permission of HarperCollins Publishers, Inc. For an excerpt from *At the Root of This Longing: Reconciling a Spiritual Hunger and a Feminist Thirst* by Carol Lee Flinders, copyright © 1998 by Carol Lee Flinders, reprinted with permission of HarperCollins Publishers, Inc. and the author. For excerpts from *It's Easier Than You Think: The Buddhist Way to Happiness* by Sylvia Boorstein, copyright © 1955 by Sylvia Boorstein; *The Last Report on the Miracles at Little No Horse* by Louise Erdrich, copyright © 2001 by Louise Erdrich; from *Glimpses of Grace: Daily Thoughts and Reflections* by Madeleine L'Engle with Carole F. Chase, copyright © 1996 by Crosswicks, Ltd.; from *Loaves and Fishes* by Dorothy Day, copyright © 1963 Dorothy Day; from Ursula K. LeGuin, *Always Coming Home* by Ursula LeGuin, copyright © 1985 by Ursula LeGuin; from *A Book of Courtesy* by Mary Mercedes Lane, copyright © 2001 by San Dominico School; from *A Manual for Living: Epictitus,* by Sharon Lebell, copyright © 1994 by Sharon Lebell; from *Teaching a Stone to Talk* by Annie Dillard, copyright © 1982 by Annie Dillard; from *The Annie Dillard Reader* by Annie Dillard, copyright © 1985 by Annie Dillard; from *Pilgrim at Tinker Creek* by Annie Dillard, copyright © 1982 by Annie Dillard; from "My True Home Is Brooklyn," by Tracy Cochran in *The Best Spiritual Writing, 1999,* ed. Philip Zaleski, copyright © 1999 by Philip Zaleski, reprinted by permission of the author.

Harvard University Press, Cambridge, MA, for excerpts from *Hypatia from Alexandria* by Maria Dzielska, translated by F. Lyra, copyright © 1995 by the President and the Fellows of Harvard College; from *A Sor Juana Anthology,* translated by Alan S. Trueblood, copyright © 1988, by the President and the Fellows of Harvard College.

The Belknap Press of Harvard University Press for excerpts from *The Poems of Emily Dickinson,* edited by Thomas H. Johnson, copyright © 1951, 1955, 1979 by the President and Fellows of Harvard College.

Hellenic College Press, Brookline, MA, for excerpts from *A Woman's Quest for Spiritual Guidance: The Correspondence of Princess Irene Eulogia Choumnaina Paliologina* by Angela C. Hero, copyright © 1986 by Angela C. Hero.

Hohm Press, Prescott, AZ, for excerpts from *The Woman Awake: Feminine Wisdom for Spiritual Life* by Regina Sara Ryan, copyright © 1998 by Regina Sara Ryan; and for selection from *Marrow of Flame: Poems of the Spiritual Journey* by Dorothy Walters, copyright © 2000 by Dorothy Walters. Reprinted by permission of the authors.

Houghton Mifflin Company, New York, NY, for excerpts from *Dakota: A Spiritual Geography* by Kathleen Norris, copyright © 1993 by Kathleen Norris.

Indiana University Press, Bloomington, IN, for an excerpt from "Prayer" by Gabriela Mistral in *Selected Poems,* trans. Langston Hughes, copyright © 1957 by The Estate of Gabriela Mistral.

Inner City Books, Toronto, Canada, for an excerpt from *The Owl Was the Baker's Daughter: Obesity, Anorexia Nervosa and the Repressed Feminine* by Marion Woodman, copyright © 1980 by Marion Woodman; and from *Conscious Femininity: Interviews with Marion Woodman* by Marion Woodman, copyright © 1993 by Marion Woodman and Daryl Sharp.

La Colomba, Paris, France, for an excerpt from *Attendant Dieu,* by Simone Weil, copyright © 1950 by Simone Weil.

Open View Press, Mill Valley, CA, for excerpts from *Torch-Bearer to Light the Way: The Life of Myrtle Fillmore* by Neal Vahle, copyright © 1996 by Neal Vahle.

Opportunity 9 (August 1931): pp. 242–243, "No. 60 in Ward 400" by Anita Scott Coleman.

Orbis Books, Maryknoll, NY, for excerpts from *Daughters of Anowa: African Women and Patriarchy* by Mercy Amba Oduyoye, copyright © 1995 by Mercy Amba Oduyoye. Reprinted by permission of the publisher.

Oxford University Press, New York, NY, for excerpts from *Mother of Bliss: Anandamayi Ma* by Lisa Lassel Hallstrom, copyright © 1999 by Lisa Lassel Hallstrom; and *Women Living Zen* by Paula Kay Robinson Arai, copyright © 1999 by Paula Kay Robinson Arai.

Parabola: Myth, Tradition, and the Search for Meaning (Summer 1999) for an excerpt from "Playing with God: A Child's Response to Religion," by Tracy Cochran, copyright © 1999 by Tracy Cochran. Reprinted with the permission of the author.

Parallax Press, Berkeley, CA, for an excerpt from *Learning True Love: How I Learned and Practiced Social Change in Vietnam* by Cao Ngoc Phoung Chan Khong, copyright © 1993 by Cao Ngoc Phoung Chan Khong; and from *World as Lover, World as Self* by Joanna Macy, copyright © 1991 by Joanna Macy.

Paulist Press (Classics of Western Spirituality Series), New York, NY, for excerpts from *Julian of Norwich: Showings* by Edmund Colledge and James Walsh, eds. copyright © 1978 by Edmund Colledge and James Walsh.

Pearson Education New Zealand, Auckland, New Zealand, for "The Healer" by Marjorie Crocombe, in *Lali: A Pacific Anthology,* ed. Albert Wendt, copyright © 1980 by Albert Wendt.

Penfold, Nita, for a poem from *Cries of the Spirit,* ed. Marylin Sewell, copyright © by Nita Penfold. Reprinted by permission of the author.

Penguin Putnam USA, Inc, New York, NY, for excerpts from *A Journey with Elsa Cloud* by Leila Hadley, copyright © 1997 by Leila Hadley. Reprinted with permission of the author. For excerpts from *The Treasure of the City of Ladies or The Book of the Three Virtues* by Christine de Pisan, tr. Sarah Lawson, translation copyright © 1985 by Sarah Lawson; from *Roots in Heaven: One Woman's Passionate Journey into the Heart of Her Faith* by Tirzah Firestone, copyright © 1998 by Tirzah Firestone; from *The Joy Luck Club* by Amy Tan, copyright © 1989 by Amy Tan; and for an excerpt from *To Be a Woman: The Birth of the Conscious Feminine* by Elizabeth S. Strahan, ed. Connie Zweig, copyright © 1990 by Connie Zweig.

Penguin Books Ltd., London, for an excerpt from *The Letters of Heloise and Abelard,* tr. Betty Radice, translation copyright © 1974 by Betty Radice.

Praying Magazine, Art Winter, editor, and The Continuum Publishing Company, New York, NY, for an excerpt from "A Beggar's Gift," in *Stories of Awe and Abundance,* by José Hobday, copyright © 1995 by Sr. José Hobday. Reprinted by permission of the author.

Princeton University Press, Princeton, NJ, for excerpts from *Passionate Enlightenment* by Miranda Shaw, copyright © 1994 by Miranda Shaw; and for three lines of "Love Song from Egypt" in *Ancient Near Eastern Texts* by J. B. Pritchard, copyright © 1955 by J. B. Pritchard.

Random House, New York, NY, for excerpts from *The Dead and the Living* by Sharon Olds, copyright © 1987 by Sharon Olds. Used by permission of Alfred Knopf, a division of Random House, Inc. *Love Is Stronger than Death: The Mystical Union of Two Souls,* copyright © 1997, 1999 by Cynthia Bourgeault. Used by permission of Harmony Books, a division of Random House, Inc. *Contemplative Living* by Joan Duncan Oliver, copyright © by The Omega Institute 2000. Used by permission of the author.

Riverhead Books (division of G. P. Putnam's Sons; Penguin Putnam, Inc.), New York, NY, for excerpts from *The Cloister Walk* by Kathleen Norris, copyright © 1996 by Kathleen Norris, and *Kitchen Table Wisdom* by Rachel Naomi Remen, MD, copyright © 1996 by Rachel Naomi Remen, and from *Walking a Sacred Path* by Lauren Artress, copyright © 1995 by Lauren Artress. Used by permission of the author.

Scarlet Tanager Books, Oakland, CA, for a poem in *Red Clay Is Talking* by Naomi Ruth Lowinsky, copyright © 2000. Used by permission of the author.

Schocken Books Inc., New York, NY, for excerpts from *Women's Diaries of the Westward Journey* by Lillian Schlissel; copyright © 1992 by Schocken Books.

Shambhala Publications, Inc., Boston, MA, for excerpts from *Visions and Longings: Medieval Women Mystics,* ed. Monica Furlong, copyright © 1997 by Monica Furlong; *Passionate Journey: The Spiritual Autobiography of Satomi Myodo,* tr. Sallie B. King, translation copyright © 1987 by Sallie B. King; *Start from Where You Are* by Pema Chödrön, copyright © 1994 by Pema Chödrön; *When Things Fall Apart: Heart Advice for Difficult Times* by Pema Chödrön, copyright © 1997 by Pema Chödrön.

Simon & Schuster, Inc., New York, NY, for excerpts from *A Woman on Paper: Georgia O'Keeffe* by Anita Pollitzer, copyright © 1988 by Anita Pollitzer.

Sri Ramakrishna Math, Mylapore, Madras, India, for excerpts from *Sri Serada Devi, the Holy Mother, Life and Teachings* by Swami Tapasyananda.

The SYDA Foundation, excerpted with permission from *Courage and Contentment: A Collection of Talks on Spiritual Life,* pp. 77–80, copyright © 1999 by SYDA Foundation. All rights reserved.

Tan Books & Publishers, Rockport, IL, for excerpts from *The Autobiography of St. Margaret Mary Alacoque: A Vision of the Divine Heart* by Margaret Mary Alacoque, copyright © 1986 by Tan Books & Publishers.

Unity School of Christianity, Unity Village, MO, for excerpts from *How to Let God Help You,* by Myrtle Fillmore, 1956.

University of California Press, Berkeley, CA, for Fragment #46 "Thank you, my dear" from *Sappho: A New Translation,* tr. by Mary Barnard, copyright © 1958 The Regents of the University of California, © renewed 1986 by Mary Barnard. Reprinted with permission of University of California Press. For four lines of a "Love Song from Spain" in *Women in Hispanic Literature,* ed. Beth Miller, copyright © 1983 by Beth Miller; for an excerpt from *Mama Lola: A Voudou Priestess in Brooklyn* by Karen McCarthy Brown, copyright © 1991 by Karen McCarthy Brown.

University of Nebraska Press, Lincoln, NE, for "Grandmother" by Marilyn Krysl, from *Prairie Schooner* 61 no. 2 (Summer 1987): pp. 56–57, copyright © 1987 by the University of Nebraska Press. Reprinted with the permission of the University of Nebraska Press.

Vincent Stuart Ltd., London, United Kingdom, for excerpts from *The One Work: A Journey Toward the Self,* copyright © 1961 by Anne Gage (Anne Baring).

Warner Books, New York, NY, for an excerpt from *A Kind of Grace* by Jackie Joyner-Kersee, copyright © 1997 by Jackie Joyner-Kersee.

Wesleyan University Press, Hanover, NH, for excerpts from *Centering in Pottery, Poetry, and the Person* by Mary Caroline Richards, copyright © 1962, 1964, 1989 by Mary Caroline Richards.

White Pine Press, Fredonia, NY, for four lines from "Those Who Do Not Dance" by Gabriela Mistral in *Gabriela Mistral: A Reader,* ed. Marjorie Agosin, tr. Maria Giachetti, translation copyright © 1993 by Maria Giachetti.

Wisdom Publications, Somerville, MA, for excerpts from *The Lives and Liberation of Princess Manadarava* by Lama Chonam and Sangye Khandro, copyright © 1998 by Nanci Gay Gustafson, aka Sangye Khandro. Reprinted with permission of Wisdom Publications. From *Be an Island: The Buddhist Practice of Inner Peace* by Ayya Khema, copyright © 1986 by Parapaduwa Nun's Island, copyright © by Wisdom Publications.

YES International Publishers, St. Paul, MN, for an excerpt from Abbess Koei Hoshino in *The Spiral Path: Essays and Interviews on Women's Spirituality,* ed. Theresa King O'Brien, copyright © 1988 by Theresa King O'Brien. Reprinted with the permission of YES International Publishers.

Zeitgeist Press, Berkeley, CA, for poems from *Ask a Mask* by Julia Vinograd, copyright © 1990 by Julia Vinograd. Reprinted with the permission of Zeitgeist Press and the author.

Extensive efforts, including Internet searches, have been made to locate copyright holders of texts reprinted in this book. If any work has been reprinted without permission, the author apologizes and would be grateful to hear from anyone who has not been consulted. Unidentified translations and adaptations in *Sacred Voices* by Mary Ford-Grabowsky.

ABOUT THE EDITOR

*M*ary Ford-Grabowsky is an award-winning writer, editor, and teacher with a specialty in the world's mystical traditions. Her publications include inspirational books such as *Prayers for All People* and *Sacred Poems and Prayers of Love,* and many essays and scholarly articles. After receiving a master of divinity degree and a doctorate in theology and spirituality from Princeton Theological Seminary, she taught in the religious studies department of Regis College, later returning to Princeton to become editor of Fellowship in Prayer. In 1995 she moved to California at the invitation of the Episcopal theologian Matthew Fox to become vice president and academic dean of the University of Creation Spirituality in Oakland, where she today serves as a member of the adjunct faculty and board. Among honors she has received are an award from the ecumenical branch of the World Council of Churches for distinguished service in interfaith work. A translator who studied Spanish in Mexico and German, French, and Italian in Europe, she has been collecting and translating prayers for many years and is currently preparing a book of women's prayers for publication by HarperSanFrancisco in 2003. She warmly invites readers of this book to send their favorite prayers to her at P. O. Box 21267, Oakland, CA 94620–1267.